A HISTORY OF JEWISH LITERATURE
VOLUME XI

Israel Zinberg's *History of Jewish Literature*

Israel Zinberg

A HISTORY OF
JEWISH
LITERATURE

TRANSLATED AND EDITED BY BERNARD MARTIN

The Haskalah Movement in Russia

HEBREW UNION COLLEGE PRESS
CINCINNATI, OHIO
KTAV PUBLISHING HOUSE, INC.
NEW YORK, NEW YORK
1978

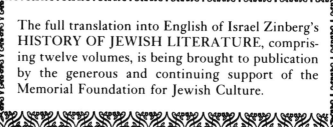

The full translation into English of Israel Zinberg's HISTORY OF JEWISH LITERATURE, comprising twelve volumes, is being brought to publication by the generous and continuing support of the Memorial Foundation for Jewish Culture.

PJ5008
Z5313
vol 11

Library of Congress Cataloging in Publication Data

Zinberg, Israel, 1873-1938.
    The Haskalah movement in Russia.

    (His A history of Jewish literature; 11)
    Translation of Di Haśkole-bavegung in Rusland, which was published as Part 12 of the author's Di geshikhte fun der literatur bay Yidn.
    Bibliography: p.
    Includes index.
    1. Haskalah—Russia—History. 2. Jews in Russia—History. 3. Hebrew literature, Modern—History and criticism. 4. Yiddish literature—History and criticism. I. Title, II. Series: Zinberg, Israel, 1873-1938. Di geshikhte fun der literatur bay Yidn; 11.
PJ5008.Z5313 vol. 11 [BM194]809'.889'24s [809'.889'24]
    ISBN 0-87068-492-2   77-24373

Printed in the United States of America

Contents

The collapse of the peaceful alliance—The "last of the Mohicans," Manasseh of Ilya—"The dreamer of the ghetto"—Manasseh on "the general good"—The tragic struggle of the dreamer—The significance of *Alfei Menasheh*—There is no absolute; the value of everything is dependent on "time and place"—Manasseh's social program—The sad fate of his *Shekel Ha-Kodesh*—The influence of the Galician *maskilim* on the *maskilim* in southern Russia—The *maskil* Hirsch Baer Hurwitz and Prince Dolgoruki—Isaac Baer Levinsohn.

Isaac Baer Levinsohn's childhood and youth—His patriotic anthem—Levinsohn's years of study in Galicia—His anti-Hasidic satires—*Te'udah Be-Yisrael* and its significance—The sources of the exaggerated patriotism of the bearers of Haskalah—*Te'udah Be-Yisrael* and the *maskilim*—The *maskilim* of Vilna and their projected *Minhat Bikkurim*—"Men of the previous century"—Levinsohn's program of reform—*Bet Yehudah* and its "adventures"—Veiled allusions to civic rights.

··❧[v]❧··

Contents

Contents

A Note on Israel Zinberg

D R. ISRAEL ZINBERG is widely regarded as one of the foremost historians of Jewish literature. Born in Russia in 1873 and educated at various universities in Germany and Switzerland, he devoted more than twenty years to the writing, in Yiddish, of his monumental *Di Geshikhte fun der Literatur bay Yidn* (History of Jewish Literature). This work, published in eight volumes in Vilna, 1929–1937, is a comprehensive and authoritative study of Jewish literary creativity in Europe from its beginnings in tenth-century Spain to the end of the Haskalah period in nineteenth-century Russia. Based on a meticulous study of all the relevant primary source material and provided with full documentation, Zinberg's history is a notable exemplar of the tradition of modern Jewish scholarship known as *die Wissenschaft des Judentums* (the Science of Judaism).

In addition to his *magnum opus*, Zinberg, who earned his living as a chemical engineer, wrote numerous other valuable monographs and articles on Jewish history and literature in Russian, Hebrew, and Yiddish. In 1938, during the Stalinist purges, he was arrested by the Soviet police and sentenced to exile in Siberia. He died in a concentration camp hospital in Vladivostok in that same year.

The reader who wishes a fuller introduction is invited to consult the Translator's Introduction to Volume I of Zinberg's *History of Jewish Literature*.

Foreword

In 1972 the Case Western Reserve University Press began publishing an English translation of Israel Zinberg's *History of Jewish Literature*. Zinberg, an engineer by profession, was a scholar by choice and inclination. In thirty years of intensive study in the great Jewish libraries of St. Petersburg (later Leningrad), he produced eight volumes in Yiddish portraying the course of literary creativity among the Jews beginning with the Golden Age of Spanish Jewry and continuing to the end of the last century. It was not until many years after Zinberg's death that a Hebrew translation was prepared and published in the State of Israel.

There has been no work of similar scope and magnitude in the English language, despite the fact that the Jewish reading public in Britain, South Africa, Canada, and the United States constitutes about half of the Jews in the world. Now, however, the Zinberg volumes have been beautifully translated into English by Dr. Bernard Martin, Abba Hillel Silver Professor of Jewish Studies and Chairman of the Department of Religion at Case Western Reserve University in Cleveland, Ohio. All the English-speaking lands are indebted to Professor Martin for his endeavor to make accessible a literary history such as Zinberg's, a history which depicts the intellectual strivings of the Jews, their aspirations, yearnings, and spiritual search in the medieval and modern worlds, in both of which they have played a not undistinguished role.

Special gratitude is due to the Press of Case Western Reserve University which inaugurated the challenging task of publishing this handsome and very important series of books. Each volume is an aesthetic as well as intellectual delight. The Case Western Reserve Press was aided in publication by a generous grant from the Memorial Foundation for Jewish Culture. The grant is, indeed, a memorial to the martyred Zinberg, who was arrested by the Soviet police in 1938 and deported to Siberia, where he died. We, for our part, are pleased with this opportunity to express our gratitude to the Memorial Foundation for the support which made possible the publication of the first three volumes.

Unfortunately, the economic difficulties from which many universities are now suffering has led to the dissolution of the Case Western Reserve Press and made it impossible for it to continue with the remaining nine volumes. That is why the Hebrew Union College—Jewish Institute of Religion, realizing the importance and cultural implications of this work, is cooperating with the Ktav Publishing House, Incorporated, in the publication of the remaining volumes.

The completion of this series will make available to the English-speaking world a magnificent account of the literary and cultural treasures created by the Jewish people during their millennial history.

Hebrew Union College—   Alfred Gottschalk
Jewish Institute of Religion   President
Cincinnati, Ohio
March, 1978

Acknowledgments

The generous support of the Memorial Foundation for Jewish Culture, New York City, of the Morris and Bertha Treuhaft Memorial Fund, the Leonard, Faye, and Albert B. Ratner Philanthropic Fund, Mr. and Mrs. John K. Powers, and Mr. Samuel Givelber all of Cleveland, is gratefully acknowledged by publisher and translator alike. Without this generosity it would not have been possible for Israel Zinberg's monumental work to reach the new audience that it is hoped a translation into English will afford. The editor and translator wishes to express his appreciation to his friend Dr. Arthur J. Lelyveld, Rabbi of the Fairmount Temple of Cleveland and President (1966–1972) of the American Jewish Congress, for his aid in securing a grant from the Memorial Foundation for Jewish Culture for the publication of this work.

The translator also wishes to express his deep appreciation to Dr. Nathan Susskind, formerly Professor of German at the College of the City of New York and Visiting Professor of Yiddish at Yeshiva University, for his invaluable help in clarifying the meaning of many terms and concepts in Zinberg's Yiddish and Hebrew text. Responsibility for any errors of translation is, of course, the translator's.

It should be noted that Yiddish books with Hebrew titles are usually rendered according to the modern Sephardic pronunciation of Hebrew.

A gift to my loyal friend
and life-companion—my wife.

—Israel Zinberg

Transliteration of Hebrew Terms

א is not transliterated

ב = b

בּ = v

גּ, ג = g

דּ, ד = d

ה = h

ו = v (where not a vowel)

ז = z

ח = ḥ

ט = t

י = y

כּ = k

כ = ch

ל = l

מ = m

נ = n

ס = s

ע is not transliterated

פ = p

פ = f

צ = tz

ק = k

ר = r

שׁ = sh

שׂ = s

תּ, ת = t

◌ָ = a   ◌ֶ = e

◌ַ = a   ◌ִ = i

◌ֹ , וֹ = o   ◌ֵ = ei

◌ֻ , וּ = u   ◌ְ = e

short ◌ָ = o   ◌ֹ = o

י◌ֵ = ei   ◌ֲ = a

vocal *sheva* = e

silent *sheva* is not transliterated

Transliteration of Yiddish Terms

א	not transliterated		יי	ey
אַ	a		ײַ	ay
אָ	o		כ	k
ב	b		כ,ך	kh
בֿ	v		ל	l
ג	g		מ,ם	m
ד	d		נ,ן	n
ה	h		ס	s
ו,וּ	u		ע	e
וו	v		פ	p
וי	oy		פֿ,ף	f
ז	z		צ,ץ	ts
זש	zh		ק	k
ח	kh		ר	r
ט	t		ש	sh
טש	tsh. ch		שׂ	s
י	(consonant) y		ת	t
י	(vowel) i		ת	s

Abbreviations

JQR	*Jewish Quarterly Review*
JQR, n.s.	*Jewish Quarterly Review*, new series
MGWJ	*Monatsschrift für die Geschichte und Wissenschaft des Judentums*
PAAJR	*Proceedings of the American Academy for Jewish Research*
REJ	*Revue des Études Juives*
ZHB	*Zeitschrift für hebräische Bibliographie*

This volume is dedicated
to
Isadore E. Millstone
Constructive, imaginative entrepreneur,
ardent Jew, creative philanthropist

THE HASKALAH MOVEMENT IN RUSSIA

CHAPTER ONE

Rabbi Manasseh of Ilya

[The collapse of the peaceful alliance—The "last of the Mohicans," Manasseh of Ilya—"The dreamer of the ghetto"—Manasseh on "the general good"—The tragic struggle of the dreamer—The significance of *Alfei Menasheh*—There is no absolute; the value of everything is dependent on "time and place"—Manasseh's social program—The sad fate of his *Shekel Ha-Kodesh*—The influence of the Galician *maskilim* on the *maskilim* in southern Russia—The *maskil* Hirsch Baer Hurwitz and Prince Dolgoruki—Isaac Baer Levinsohn.]

T THE close of Part Nine of our *History* we noted the factors that brought a definite change in the spiritual and intellectual moods within Jewish learned circles in Lithuania and White Russia at the beginning of the nineteenth century. The amicable bond between Torah and science, piety and enlightenment, which was discernible among the pioneers of Haskalah, fell apart. The principle set forth by the Gaon of Vilna—that every deficiency in knowledge of the secular sciences produces a hundredfold deficiency in study of the Torah—was categorically rejected. Every branch of knowledge, all secular sciences, were declared nothing but heresy. For this reactionary mood, the triumphant growth in strength of the

Hasidic movement was more than a little responsible. This movement, as we have observed, was extremely hostile to everything having the slightest relationship to European culture. Highly characteristic in this respect is the tragic fate of one of the youngest disciples of the Gaon of Vilna, Manasseh of Ilya.

Manasseh ben Joseph was born in 1767 in Smorgon into the family of the local *dayan*, or rabbinic judge. It is related that, because of his great ability, at the age of ten he could no longer find a suitable teacher in Smorgon and began from that time on to study "on his own" in the *bet ha-midrash*, along with the older youths. At fifteen he was already renowned as a scholar. After his marriage, when he went to live in Ilya with his father-in-law, who supported him and his wife, he would spend day and night studying in the *bet ha-midrash*. When his father-in-law lost his fortune and could no longer provide for Manasseh, his wife became the breadwinner. She maintained the family, while he continued to pore undisturbed over his books.

Two men had a great influence on the youthful Manasseh and his intellectual and spiritual development. The first was the Gaon of Vilna, whom he would frequently visit and with whom he spent whole years.[1] Of no lesser importance was his relationship with his kinsman, the well-known bibliophile, Joseph Mazal, who lived in the nearby village of Viasyn and acquired renown for his remarkably rich library. With his thirst for knowledge, the young Manasseh used to spend months in his relative's library. There he became familiar with the medieval Jewish philosophical works and also with such "external wisdoms" as mathematics, astronomy, and physics—to the extent that these are dealt with in medieval Hebrew literature.

The young scholar became a "seeker" for knowledge and set out to look for larger centers of science. Like all the other pioneers of Haskalah, he dreamed of the Prussian capital, Berlin. After many trials Manasseh arrived in Königsberg and from there hoped to go to Berlin. In Königsberg, however, he encountered some merchants whom he knew from Lithuania. These men were enraged that such a distinguished scholar should go to the major seat of heresy, where he might—God forbid—be led astray from the right path. They admonished him severely, and when he persisted, the pious merchants attempted to save him from the demonic "other side" through a secret denunciation to the government authorities. Manasseh was refused the required passport and had to return to Ilya.

1. *Ben Porat*, 14.

Manasseh's unsuccessful journey intensified his thirst for knowledge, because on the way to Berlin he met several persons with some European education who explained to him that the information about the "external wisdoms" he had drawn from medieval Hebrew literature was quite outdated and insufficient. Through great effort he managed to obtain several German and Polish scientific books, but he had a very poor understanding of the languages in which these were written. Moreover, the books themselves were somewhat obsolete. Nevertheless, these works apparently gave Manasseh more or less familiarity with the rationalist and humanitarian ideas of the eighteenth century. They also aroused his interest in social problems. All this had an immense influence on his world-outlook. With all his strict religiosity, Manasseh of Ilya became a convinced rationalist. Since his was a deeply ethical nature, however, his rationalism assumed very unique forms, and he represents one of the most typical and noblest of the "dreamers of the ghetto" whom years later Israel Zangwill celebrated so beautifully.

The basic principle of Manasseh's philosophy is "the general good." "If God Blessed be He," he declares in the introduction to his work *Ha'amek She'elah*, "would wish to endow me and mine eternally with everything good but allow evil to prevail in the world, i.e., permit living creatures to continue to suffer and men to go on living in pain, I would reject the gift. I do not wish to be an exception to other creatures."[2] "What value," he asks further, "can personal, individual good have over against the general good? My only desire and hope is that perhaps somehow I may contribute to the improvement of the existing order."

"I have considered what takes place all around," he writes in the introduction to another work, *Tikkun Kelali*.[3]

I do not speak of the outright robbery that occurs in the world, how the stronger always swallows the weaker. It is clear to me that the chief cause of all the ills of the world is material distress and insecure sources of livelihood. Only a few are provided with a secure living; the great majority are burdened, poverty-stricken men who go about naked and bare, have no roof over their heads, and literally perish of hunger, cold, and all kinds of sicknesses . . . I am ashamed to be concerned about myself and the needs of my household when I see that the whole world is in pain and want. I cannot forget this great distress. I see it constantly before my eyes,

2. This work, like many other of Manasseh's writings, remained unpublished. Only fragments are presented in the introduction of the publisher of the second part of *Alfei Menasheh*, 1904.
3. This work itself has not been preserved (see M. Spalter's introduction to the second part of *Alfei Menasheh*).

and I cannot be at peace. I must expose the order of the world, show how people live, how they support themselves; I must reveal their needs and sufferings. Perhaps God will enlighten my eyes and show me the right way for the improvement of the world, and I shall be privileged to bring benefit and relief to the world.

Manasseh believed firmly in the power of common sense. He was strongly persuaded that if only men's eyes were opened, if they were given to understand through common sense how greatly they have erred, followed false paths, and not grasped what is useful, they would at once repair to good sense, set out on the right way, and salvation would promptly supervene. In the course of several decades Manasseh, with tireless energy, wrote one work after another. A typical autodidact, he was thoroughly convinced that he had accumulated great knowledge in many branches of science and could thereby be of much use to the Jewish community.[4]

Here the tragic battle of the "dreamer" with dreary, gray, everyday reality began. For many years this battle—the battle of an individual who, with enormous obduracy, wished to alleviate distress, to bring light and salvation to darkened souls, and obtained as his reward only hatred, wrath, and disappointment— continued. In 1807 Manasseh's little composition *Pesher Davar* appeared in Vilna. In the introduction he declares that his aim is to serve as a compromiser, to effect a reconciliation between the factions or sects[5] that have arisen among the Jews, to demonstrate that science is absolutely compatible with faith, that imagination without the control of reason leads men on false paths. In this connection he reproaches the Hasidim who refuse to acknowledge the demands of cold reason and always soar on the wings of overheated fantasy. He reproaches the Mitnagdim for their arid formalism and for their worship that is conducted so mechanically and without fervor. He also complains strongly of those who have obtained knowledge but do not deem it necessary to bestow what they have achieved on others.

But Manasseh is not content with this. He wrote shortly after the publication of the notorious Statute of 1804 with regard to the Jews, in which the Russian government expressed its decision to expel all the Jews in the western provinces from the villages. Manasseh points out that the major cause of the economic decay among the Jews is their choice of insubstantial occupations, the fact that they do not engage in productive work. Jews must betake

---

4. In *Ha'amek She'elah* Manasseh notes: "And with the help of God there is hope, following the mass of new and clear knowledge with which the Lord favored me after much labor and searching on my part, that there is much benefit in them."
5. A reference to the Mitnagdim and Hasidim.

themselves as quickly as possible to essential crafts and useful vocations. Much in Jewish life, Manasseh declares, must certainly be changed. The Torah, after all, teaches that we should obey everything that the leaders of the generation command. The sages and leaders ought to convene each year, make decisions, and indicate the ordinances that ought to be instituted for the general good.

But the leaders of that generation were fearful of all new "ordinances." In everything "new" they saw either "oppressive decrees," on the one side, or "heresy," on the other. Thus they also perceived in Manasseh's *Pesher Davar* dangerous heterodoxy and promptly took measures to prevent the work from reaching the reader. The destruction of *Pesher Davar* was carried through so thoroughly that only a single copy, located in the British Museum, has been preserved.[6]

But Manasseh of Ilya did not lose courage. He composed one work after another, all on the theme of "the general good." However, he found great difficulties in getting his works published. It was not merely that he lacked the necessary resources. After his sad experience with *Pesher Davar*, he decided not to publish any longer in Lithuania but to conduct negotiations with printers in Volhynia. Only his work *Binat Mikra*, on the accents and cantillation of the Torah, was published in Grodno in 1818. In this work also, however, traces of heresy were discovered. Manasseh's explanation that the ancient accents and notations served the same purposes as modern musical notes aroused strong resentment in orthodox circles. "How," they indignantly asked, "can one explain in such a common and secular way the sacred notation, in which every crownlet contains the profoundest mysteries?"

This persuaded Manasseh even more strongly of the necessity for "opening the eyes of his brethren," enlightening them, and convincing them that the most proper way of interpretation is the literal one, to which common sense leads. He traveled to Volhynia, determined to publish there his major work, *Alfei Menasheh*, which he firmly believed would be the guide and spiritual leader of his generation.

But Manasseh was soon persuaded in the most melancholy way that he was mistaken in thinking that Volhynia was more modern and secular than Lithuania. He came to terms with the owner of a press in Volhynia, who promptly undertook to print his work. When the first sheets were already printed, a man with whom the

---

6. We have employed only the extracts that are presented in M. Plungian's *Ben Porat*, Vilna, 1858, pp. 90–94 and in S. J. Stanislavski's article in *Ha-Shiloah*, XVIII (1908) 474.

printer was acquainted, a great pietist, came to visit him. As soon as the latter read the part of *Alfei Menasheh* that had already been printed, he raised a great outcry: How can a God-fearing Jew print such a heretical book, which undermines the pillars of the sacred Torah? To atone for such a grievous sin, the frightened printer burned the printed sheets and the manuscript as well.

Manasseh returned to Ilya and from memory rewrote the work that had been destroyed and had it printed in Vilna. But in Vilna also the printing did not go smoothly. While *Alfei Menasheh* was still on the press, the rabbi of Vilna, Saul Katzenellenbogen, became aware of the fact that in a certain passage (No. 129) the author permitted himself to assert that the rabbis of the generation have the right to nullify certain laws when they are convinced "that the hour requires it" and that these laws are overly burdensome and harmful. The enraged rabbi at once summoned Manasseh and informed him that if he did not remove this heretical statement, he, the rabbi, would order the book burned publicly in the courtyard of the synagogue.[7] Manasseh obeyed the rabbi's command; he could do so quite lightheartedly, since numerous other passages of *Alfei Menasheh* were permeated with the very idea which so irritated Rabbi Saul Katzenellenbogen.

In 1822 Manasseh's major work was finally published. He was so strongly persuaded of its great importance that he allowed himself to state in the introduction that the book was quite as essential to everyone as a prayerbook. He further expressed the hope that he would be requested to publish the subsequent part of his work, because he had, for the time being, "on account of the expenses of printing," published only the least part of that with which God had blessed him.

Manasseh's chief work makes a very odd impression on the modern reader. While the other pioneers of Haskalah in Russia— such as Dr. Hurwitz, Jehudah Loeb Margolioth, and Baruch of Shklov, not to mention Mendel Levin (Lefin)—attempted to write in an accurate, more modern style, Manasseh of Ilya represents utter lack of style. His wooden, cumbersome language is at a not much higher level than that of most of the rabbinical compositions of his time. In addition, the author of *Alfei Menasheh* is also a very unskilled systematizer. To be sure, he himself, is staunchly committed to the clear, literal interpretation and asserts that, were it not for the Gaon of Vilna, "the Torah would have been forgotten in Israel," and that only the Gaon, who with his tremendous genius always endeavored "to explain everything literally and simply,"

7. *Ben Porat*, 99–100.

managed "to restore to the crown [of the Torah] its ancient splendor."[8]

But in this respect Manasseh was hardly one who practiced what he preached. He asserts "that he writes in concise and easy language." In fact, however, his *Alfei Menasheh* is written without any system. He mixes together subjects that actually have no connection whatever with each other. Indeed, at times he himself admits that "this matter has no relationship to the theme of my work," but he defends himself by saying that "this information may also be useful."[9]

Proceeding from the idea that extraneous information "may also be useful," the author dwells in the first chapters of his work on problems of natural science, chiefly on the fundamental principles of chemistry and physics. Here it is very apparent how backward the self-taught Manasseh was in these matters. Fifty years after Lavoisier's brilliant discoveries, the author of *Alfei Menasheh* still operates with the four elements of the Middle Ages: fire, water, air, and earth. He asserts that fire and air are identical, that fire is merely more compressed air, and that when one strikes flint with steel the atoms of the air are so pressed together that sparks appear and flame arises. He also has a very slight notion of Isaac Newton's basic laws and speaks at length of "thunder stones."[10]

In this connection the remark of the acute Naḥman Krochmal after spending several hours with Manasseh of Ilya is characteristic: He is certainly a remarkable Torah scholar, a good grammarian, and a competent mathematician. But he is mistaken in believing that he discloses the profoundest mysteries, which have been unknown until he came along, and that the most important discoveries are due to him. Unfortunately, he does not realize that these mysteries and discoveries have been known for a long time to every enlightened, thinking person.[11]

Nevertheless, *Alfei Menasheh*, with all its old-fashioned, crude form, is an interesting memorial of that era, and a lovely, romantically dreaming personality shines through the awkward, unpolished substance.

Manasseh of Ilya does not grow weary of pointing out to his readers that the finest goal and highest good can be attained by men only if they allow themselves to be led, not by imagination or blind feelings, but by common sense.[12] There is no clear and correct knowledge, he declares, except that obtained through true

8. *Alfei Menasheh*, No. 102, folio 38.
9. *Ibid.*, No. 45, folio 15.
10. *Ibid.*, I, Nos. 1–5, 64: II, Chapter Seven.
11. *Tziyyun Le-Nefesh RaNaK*, 61.
12. *Alfei Menasheh*, No. 140.

understanding.[13] The author of *Alfei Menasheh* is thoroughly persuaded that common sense and truth "are twins that can never be separated,"[14] and that it is inconceivable that the Torah should be inconsistent with true reason, for human reason is, after all, clearly "a part of God on high."[15]

Only with the aid of knowledge obtained through reason can one fulfill the basic commandment: "And thou shalt love the Lord thy God." And the more knowledge and understanding there is, the more love there is. Only through knowledge does one grasp the fact that the purpose of the world is the attainment of good, that God created the world "to do good consummately."[16] The most important thing Manasseh wishes to show, however, is that only he who allows himself to be guided by common sense properly realizes that the welfare of the individual is strictly bound up with the welfare of the community,[17] just as the wellbeing of each individual limb or organ is the consequence of the healthy condition of the whole body.[18] Whoever examines the "ways of the world" quickly realizes that the interests of the individual are inextricably associated with the interests of the community, and that when some disorder occurs in the community, this affects the individual more than when his private affairs are disturbed. Hence, the individual must suppress and annul his own will before the "benefit of the community."[19]

From these theoretical premises, Manasseh of Ilya comes to some very practical conclusions. In the grievous and abnormal social condition of the Jewish community, he sees two major factors operative: (1) the fact that Jews engage so little in productive work, and (2) that they are so frightfully deficient in elementary secular knowledge. All the troubles in the world, he declares, derive from the fact that men decide to live off the gifts of mortals, the charity of others, and give no thought to means whereby they might live from their own labor.[20]

He addresses the "capable men," the leaders and men of wealth, in an attempt to explain to them through common sense that they must not be content with accumulating fortunes for themselves; they must bear in mind that "the good of individuals is dependent on the general good." We observe, Manasseh points out, that in our

---

13. *Ibid.*, II, Chapter Nineteen; see also *ibid.*, I. No. 104.
14. *Ibid.*, No. 129.
15. *Ibid.*, No. 149.
16. *Ibid.*, No. 90.
17. *Ibid.*, No. 98.
18. *Ibid.*, No. 71. See also *ibid.*, No. 85, and *ibid.*, II, Chapter Twenty-Three.
19. *Ibid.*, II, Chapter Twenty-Three.
20. *Ibid.*, No. 110.

times so many rich men have lost their fortunes and their children are poverty-stricken;[21] this is a consequence of the fact that the social foundations of the Jewish community are rotten. Hence the "capable men" ought, out of purely utilitarian motives, to be concerned for the general good and see to it that their brethren occupy themselves with productive labor.

For this, however, Manasseh emphasizes, it is necessary to disseminate as much knowledge as possible and to familiarize the people with the natural sciences. Like Moses Marcuse in his day,[22] Manasseh notes, incidentally, how many misfortunes occur and how many persons depart from the world prematurely only because men do not properly appreciate the value of "the science of healing." The well-known Talmudic dictum, "Ninety-nine die from the evil eye and one through ordinary causes *(bi-derech eretz),*" he interprets as meaning: Only one person out of a hundred dies a natural death; the remaining ninety-nine die simply as a result of improper care, because, out of ignorance, they are not treated as they ought to be.[23]

Manasseh, however, realizes quite well how hostile to all reforms both the "capable men," the rabbis and leaders, and the unlettered masses are. Here we encounter the most interesting aspect of his philosophy. We have noted how deficient Manasseh was in the realm of secular knowledge. The rationalist and humanitarian ideas of the *Aufklärer* and Encyclopedists came to him from dated sources, and this indirectly. But the old-fashioned Torah scholar of Smorgon expresses, in his *Alfei Menasheh*, ideas that were still alien to the rationalists of the eighteenth century. The latter always operated with absolute concepts, determined once and for all. They fought for an absolute (in fact, for the bourgeois-middleclass) rationalist order that they believed valid for all time and best suited to human nature, which they conceived as good and just by nature but as having gone astray on crooked byways through ignorance, misled by false guides.

Manasseh of Ilya, however, was quite far from such a view. He does not grow tired of repeating the fundamental idea that "there is nothing in the world absolutely good or bad, but everything that is in its time and place is good, and what is not in its time and place is bad,"[24] meaning that all things are relative to time and place and what, under certain circumstances and at a definite moment, is good and useful may, under altered conditions, become bad and harmful. The God-fearing Torah scholar of Smorgon is firmly

21. *Ibid.*, No. 96.
22. See our *History*, Vol. VIII, Chapter Six.
23. *Alfei Menasheh*, No. 86.
24. *Ibid.*, I, Nos. 20, 124, 129, etc.

persuaded that everything—all values, all qualities—are judged according to "time and place"[25] and "are changed according to the generation,"[26] i.e., evolve from generation to generation. He has the courage to declare that, even in the case of religious rules governing the relationship between man and God and of positive, practical commandments, the same principle applies; these, too, are dependent on time and must evolve in the course of generations.

Manasseh declares that only after taking account of the law that there is nothing in the world absolutely good or absolutely evil but that, depending on time and place, the good may be transformed into its utter antithesis, do we properly understand that there are two kinds of order of behavior, the general *(hanhagah kelalit)* and the particular *(hanhagah peratit).* The general order is for the ignorant masses, for those who are "scantily endowed with reason;" for them, general rules and laws that may serve as necessary support and restraint have been provided. The second order of behavior, the individual, however, is for "those who comprehend science and knowledge," for the intelligent and critically reflective who know "how to conduct themselves in everything according to time and circumstance."[27]

It is clear that Manasseh of Ilya cannot be content with the ancient principle, "Follow the majority." We observe, he points out, that the truly wise are a very small minority, and the higher a man is in knowledge and understanding, the smaller the number of those like him. Hence, he concludes, when a rabbinic judge sees that "the majority of the judges are minded to issue an incorrect legal judgment," he should not say: Since the majority so decides, I will concur; rather, he must express his own proper view.[28]

Manasseh also refuses to acknowledge the old dictum that no rabbinic court can nullify the decisions of an earlier court unless it be greater than its predecessor in numbers or in wisdom. He declares explicitly that the practical commandments are dependent on the temporal situation and on the court and judge of each generation.[29] The author of *Alfei Menasheh* repeats the admonition that one must not rely blindly on what others bid him do or fulfill the laws and customs automatically, only on the authority of the fact that such has been the previous custom.[30] One must remember

25. *Ibid.,* No. 124.
26. *Ibid.,* Nos. 129–130.
27. *Ibid.,* No. 166.
28. *Ibid.,* No. 125.
29. *Ibid.,* No. 129, folio 48.
30. *Ibid.* 144. See also *ibid.,* II, Chapter Thirty-Two: "From the time that the hands of those who are drawn after the custom and the commandment of men, without paying any attention to all of the act, whether it agrees with right and true common sense, have increased and grown."

that many of the "great codifiers and decisors" who were worthy of "teaching and deciding" also allowed themselves to be led astray by someone. "I can cite numerous examples of this," Manasseh adds.[31] One ought not to tremble so, he states elsewhere, before the tradition of the fathers and blindly imitate what was accepted among one's ancestors. We must take a lesson from the patriarch Abraham; he did not rely blindly on the tradition of his fathers but issued forth with axe in hand against the idols.[32]

At the end Manasseh proposes[33] that the great scholars of the day should convene and, with their authority, institute all the reforms in the life of the Jewish community which the time and conditions require.

The dreamer of Smorgon was sure that his work would be as highly venerated and loved by the reader as the Jewish prayerbook, but he was mistaken. His book was coldly received, and it provoked no such indignation as his *Pesher Davar* only because of the fact that it was written in a difficult and obscure language and mixed with novellae on the Torah and commentaries on various puzzling passages in the Babylonian Talmud.

When Manasseh of Ilya realized that his work had obtained a very limited circle of readers, he hit upon a new idea. He observed that in his time Hasidic literature in Yiddish had grown greatly. "In our generation, when books printed in Yiddish and made available to women and unlettered persons have multiplied," he notes in *Alfei Menasheh*,[34] he has arrived at a new decision: he, too, will address the Jewish masses in their own language, to explain to them "how human life ought to be alleviated and improved." And in order that his work might be easily distributed, he decided to issue it in printers' sheets (a sheet each week) in two parallel texts: *Samma De-Ḥayyei* in Hebrew and *Lebens-Mitl* in Yiddish. "The little which God has enlightened my eyes to understand in the world," he declares in the introduction to the first part, which appeared in 1823, "I now write down, so that all men may know it; and I write it in simple language, so that all, even common persons, may understand it."

In *Samma De-Ḥayyei* Manasseh also attempts to show the ordinary public how strictly the interests of the individual are bound up with those of the community. Everyone ought to be concerned about the general good, for his own happiness and welfare are indissolubly connected with it.

31. *Alfei Menasheh*, No. 145.
32. *Ibid.*, II, Chapter Thirty-Six.
33. *Ibid.*, I. No. 180.
34. *Ibid.*, No. 179.

Once again Manasseh was mistaken. His "simple language" was actually an overly difficult and aridly pedantic one.[35] He was certain that, because of the fact that he produced his work in single printers' sheets, "people would certainly read it through and would thirst for the coming sheets, and when they received them, these would be like cold water on a weary body." But his publication had very little success, and the first booklet was also the last. But Manasseh did not lose courage. In the same year (1823) that his *Samma De-Hayyei* was printed,[36] he published his tract *Shekel Ha-Kodesh*. Here he addresses only the Hebrew reader. The little brochure, however, was not composed in the cumbersome and pedantic rabbinic language of *Alfei Menasheh*, but in simpler and clearer fashion. The structure of the work is also significantly improved; it lacks the sea of extraneous speculations and subtle novellae on the Torah.

In simple words Manasseh notes the economic decline of Jewish life and endeavors to set forth the ultimate causes of the decay, for which the Jews themselves are responsible. He especially deplores the fact that parents are eager to marry off their children as early as possible and do not stop to consider that their young sons-in-law are not at all suited to lead an independent life, to support themselves and their families with their own hands. Thus, we see how miserable the young people are when they leave the arrangement whereby their in-laws provide them with food and lodging. Since they are not qualified for any productive work, all of them go into trade, which is mainly swindlery and robbery, and engage in insubstantial, non-dependable occupations that are a plague both for themselves and others.

Whereas, in *Alfei Menasheh*, Manasseh had concerned himself much with the problem of raising children and reforming the educational system in the elementary schools, in *Shekel Ha-Kodesh* he places on the agenda the battle against insubstantial ways of earning a living and the matter of preparing the young for productive labor. Parents must be concerned, above all, that their children be made ready from childhood on to become useful, contributing members of society.

The sharp tone in which *Shekel Ha-Kodesh* was written and the bitter truth expressed in it greatly irritated the public. Hence they

---

35. It is sufficient to present the beginning of the introduction: "Because, when one opens his eyes only a little bit, he sees that the usefulness of all of the limbs of a person, despite the fact that one knows—apparently—for what they are needed, but one must nevertheless find in them a higher use, as I shall, if God be willing, demonstrate when I come to the matter, and now I will write only what I need for my subject."

36. *Samma De-Hayyei*, which is a rarity, was reprinted by Zalman Rejzen in his *Fun Mendelssohn Biz Mendele*, 199–206.

decided to fight against the "heretical" brochure with the ancient, long-tried method of fire. *Shekel Ha-Kodesh* was burned in heaps, and this was done so thoroughly and systematically that Manasseh's little book is now extremely rare.[37]

Shekel Ha-Kodesh was the last work that Manasseh of Ilya published. The expenses incurred in printing his works entailed such hardship for him, and the results were so sad, that his numerous other writings remained in manuscript.[38] But the basic principle that the author had preached so frequently—that the individual is obliged to think about and be concerned for the general good—did not let him rest. Hence, in 1827 he gladly accepted the position of rabbi that was offered to him in his native town of Smorgon. He was certain that, as leader of the community and one of the "capable men," he would be able to accomplish much for the general good. But he was soon persuaded that here again he was grievously mistaken.

In that very year the notorious ukase concerning Jewish recruits for the Russian army was issued. Associated with this ukase is one of the most melancholy and shameful pages in the history of the Jewish *kahal*, or community council. Now began the nightmarish epic of the *khapers* (kidnappers) and the "gang of city benefactors" with their terrible, bloody deeds. Manasseh could not bear this, and from the pulpit endeavored to expose the vile deeds crying to the heavens and contended that the base men who committed them should be excommunicated from the congregation of Jewry. But friends and acquaintances explained to him that such sermons may not be delivered publicly, since they smack of "sedition" and touch upon the czar's ukase. The dreamer realized how seriously mistaken he had been and how powerless he was to battle for the general good, and at once resigned from the rabbinate (1829).[39]

Two years later a cholera epidemic broke out. Among its numerous victims were, as we have already noted, the *maskilim* Samuel Jacob Bick and Jehudah Miesis. The epidemic also made an end of Manasseh's sorrowful life-path. In July, 1831, in the sixty-fourth year of his life, he died.

This last of the Haskalah pioneers of the nineteenth century ended his life solitary and forgotten. However, at the same time that Manasseh, after the failure of his *Shekel Ha-Kodesh*, gave up the

37. We have employed the autograph copy which was found in the library in Leningrad of the Society for the Promotion of Culture and Enlightenment among Jews, bound together with several manuscripts of Manasseh's that have been preserved.
38. In the home of Manasseh's grandson, Abraham Blitstein, a large chest filled with his grandfather's manuscripts was kept. During a great fire in 1884 all these manuscripts were burned (*Alfei Menasheh*, II, 1904, 13.)
39. See *Alfei Menasheh*, II, 1904, 10.

struggle and no longer made any attempt to appear in public, a younger representative of the new generation issued forth on the field of battle. He became, for several decades, the standard-bearer of the Haskalah movement in Russia. His battle was of a different character, and in it he sought support in spheres of which Manasseh of Ilya had never dreamed. This battler was named Isaac Baer Levinsohn, and he lived and fought not in Lithuania but in Volhynia.

The Haskalah movement in southern Russia is closely associated with the Haskalah of Galicia. The influence was a twofold one. Not only did the pioneers of enlightenment in the southwestern provinces of the erstwhile land of the czars draw their intellectual nourishment from the Galician centers of Haskalah, but the Russian government, in its plans for "enlightment" and projects for reform in regard to the Jewish populace, also faithfully copied the "edicts" and decrees that Joseph II and his successors bestowed on the Jewish community in Galicia.

We noted previously that Brody was closely connected with southern Russia through its commercial enterprises. Merchants from Brody would come to Odessa and other centers and bring with them not only material merchandise but intellectual and spiritual goods as well. "Wherever a Brody merchant would come," Gottlober relates in his memoirs,

he would captivate the young with his eloquent speech; their eyes would be opened and they would realize that they were stark naked and void of all culture and knowledge, and they would betake themselves to education. In this respect the merchant of Brody was for them a guide and leader. Because of this, the Hasidim could not bear the Jews of Brody, and the rabbi of Apt cursed them with bitter anathemas and declared that they brought heresy into Russia.[40]

Outside of Odessa, of which we have spoken in the previous volume,[41] the enlightened merchants of Brody also exercised their intellectual influence on the larger centers of the Kiev region, in which there were many wealthy Jewish lessees and large-scale merchants who used to export the products of the enormous farm and forest estates of the Polish magnates and nobles in that area.

40. A. Fridkin, *Avrohom Ber Gottlober Un Zayn Epokhe*, 84. See also Gottlober's travel account ("Michtav-Massa") in *Ha-Maggid*, 1874, No. 25, p. 222: "In every place where the Jews of Brody landed, the Jews there had light and enlightenment, and their eyes were opened to see that the preeminence of man lies only in wisdom and knowledge. I know many towns in my land where in the beginning it was pitch dark, and one enlightened man came from Brody and established his residence among them and it was not many days before numerous persons came to his light, began to teach their children language and books, and there was relief and comfort."

41. Pp. 000–000.

Russian Jews in the Textile Industry

The court lady Smirnova-Rosset of the era of Nicholas I describes in her well-known memoirs[42] how, at the end of the second decade of the nineteenth century, people would come together in Kiev from the whole region for "contracts." There, she relates, one could find all the higher Polish nobility. The Polish noblemen would hand over their estates to Jews on lease contracts and in this way dissipate their fortunes. With the frivolity so characteristic of them, they would sing the little song:

> Jak przyjechal do Zlotonosz
> Tak do Zyda w arende.

Jews of the western region of Russia also played a considerable part in the emergence of the factory industry which occurred at just that time. They were especially conspicuous in the textile industry which then began to develop in Russia for military reasons, chiefly the demand for providing the army with the necessary amount of domestically fabricated cloth. The province of Volhynia became the largest center of the textile industry among Jews in the western region. At the end of the 1820s there were already in Volhynia scores of Jewish-owned cloth factories. In 1828 the Volhynian merchant Yosel Bernstein owned seventeen cloth factories, and in 1832, twenty. After Prince Sangushko, Bernstein was the most important manufacturer of cloth in all of the Ukraine.[43]

At that time, the city of Berdichev especially burgeoned as a commercial center.[44] Prince I.M. Dolgoruki relates in his travel account of 1810: "I wanted very much to run down (from Uman) to Berdichev, a city renowned throughout the region for its fair, its great church, and its trade. If a young man has completed his education but has not visited Berdichev, he loses one hundred percent in the larger world."[45] Smaller towns in Volhynia also were under the strong influence of the *maskilim* of Brody. Interesting in this respect is the following passage from Gottlober's memoirs about Dubno in the 1820s:

Dubno is not far from Galicia, from Brody, and it was thence that the sun of Haskalah shone upon me. At that time, even before the morningstar rose over our land, some Galician Jews who could not settle in their

42. A.O. Simirnova–Rosset, *Avtobiografiya*, 1931, 153.
43. See A. Yuditzki, *Yidishe Burzshvazye Un Yidisher Proletariat*, 29–37; S. Borovoi, in his Russian work on Jewish colonization, 125.
44. For the figures and statistics on the powerful growth of Berdichev in the first half of the nineteenth century, see Jacob Lestschinsky's article in *Bleter Far Yidishe Demografye . . .*, 1923, No. 2, 37–48.
45. I.M. Dolgoruki, *Slavnï bubnï za gorami*, 252.

country with the knowledge they had there obtained, came to Dubno and became Jewish teachers. For this reason the first thing that the Jewish children of Dubno began to study was German, and the works of Schiller and Goethe were extremely popular in Dubno. To it all those who suffered for the sake of Haskalah began to come from all the benighted little towns.[46]

Characteristic of the influence of the Galician *maskilim* in the southwestern region is the following point. As early as the 1820s the first two attempts were made to establish model Jewish schools following the pattern of Joseph Perl's academy in Tarnopol. Heading both schools were Galician *maskilim*, Meir Horn of Brody, and Joseph Perl's friend and admirer, Bezalel Stern of Tarnopol. The first of the two model schools was established in 1822 in Uman by the *maskil* Hirsch Baer Hurwitz,[47] son of the wealthy merchant Chaim Ḥaykl Hurwitz (author of *Tzofnas Pane'akh*).[48]

Ḥaykl Hurwitz provided his son with a European education. Hirsch Baer spoke and wrote Russian, German, and French fluently. Because of his father's extensive commercial interests, the young man had occasion to make frequent journeys to Leipzig and there had opportunity to become closely acquainted with the Berlin Haskalah. Thanks to Dolgoruki's abovementioned travel account, we have a relatively clear picture of the young Hurwitz's world-outlook. Prince Dolgoruki spent some time in Hurwitz's house and used to spend entire evenings with this young Jew of European education. He even wrote down one of his conversations with him verbatim and included it in his travel account.[49] This conversation between the young Jewish *maskil* and the Russian prince is an interesting *document humain* in which the ideals and yearnings of the first *maskilim* in Russia are presented quite openly and without fear of the environment.

Dolgoruki stresses that, through his conversations with the young Hurwitz, he became convinced that the latter "loves his people ardently, defends their interests passionately, and is prepared to sacrifice himself for the welfare of his brethren." But when we study the content of the conversation Hurwitz carried on with the Russian prince in French, two characteristic details which sharply distinguish the *maskilim* who were raised on the Berlin

46. A. Fridkin, *Avrohom Ber Gottlober Un Zayn Epokhe*, 218.
47. Born in 1785, died in Cambridge in 1857.
48. See our *History*, Vol. IX, pp. 225ff. The following characteristic detail is worth noting. Shortly after the opening of the new school, one of its pupils was drowned. Following the initiative of the teacher and director of the school Horn, the friends of the dead student composed a dirge according to the pattern of a poem by Schiller and sent it to the editors of *Bikkurei Ha-Ittim*. Part of this very long elegy is printed in the second volume of the journal.
49. I.M. Dolgoruki, *Slavnï bubnï za gorami, pp.* 222–23.

Haskalah from the pioneers of Haskalah in the nineteenth century become very obvious.

Manasseh of Ilya, for instance, upon reading the text of the Statute of 1804, in which the Russian government takes measures to liberate the Jews from their "prejudices" and "wild superstition," at once wrote a special composition in which he attempted to show the government that it was mistaken, that Jews are no more barbarized and ignorant than other peoples.[50] In Hurwitz, however, we already encounter the strong faith, so characteristic of the Berlin *maskilim,* in the "enlightened absolutism" with the aid of which alone Jews will be able to free themselves from their "superstition" and enjoy the illumination of "enlightenment" and culture. Like the *Aufklärer* of Berlin, Hurwitz is distinguished by his profound hatred for the Talmud, in which he sees the chief cause of Jewish intellectual barbarization. To Dolgoruki's question, "What do you lack that keeps you from feeling happy?," Hurwitz replies:

I would wish that we might, first of all, be forbidden to wear our scandalous costume, for this dress places upon us the mark of shame and contempt. One who is despised loses his feeling of self-respect. It is for this reason that our people is now so contemptible, foolish, and ignorant. Whoever sees me now in my long frock coat at once wags his finger at me and says, "This is a Jew!" But I feel myself so human that I cannot be indifferent to such unmerited contempt, which bars for me entrance to the larger world. .

"Why, then," Dolgoruki asks Hurwitz, "do you not change your dress?" To which the latter replies that he has a very pious old mother whom he does not wish to grieve. But if a ukase were issued on the subject, "no one would be so eager to obey the ukase as I."

Later on Hurwitz expresses his firm conviction that "sooner or later they [the Jews] will have to be made happy by force" (*nasilno oschastlivit*). Like Aaron Wolfsohn-Halle in his day, so Hurwitz expresses his great delight with the ethics of the New Testament.

The morality of the evangelists is the best system of ethics in the world. I wish to acquaint my brethren with it; I desire that they read it. We may or may not believe in the Gospel, but to profit from what is noble is so pleasant. It is time now to burn our Talmud which represents a book filled with stupidities that corrupt the Torah of Moses. Let them leave us only the Five Books of Moses in their original appearance; their laws and ordinances are the most suitable for us.

50. *Ben Porat,* 73–74.

"Why," he argues further, "should not all absurdities be destroyed? The Jewish people will not have the courage to set itself against this. All these follies and stupidities are bound together like links of a chain. Destroy the first link—I mean the Talmud—and all the other follies will disappear of themselves. And only in this way will the fetters of our foolish prejudices, which bring us so much misfortune, be set aside."

From the cultural-historical point of view, it is interesting to compare these words of the young Jewish *maskil*[51] with the ideas that the chief inspector of the Vilna district, Prince A. Chartoriski, expressed seven years later in regard to the Jewish question:

Coming closer to the Christians, they [the Jews] would be able to free themselves from superstition, forget their avarice, raise themselves to the proper level, and assume the morality of the Christian religion, which is opposed to all egotism. Only then would their true education begin, for under present conditions of society, no culture and education can be conceived for any European people other than Christian morality and on the foundation of Christianity, to which the enlightened peoples are indebted for their progress.[52]

These ideas of the Russian official are not, we note, greatly inconsistent with the point of view of the first Jewish "enlighteners" who were raised on the Berlin Haskalah. And indeed, these men—the Franks, the Hurwitzes, and others like them—undoubtedly had a certain part in the "enlightenment" policy of the Russian government in regard to the Jews in the era of Nicholas I.

This must be taken into consideration if one wishes to have an objective understanding of the literary and social activity of Isaac Baer Levinsohn.

51. In 1825, several years after his father's death, Hirsch Baer Hurwitz went bankrupt and had to flee from Russia. After long sojournings, he settled in England and eventually, under the name of Herman Berman, became a lecturer in Hebrew language at Cambridge University.
52. J.I. Hessen in *Dos Lebn*, 1906, 86; Zinberg, *Istoriya yevreyskoi pechati*, 12.

CHAPTER TWO

Isaac Baer Levinsohn

[Isaac Baer Levinsohn's childhood and youth—His patriotic anthem—Levinsohn's years of study in Galicia—His anti-Hasidic satires—*Te'udah Be-Yisrael* and its significance—The sources of the exaggerated patriotism of the bearers of Haskalah—*Te'udah Be-Yisrael* and the *maskilim*—The *maskilim* of Vilna and their projected *Minḥat Bikkurim*—"Men of the previous century"—Levinsohn's program of reform—*Bet Yehudah* and its "adventures"—Veiled allusions to civic rights.]

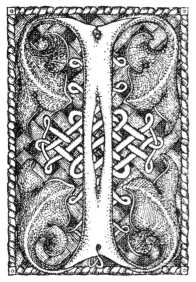 SAAC BAER Levinsohn was born September 2, 1788, in Kremenets, Volhynia into a well-to-do, prominent family.[1] His father Jehudah Levin, who carried on extensive business with the Polish landowners, knew Polish quite well. He was also reputed to be a grammarian and "linguist," and would not only frequently study a page of the *Gemara* but also refresh himself with the mighty, polished rhetoric of the Hebrew prophets. While still a child the young Levinsohn acquired renown for his brilliant capacities. At the age of nine he wrote a complete essay on Kabbalah. The proud father showed his child's composition to the scholars of his city who were delighted with it.[2] Levinsohn especially distinguished himself with his extraordinary power of recollection. Every book that he ever read remained inscribed in his memory, and even in later years he

---

1. Levinsohn himself in his old age mentions in one of his letters: "For from my youth on I was raised in delight and tenderness like one of the wealthy, and I had everything that my eyes asked for" (*Sefer Ha-Zichronot*, 109). There is still no exhaustive monograph on this important battler for Haskalah. The most significant works are B. Nathanson, *Sefer Ha-Zichronot*, and I. Zinberg's Russian work, "Isaac Baer Levinsohn and His Time," in *Yevreyskaya Starina*, 1910.
2. See *Bet Yehudah*, 343.

mentions with great self-satisfaction the "remarkable power of recollection with which God has blessed me."[3]

Thanks to his father the "linguist," Levinsohn at the age of ten was already quite proficient in the whole of the Hebrew Bible. His father was also concerned that his son should study the language of the country, not so much Polish as Russian itself.

This is a characteristic feature of definite cultural-historical significance. Volhynia had then just come under Russian dominion. Jehudah Levin and his family retained extremely tragic memories of persecutions and oppressions by the Polish *szlachta*, or nobility, which assumed literally pathological forms in the years of the Polish kingdom's death-agonies. Jehudah Levin's brother Hayyim, a wealthy merchant, carried on business with a Polish landowner who owed him a substantial sum of money. In order to rid himself of his creditor, the landowner instituted judicial proceedings against Levin on a blood-libel, and the innocent defendant languished in prison for all of twelve years.

Levinsohn's father also remembered throughout his life his encounter with a Polish count. He once rode in his little cart through a narrow street, when a carriage bearing a Polish count was coming the opposite way. The street was too narrow, and Levin's Christian servant who led the horse and cart was not very skilled, with the result that the little cart struck the carriage. The terrified servant immediately fled, and Levin remained sitting in the cart. The count, maddened with fury that a Jewish droshky should strike his carriage, at once fell upon the unfortunate Levin and battered him so furiously with a stick that he remained a cripple throughout his life.[4] Hence, it is not surprising that a Jew such as Levin and others like him regarded the new Russian government as a powerful restraint capable of holding in check, through fear, the debauched and degenerate *szlachta*. From this derives the ardent Russian patriotism of the young Levinsohn which, as we shall see further on, grew significantly as time passed.

Of Levinsohn's youth we have very few details. We know only that while still a young man he wrote numerous poems. A love poem of his, written in 1804, in which the sixteen-year old poet addresses his beloved with the following reproach has been preserved: "When one wounds another, the latter hates him and considers him his enemy. You, my lovely one, have wounded my heart, but how can I hate you? And even if you should double the

---

3. See the introduction to *Eshkol Ha-Sofer.*
4. *Sefer Ha-Zichronot*, 5.

wounds, my love for you will grow even stronger."[5] When he reached the age of eighteen, Levinsohn's parents married him off, and he moved to Radziwill. The match, however, was not a successful one. Levinsohn became displeased with his wife, and after their only child died she became even more repugnant to him. The offended woman, out of desire for revenge, attempted to poison him. Fortunately, Levinsohn survived and immediately afterwards divorced his wife. At this time his parents became impoverished, and Levinsohn earned a living through giving lessons.

At the time of the Napoleonic war Levinsohn carried through some translation activities on the Austrian border and celebrated the definitive triumph over the French in a poem of praise entitled "Kol Anot Gevurah." The commandant of Radziwill, Giers, who was personally acquainted with Levinsohn, sent this poem to the minister of the interior as evidence of the patriotism of the Jews.

Levinsohn occupied himself with self-education in extremely diligent fashion. Day and night, tirelessly, he gathered information and knowledge from the most varied branches of science. His youthful physical constitution, however, could not endure such overly strenuous mental effort, and he was stricken with a severe nervous disease. He thereupon decided to travel for a cure to Brody, which was on the other side of the border, eight versts from Radziwill. But the young man decided to go to Galicia not merely because of the doctors of Brody; he was also attracted to it because it was an important cultural center where he might be able to obtain the requisite armor to battle for light and enlightenment. The years he spent in Galicia constitute, in fact, one of the most important stages in his life.

Shortly after his arrival in Brody, Levinsohn became acquainted with the circle of *maskilim* there, and made friends with the aged Mendel Levin (or Lefin), Samuel Jacob Bick, Isaac Erter, and Berish Blumenfeld. To earn a living, he at first served as a bookkeeper in a commercial establishment and later passed the teacher's examination at the Tarnopol school. There he became acquainted with Joseph Perl and, thanks to the latter's patronage, obtained a position as a teacher of the Hebrew language in the newly

---

5. Throughout his life Levinsohn eagerly wrote poems, and his translations of Schiller ("Der Täucher" [The Diver] and others) which he wrote in his old age have been preserved. However, he himself noted that he absolutely lacked poetic talent (see his preface to *Eshkol Ha-Sofer*). In another place (*Bet Yehudah*, 366) he complains strongly of the fact that virtually every *maskil* who had studied just a bit of grammar already scribbles poems, and none of them is willing to understand that everyone can write rhymed lines but that, of genuine poets, there is barely one in a whole country.

established *Realschule* in Brody. At the same time he published his first work, a Yiddish translation of the tax schedule, *Luah Ha-Meches*.[6]

This work was published by Levinsohn in Zolkiew, where he became acquainted with Nahman Krochmal. Krochmal made an enormous impression on him both as a personality and as a thinker. He remained for Levinsohn, to the end of his life, "my friend, the delight of my soul, my master, and the lifter up of my head."[7] Many years later, Levinsohn recalled with enchantment: "The months I spent in Zolkiew are more precious to me than anything in the world." In Krochmal he saw the teacher and guide of his generation. "From the crumbs that fell from Krochmal's literary table," he declares, "many *maskilim* of our time wrote entire books."[8]

Levinsohn showed Krochmal his first scholarly work, *Ha-Mazkir*, a collection of learned articles on philology and history.[9] Krochmal was pleased with the work, and was even prepared to contribute financial assistance for its publication. For reasons that are unknown, *Ha-Mazkir* remained in manuscript.[10] Also unpublished is Levinsohn's textbook of the Russian language, *Yesodei Leshon Russiyah*,[11] which he composed in 1820 "for the benefit of the young." His satire *Divrei Tzaddikim*,[12] written in the same year, had better luck. *Divrei Tzaddikim* is a kind of epilogue to *Megalleh Temirin* which had just appeared. Three Hasidim, Reb Yekel Hanipoler, Reb Elijah Sokulipker, and Reb Leib Kremenetser cudgel their brains in an attempt to figure out in their letters who the author of *Megalleh Temirin*, the pseudonymous Obadiah ben Petahiah, can be. Kremenetser reports in his letter, word for word, a long conversation on this subject between two Hasidim which he overheard in a Hasidic prayer-house in Olik. These Hasidim arrived at the conclusion that *Megalleh Temirin* was undoubtedly written by one of the great *tzaddikim*, for in the book the profoundest mysteries are concealed. Levinsohn attempts in this connection to present in very witty fashion the way Kremenetser translates into Hebrew the unique Yiddish conversation of the two Hasidim of Olik. He deliberately reports this conversation in

6. This edition has not been preserved.
7. See his letter of 1851 to S.J. Fuenn (*Yalkut Ribal*, 76).
8. *Tziyyun Le-Nefesh RaNaK*, 61.
9. See *Bet Yehudah*, Chapter 118, 287.
10. Levinsohn later used only a few fragments of *Ha-Mazkir* in his *Te'udah Be-Yisrael* and *Bet Yehudah*.
11. *Sefer Ha-Zichronot*, 7; *Te'udah Be-Yisrael*, Gate Two, Chapter 4.
12. At first this work was entitled *Megalleh Sod* (for a discussion of this, see Perl's letter to Levinsohn, *Be'er Yitzhak*, 11, 39–40).

caricatured form. The speech of the Hasidim is given in expressions such as the following: "So should you know to say of your life as you know," "The rest you will knock up against yourself;" "How am I responsible for the fact that you have no eyes?"; "Probably, when I give advice, it is not wrong;" etc.

Levinsohn transmitted his satire to Perl who, after much difficulty,[13] published it in Vienna in 1830, along with another anti-Hasidic tract by Levinsohn entitled *Emek Refa'im*. This tract has a certain affinity with Isaac Erter's *Gilgul Nefesh*. One must take into consideration, however, that Levinsohn's work was written considerably before Erter's renowned satire. Through the power of hypnotism (which at that time was known as mesmerism, or magnetism), the soul of a miracle-working *guter Yid*, or Hasidic *rebbe*, that is already in the "other world" and is being judged in the lowest level of hell relates everything that transpired with it in its sinful life. Like Erter, Levinsohn is not chary in employing black colors to portray the way of life of the miracle-working *rebbe*.[14] The latter is a scoundrel—a terrible ignoramus, a base swindler, a guzzler, a glutton, an avaricious liar who robs the people and with utmost cruelty persecutes everyone who thirsts after knowledge. As in Erter's satire, so also in *Emek Refa'im* the social element, the protest against the oppression of the masses of the people, resounds powerfully.

One characteristic feature, however, is worth noting: Erter the purist, the "watchman of the House of Israel," endeavors to write in a purely Biblical style, polishing every word, but Levinsohn deems it necessary to rework his satire into Yiddish in order to make it available to the masses.[15] It is a bit reminiscent of the style of Grandfather Mendele (Mendele Mocher Seforim) when the bloodsucker, the miracle-worker, tells his son:

You should not regard the preachers who admonish the tax-collectors and the city councilors and the like, the other officials and the rich men, that they should not rob the poor people, not place upon them various tax arrears from which the men of wealth themselves are free. Their sermons in general consist only in admonitions not to pursue wealth and power,

13. *Be'er Yitzhak* 39, 40.
14. In Levinsohn the colors are even thicker, but the power of portrayal is less artistic than in Erter.
15. It forms the second part of *Di Hefker-Velt*. Zalman Rejzen in his book *Fun Mendelssohn Biz Mendele*, p. 250, poses the question: "Did the author himself rework this into Yiddish, or did his publisher do it?" That Levinsohn himself reworked his *Emek Refa'im* into Yiddish is clear not only from the pithy Volhynian language (so strongly distinguished from Nathanson's Judeo-German) in which the work is written, but also from the brief introduction, where it is noted explicitly: "It is said that this composition has a completely different title and is written in the language of the Hasidim, but the author is the same" (*Di Hefker-Velt*, 41).

whereas the majority of the people are very enamored of these things. You, my son, should, however, avoid this way. Let such sermons not be heard from you if you wish to be liked and to have people favorably disposed toward you. On the contrary, you should always yield to, and side with, the powerful men of the city. You should accord honor to the rich, and you should also honor the officials, the councilors, and the presidents of the community, the *otdatshikes* who deliver recruits, the farmers of the religious taxes, general tax-farmers,[16] and the like; you should always be a seeker of peace with these and desire only their good. You should also not remove yourself from the agents and brokers; you should be close to them, for through them you will secure your position, accumulate much money, enjoy high honor, and grow ever stronger and greater.[17]

But Levinsohn was unwilling to content himself merely with mockery and satire. During the years he spent in the Galician centers of Haskalah his decision to return to his home and there devote all his powers and knowledge to "the general good," to a struggle, carried on according to a systematically worked-out program, for the material and intellectual renewal of Jewish life in Russia, matured. In 1820, the year that he wrote his satire *Divrei Tzaddikim*, he left Galicia[18] and returned to his native town of Kremenets.

16. In the Hebrew text, among the list of the "powerful men" are also mentioned *kvartirne komisaren* (billeting commissars) (*Yalkut Ribal*, 127). Also further on (*ibid.*, 137) there is a discussion of one who is "appointed to be *kvartirne komisye*."

17. *Di Hefker-Velt*, 1896, 49. In 1904 Ephraim Deinard published a third satire of Levinsohn's entitled *Megillah Efah* which was preserved among Levinsohn's manuscripts. The literary historian F. Lachover (*Toledot Ha-Safrut Ha-Ivrit Ha-Hadashah*, II, 84) expresses his doubts that Levinsohn was really the author of this satire. In fact *Megillah Efah* does not derive from Levinsohn's pen, and A.B. Gottlober even gives precisely in his memoirs (*Ha-Boker Or*, 1879, 782) the name of its author. This was Levinsohn's relative Solomon Isaiah Landsberg of Kremenets. "In 1827," Gottlober relates, "Landsberg, who then lived in Korets, composed a satire *Megillah Efah* against the *gute Yidn* and the false leaders. To my knowledge, this was the first satire with which a Jew dared openly to issue forth against these deceivers . . . Many copies of it were made and it was read publicly in the streets in many towns. However, it was not printed and eventually it was lost." Gottlober, however, was mistaken Levinsohn, apparently, provided himself with a copy of Landsberg's satire, and consequently it was preserved and appeared in print.

18. Regarding the date of Levinsohn's return from Galicia there is a bit of confusion among his biographers. B. Nathanson indicates (*Sefer Ha-Zichronot*, 7) that Levinsohn is supposed to have returned to Kremenets in 1817, and according to F. Alabin (*Russkaya Starina*, 1878, V) this happened only in 1823. It is easy to persuade oneself that Nathanson's assertion is incorrect from the following points: (1) under Levinsohn's article "Shem Ha-Mispar" (*Bet Ha-Otzar*, 191–195) is noted the following date: "the first day of Nissan 5579, here in Brody;" (2) M. Letteris notes in his *Zikkaron Ba-Sefer:* "In 1819 I traveled to Brody because my friends Erter, Isaac Baer Levinsohn, and others wanted to visit with me;" and (3) it is known that in 1820 Levinsohn reprinted in Lemberg Tropplowitz's drama *Meluchat Sha'ul*. In the same year Levinsohn sat for examinations in the Tarnopol *Israelitischer Hauptschule* and obtained from

His Attack on the Community Leaders

After the years Levinsohn had spent in the commercial city of Brody in the milieu of a large circle of *maskilim*, his native town made a very unpleasant and painful impression on him. Kremenets was isolated, hidden among the mountains, and had very little connection with the outside world. Its commerce was quite limited and the populace was terribly impoverished. The few wealthy people in the city were mostly money-lenders, general agents for the government administration (*nachalstvo*). They were the powerful men, the leaders of the town, and ruthlessly oppressed the poor masses. One of these "leaders" was portrayed by Levinsohn many years later in his incisive double tract, *Toledot Peloni Almoni Ha-Kozevi* and *Masechet Oto Ve-Et Beno* and in his venomous satire *Purim-Shpil Oysgerufn In Shul*, which he apparently composed on first hearing the news that the *kahal* organization had been abolished (1843):

> The good times are ending
> When I used to ride on the community—
> They ate with spoons,
> And I with bushels.
>
> . . . .
>
> *Kahal* will also soon disappear,
> And my income will cease completely;
> I will remain without money,
> Be looked on as a clown by the world . . .

In this backward environment the most extreme tzaddikism, with its virulent hatred for everything that might bring light and knowledge, ruled without restraint. "I live," Levinsohn laments,

in a benighted, obscurantist town. One sees there no new people. There are no writers, no books; there is no one to report the events that occur in the world. No one reads books, no one is interested in newspapers. I hear around me every day the cry of the poor who are, unfortunately, robbed by those who rule over the people, our Jewish leaders and commanders. There comes to me also the great clamor of the besotted Hasidim, who dance over the streets in hordes, sing out loud, and bring into the city new *rebbes* who ride in coaches. This one comes, and another departs. The ardent Hasidim guzzle liquor and shout "Holy!"[19]

Shortly after returning to Kremenets where his father and sister

there a "certificate" attesting that "he is proficient in all branches of Hebrew, Talmudic, and Syriac literature" (see *YIVO-Bleter*, IV, 82). That Levinsohn left Brody in 1820—not, as Alabin asserts, in 1823—is clear from his statement in his article about the Jewish schools which he wrote in 1857: "It is now thirty-seven years since I left Brody." In 1823 Levinsohn visited Brody only for a short time. Of this we have an indication by Levinsohn in *Yalkut Ribal*, 49.

19. *Yalkut Ribal*, 72, 75; *Sefer Ha-Zichronot*, II. See also the preface to *Bet Yehudah*, XXIII.

lived (his mother had died several years previously) Levinsohn began to write his first important work, *Te'udah Be-Yisrael*.[20] He refused, however, to be content with purely literary activity. With youthful energy he took part in the social life of the community and propagandized among the young for education and science.[21] This produced many enemies for him among the communal leaders. The local Hasidim got wind of the fact that Levinsohn was writing a book full of heresy and began to persecute him. His native town became repugnant to him, and he moved to the large commercial city of Berdichev, where he soon obtained a position as teacher in the wealthy home of Anton Rubinstein's grandfather. There also he devoted himself to social activity and attempted to organize a circle of *maskilim*. But he refused to remain for a long time in any one place, desiring to spread his propaganda activity to other centers as well. From Berdichev Levinsohn went to Ostrog, where he found a position as teacher in the house of the wealthy timber merchant Zussman. From there he moved again to Nemirov, and then to Tulchin.[22] It was at this time that he completed *Te'udah Be-Yisrael*[23] and issued a "proclamation" in which he announced that his work would appear in 1823.

The intensive, strenuous labors of the previous years, however, were beyond the capacities of Levinsohn's weak constitution. Worn out, he returned to Kremenets to his own family. There he again fell victim to his previous nervous disease, which this time did not leave him for twelve whole years. Even afterwards, when the sickness was over, Levinsohn remained throughout his life a "broken vessel." Weak and emaciated, he would not for years pass the threshold of his little house located at the very edge of the town.[24] His physical sufferings, however, did not diminish his interest in social problems and his great thirst for knowledge. In this connection the large scholarly library of the Polish historian Tadeusz Czacki,[25] which was located in the lyceum of Kremenets, was of great use to him.

With tireless diligence Levinsohn, despite his illness, studied

20. That Levinsohn was already writing his *Te'udah Be-Yisrael* in 1821 is noted by the author himself in a letter of his of 1843 to Jacob Reifmann: "It is now twenty-two years since I wrote this book of mine *Te'udah Be-Yisrael (Be'er Yitzhak*, 97).
21. This period of Levinsohn's life is recounted many years later with great enthusiasm by his friend, the *maskil* of Kremenets, Leon Landsberg (see I. Zinberg, *Isaak Ber Levinzon* [Russian], 1910, 22–23).
22. See *Bet Yehudah*, 327.
23. Levinsohn finished *Te'udah Be-Yisrael* in 1822 (see *Be'er Yitzhak*, 12).
24. In 1848 Levinsohn wrote to his friend Reuben Kulisher: "It is now twenty-five years that I have not stepped across the threshold of my house and lie most of the time in bed" (see also his letter to Zeiberling in *Sefer Ha-Zichronot*, 109).
25. Alabin and, basing himself on him, Nathanson assert that Levinsohn was on friendly

Arabic, Syriac, Aramaic, and Latin. He also devoted himself extensively to the Greek classics and to European philosophical and theological literature. But he considered his self-education simply a means to his life-goal: to reform Jewish life, to renew its material and spiritual foundations. Levinsohn appreciated quite well the great difficulties that lay before him. Of these he had already become persuaded at the time of publishing his *Te'udah Be-Yisrael.* In his original "proclamation" he announced, as we noted, that his work would appear in 1823. But five whole years later his work was still in manuscript, and the reason for this was not merely the author's material poverty.[26]

The major cause was the fact that the pious printers refused to publish such a heretical work with their "kosher" hands. At that time, a considerable number of Jewish presses functioned in Volhynia—in Berdichev, Slavuta, Ostrog, Zaslav, Sudylkow, Polonnoye, Korets, Belaya Tserkov, etc.—and not one of them was willing to print *Te'udah Be-Yisrael.* Levinsohn understood quite well that through propaganda activity alone it would not be possible to realize the necessary reforms in Jewish life. In this respect, he was considerably more practical and "this-worldly" than Manasseh of Ilya. He realized that the *maskilim* were too weak and too few in number to be able to effectuate their program of reform with their own powers. It was self-evident to him that one must turn to the external power, to the "enlightened" government authorities. Here we encounter a very interesting and, from the cultural-historical point of view, extremely important consideration in the entire Haskalah movement.

We noted above the reasons why the young Levinsohn, in whose family the memory of the persecutions and oppressions inflicted by the degenerate and debauched Polish *szlachta* were fresh, was so patriotically inclined toward the new Russian government. When Levinsohn was sixteen years old, the famous "Principles Concerning the Jews" of 1804 were published by the authorities. Chief among these were the points "about education" (*o prosvestchenie*) that were set forth in such liberal and humanitarian-sounding phrases. It was proclaimed that all Jewish children are to be accepted and educated, without any distinction from other youngsters, in all Russian schools, gymnasia, and universities. There was also an admonition that "no Jewish child, while being educated in school,

---

terms with Czacki himself, and the latter is supposed to have greatly esteemed the Jewish scholar. This, however, is not correct, since Czacki died in 1813.

26. On Levinsohn's intercession, which had no results, with the Warsaw Committee for Jews (*Komitet Starozakonnych*) about providing the necessary costs of printing, see *YIVO-Bleter*, IV, 81–82.

may be in any way removed from his religion and compelled to learn what is inconsistent with his religion." And if the Jews will not eagerly send their children to the general schools, then, according to the "Principles," special schools should be established for them in which, besides other studies, the children are to learn one of three languages—Russian, Polish, or German. To be sure, these points about education are followed by some extremely harsh decrees, among them one concerning the expulsion of all Jews from the villages in the western region. The statutes on education, in fact, remained on paper,[27] but the banishment from the villages, especially from those within an area of fifty versts from the border, was carried through with relentless cruelty. Even such a patriotic Russian historian as Prince N. Golitzin, when dealing with the situation of the Jews under Alexander I's regime, must confess: "One cannot deny that during that time the Jews suffered a great deal, and Jewish tears were shed."[28]

Levinsohn himself had opportunity to see the catastrophe through which the village Jews lived, for in 1816 the decree was applied to the Volhynia region; there, too, the Jews were driven out of the villages. Men, however, see only what they wish to see. As we shall note later, Levinsohn does, in fact, touch upon this point in his *Te'udah Be-Yisrael;* nevertheless, it does not weaken his faith in the "kindness" of the "enlightened" government and its high officials. He *had* to believe in this, for the government was his only hope, the only support in his struggle for a new way of life for Jews. Levinsohn believed firmly in the power of the idea, of common sense. Hence, he had no doubt that it sufficed merely to "enlighten" the government, to make it understand through logical arguments what is required to fulfill the spiritual and material needs of the Jewish populace, for it at once to fulfill these needs, for—after all—its concern is for the "general good."[29]

Shortly after Levinsohn completed his *Te'udah Be-Yisrael* he composed a lengthy "proposal" about the establishment of Jewish schools and seminaries, and sent it to the then heir to the throne, Konstantin Pavlovich. To the "proposal" he added a historical overview regarding the Jewish sects of former ages up until modern times. In this connection, an interesting point must be noted: Levinsohn did, indeed, compose a textbook on the elements of the Russian language; nonetheless, he did not feel sufficiently familiar

27. For a discussion of this, see S. Ginsburg's introduction to *Kazyönnoye yevr. uchilitscha,* 1920, XII–XVII.

28. See N. Golitzin, *Istoriya russk. zakondatelstva o yevreyakh,* 903.

29. "I know," Levinsohn writes to the *maskil* of Vilna Isaac Benjacob, "that the government seeks only our good and our peace." Such quotations can be produced in large number from Levinsohn's correspondence.

with the language, and all the proposals and petitions he dispatched to the government were written in German, a language of which he had a quite adequate command. The proposal he sent to Konstantin is also written in German. However, it had no practical result, for Konstantin Pavlovich at that time had already decided to renounce the throne and not concern himself with government matters. Despite the fact that his first work was still in manuscript, the sickly Levinsohn undertook another work of greater compass, *Bet Yehudah*, and only when this work was completed (1828) did he finally manage, with the aid of several friends, to publish his *Te'udah Be-Yisrael*—not in Volhynia, however, but in Vilna.

"My youthful friends of old, whom I have not seen for a long time, honorable men who hate falsehood and deception," Levinsohn declares in the introduction,

addressed me in writing with the request that I point out to them the right way of life, explain to them what studies, aside from the Talmud and rabbinic codes, are necessary for perfection as a man in general and as a Jew in particular. This question which my brethren posed to me is, in fact, bound up with a great many problems. These, however, can be reduced to the following five fundamental questions: (1) Is it the duty of an adherent of the Jewish faith to study the Hebrew language perfectly, according to the principles of grammar? (2) Is it permitted to study other languages as well? (3) May a Jew occupy himself with secular sciences? (4) If so, of what use can they be? (5) Is this utility worthwhile if the secular sciences entail, as many believe, great harm to religion and faith?

A reply to these questions is provided in *Te'udah Be-Yisrael*. The book was written at the same time as *Alfei Menasheh*. Both deal very frequently with the same questions but, in structure and style, they belong to two different eras. In its formlessness and lack of system, *Alfei Manasheh* belongs to the old rabbinic responsa literature. Levinsohn, however, did not spend many years with such a distinguished stylist as Mendel Levin in vain. He categorically rejects the rhetorical flourishes of the Meassefim[30] and writes in a clear, simple, and fluent language. Since he had a spark of the gifted journalist, there is discernible in his style at times the emotion of a tribune and preacher. In this respect he frequently reminds one of Eliezer Liebermann and his *Or Nogah*.[31]

At the beginning of his work Levinsohn placed a poem of praise to Pallas Athena, the goddess of wisdom, requesting her to guard

30. In his introduction to his *Eshkol Ha-Sofer* Levinsohn declares that "it is a great wickedness and a great foolishness and also a great evil" that the Haskalah writers refuse to make use, in their rhetorical writings and poems, of the Hebrew words created by the men of the Mishnah, the Talmud, and the Midrashim.
31. See our work, Vol. IX. pp. 248ff.

him with her armored hand from his ignorant opponents as he ventures to unfurl her banner amidst the tents of Israel. Calmly and systematically, Levinsohn shows in the first *sha'ar*, or gate,[32] of his work, with a plethora of quotations from the Talmud, Midrashim, and rabbinic literature, that it is a great duty to know the Hebrew language, and that, before seeking esoteric allusions and all kinds of homiletical meanings in the Biblical word, one must understand the literal significance of the word and its grammatical structure. Here he touches upon the question of the method of study and gives his reader to understand how one ought to learn the Biblical language systematically, not as is done in the traditional elementary schools. Again with quotations from accepted authorities, such as Rabbi Sheftel Horowitz, the author of *Vavei Ammudim*, Rabbi Jacob Emden, and others, he portrays the model schools that once existed among the Sephardim. "Now," Levinsohn feelingly exclaims, "come, my dear readers, with me into the dark and desolate valley, into the chambers of death that are called among us schools for children (*ḥadarim*)." And in pitch black colors he portrays the mode of study and the elementary teachers—"all of them great ignoramuses, whose like in evil is not to be found in the entire land" (Chapter Fifteen).

Levinsohn, however, does not consider it sufficient merely to show that one must know the Hebrew language in order to understand the text of the sacred books well. As Krochmal's faithful disciple, he particularly stresses the nationalist motif, the purely national significance of Hebrew. "Wherewith," he asks, "does one first of all recognize every nation or individual, if not through language? Language is, after all, the major distinguishing mark of every people." Not for nothing, he notes, is language set forth in the ancient Jewish literature as synonymous with people. "All the nations and tongues" (*kol ha-goyim veha-leshonot*), we read in the Bible. "Every people and tongue" (*kol ummah ve-lashon*), the Talmud many times repeats. And how can one who bears the name *Ivri* not be ashamed that he lacks knowledge of *Ivrit*, the Hebrew language?[33] Hebrew, Levinsohn concludes, is the factor that guarantees the "survival of the people." It is the bond that unites the people dispersed throughout the world; only with its aid can the Jewish inhabitants of the most varied countries and lands communicate with each other.[34]

In the second "gate," or *sha'ar*, Levinsohn deals with the question whether one may also study foreign languages. He knows his

32. *Te'udah Be-Yisrael* is divided into four "gates."
33. *Te'udah Be-Yisrael*, Gate One, Chapter 6.
34. *Ibid.*, Chapter 11.

readers quite well and realizes that they regard such a question as pure heresy. It is, after all, generally known that with every word an Israelite takes over from the nations of the world he forgets a word of the sacred Torah. Levinsohn therefore approaches this question with particular caution. First of all, he considers the problem "through reason" (*al pi derech ha-sechel*). Not without cause, he declares, is the Biblical statement that man became a "living soul" (*nefesh ḥayyah*) rendered in the Targum Onkelos by the words *ruaḥ memalleh*, "a speaking soul." The most precious treasure with which man is endowed is the living word, with the help of which he creates his world-view, his consciousness and culture. The more perfected this instrument is, the greater perfection does man attain through it. Hence, every cultured person must have a perfect command of at least one language. But we Russian-Polish Jews, Levinsohn points out, are without a language. Our Hebrew has for many generations ceased to be a living tongue. Its entire vocabulary is preserved in the Bible, and this vocabulary is quite limited. The language which the Jewish community in our lands speaks, the so-called "Judeo-German," is for Levinsohn, as for most of the *maskilim* of his generation, not a language at all, but a mixture of corrupted and error-filled German, Hebrew, Polish, Russian, French, and other words, in which one can express only ordinary concepts of the marketplace and of weekday life, but not noble, exalted ideas.[35] And as is the language, so is the man.[36] We cannot even understand the beauties of the Bible, the author contends, for it is impossible to render these in the distorted jargon that we speak.

With a whole arsenal of arguments and quotations from the Talmud and from later recognized authorities, Levinsohn shows that since Hebrew ceased to be a living language, our scholars and sages, and—along with them—the people, employed the language prevalent in the countries where they lived. In these languages they composed books of moral instruction and speculation, wrote rabbinic responsa, and produced prayers. And again relying on acknowledged authorities, Levinsohn shows that it is even permitted to pray in any language,[37] for in language itself there can be nothing prohibited. "There is no holiness and no uncleanness in

---

35. *Ibid.*, Gate Two, Chapter 3.

36. Because philology at that time had not yet reached a sufficiently scientific level Levinsohn concludes (he relies in this connection on Fichte) that a developed language influences the cultural growth of the community, not vice versa, namely, that with cultural growth the development of the language also grows.

37. However, like Eliezer Liebermann, Levinsohn also considers it necessary to stress that one ought to pray "in a pure and lucid language," i.e., not in jargon (*Te'udah Be-Yisrael*, Chapter 7).

writing and language," he urges, but only in content. The Hebrew language in and of itself is not holy; it became *leshon kodesh*, the holy language, only because sacred and divine things were composed in it. Every book, whether it be written in Russian, Polish, French, or any other language, as long as it contains words of Torah and morality and right conduct, is a "proper and pure book," and one ought to regard it with the greatest respect. But books, even if they are written in the Hebrew language but filled with follies and wild fantasies, as for example, Rabbi Naḥman of Bratzlav's *Sippurei Maasiyot* and the *Shivḥei Ha-Besht* which the "liar and false rabbinic judge of L—ts" has composed, are certainly forbidden reading. They are worse than the most cutting heretical works, and those who print such books will be required to give account therefor.[38]

Why, Levinsohn summarizes, do you need the distorted Judeo-German? Either speak pure German or the language of the country—the pure, lovely, and rich Russian tongue.

Command of the language of the country, Levinsohn notes, will also bring great material benefit in commerce and in dealings with officials. In addition, we will thereby rise in the esteem of other peoples and they will not regard us with contempt.

After considering the matter of languages, Levinsohn proceeds to the other questions: whether Jews may occupy themselves with secular sciences and, if so, what use these may bring. Again, with numerous quotations from the Talmud and medieval literature, he shows that the secular disciplines, such as the natural sciences, medicine, mathematics, and the like, are not only permitted but absolutely necessary and useful, and that only barbaric fools whose sense and reason God has taken away can be opposed to them.[39]

To clinch his argument, Levinsohn also sets forth in chronological order, from ancient times to the generation of the Gaon of Vilna, a long roster of Jewish scholars who were comprehensively equipped with the knowledge of their time and proficient in all the sciences. He deems it necessary, however, to note in this connection that the scientific knowledge of our sages and scholars of former generations was self-evidently, from the present-day point of view, very limited and insufficient, for all sciences develop further with each passing generation. Hence, at present one must draw knowledge of science from modern European sources, as our great sages did in their day.[40]

38. *Te'udah Be-Yisrael*, Chapter 8. His sharp hostility to the Hasidic movement is expressed by Levinsohn in other passages of his work as well. See especially Gate Four, Chapter 1, where the author ridicules the *rebbes* in the same fashion as he does this in his abovementioned satires.
39. *Te'udah Be-Yisrael*, Gate Three, Chapter 16.
40. *Ibid.*, Chapter 14.

Like the author of *Sefer Ha-Berit* and Manasseh of Ilya, however, Levinsohn understands quite well that knowledge and education alone cannot save the Jewish community. The abnormal social foundations of Jewish life must also be radically changed. Here Levinsohn again issues forth very sharply against the Hasidim and their spiritual leaders, but not merely because these men are opposed to all science and mislead the common people so that they do not, for instance, seek cures from doctors but rather from "masters of names and amulets" who "swindle men with their lies." He attacks them mainly because they paralyze the will of the people, develop in their followers a fantastic and pathological trust and confidence, destroy their desire for useful work, and teach them, instead, to rely on the *rebbe*, who will, in exchange for a fine gift, bestow upon them all kinds of good without effort and without labor.[41]

"Awake my brethren," Levinsohn calls out,

awake from your fantastic slumber! Enough sitting with folded hands and relying on miracles! Enough of being *Luftmenschen*, living from shady dealings, from tavernkeeping and petty trade. We must betake ourselves to productive, useful work, to craftsmanship and agriculture. We must establish special schools for artisans, in order to learn the trade well.

Again Levinsohn bases himself on the authority of the sages of the Talmud who declared that he who does not teach his son a useful trade betimes is "as if he taught him to rob." He presents, in this connection, a quite long list of famous Tannaim and Amoraim who occupied themselves with common forms of labor and earned a living thereby. There were among them shoemakers, smiths, woodchoppers, porters, tanners, etc.[42] "And we allow ourselves to regard artisans with contempt!" Basing himself on the Bible and on the historian Flavius Josephus, Levinsohn shows that in ancient times the Jews were not a people of trade but an agricultural people. To be sure, in this connection, he naively confuses two different categories—agricultural workers and landowners. With quotations from the Bible, the Iliad, and various Latin sources, he endeavors to show that in antiquity even kings and nobles were "tillers of the soil and shepherds of flocks."[43]

After a long historical excursus Levinsohn reaches the following conclusions: (1) In ancient times the Jews were exclusively a people of farmers; (2) the Jewish religion is not merely unopposed to agriculture but, indeed, considers it the most desirable and

41. *Ibid.*, Chapter 56.
42. *Ibid.*, Chapter 54.
43. *Ibid.*, Chapters 57, 58.

acceptable of occupations; (3) Jews at the present time are also suited to agriculture, along with all other nations; and (4) in antiquity, when the Jews lived on their own land, trade was altogether foreign to them. Only in later generations, when they were dispersed among various peoples, especially in the dark era of the Middle Ages when they were so persecuted and their human rights so restricted, were they compelled to occupy themselves with trade and monetary business and only then did they become specifically a commercial people. But now, Levinsohn emotively exclaims, the rays of the enlightenment have driven away the dark shadows of the Middle Ages. Humane ideas have permeated all strata of the people. The power of religious fanaticism has been weakened. Gracious and merciful kings have arisen. All the peoples of Europe preach love for mankind in general, without distinctions of nationality and religion. In certain European nations the Jews have already obtained freedom and rights, especially in our land, in the Russian empire, which, since it became independent, has never done any harm to the Jews. We have never heard or seen in any chronicle or historical book that the Jews were ever persecuted in this kingdom. Our ancestors lived quietly and peacefully with the inhabitants of the land and, even when the Russians later carried on war against Poland and invaded the Polish lands, we continued to live in peace and remained in our places without hindrance. Especially since the time we passed over under the sovereignty of Russia "we enjoy only goodness and graciousness."

Bearing in mind the Statute of 1804, Levinsohn declares:

The Russian government desires only our happiness and welfare and is applying all its strength to improve our situation. It grants us many civic rights along with the native-born citizens of the land. We are permitted to worship God freely and openly, according to the dictates of our religion. A Jew has the right to engage in any work or occupation he wishes. He is permitted to study in all middle and high schools, along with the children of the nobility and the officials. Jews also have the right to build their own schools and vocational institutes, to establish factories, to plant vineyards, to purchase fields and till them, and to enjoy their fruits.[44]

We have deliberately presented this quotation because it is characteristic in many respects. Sitting locked up in his little room at the edge of Kremenets, the battler for Haskalah lived with the humanitarian ideas of the *Aufklärer* of the eighteenth century and apparently had no conception of the fact that, in Europe, the era of the Restoration, with the oppressive regime of Metternich and the Russian czar, had just begun. Levinsohn was quite at home in the

44. *Ibid.*, Chapter 65.

"chronicles and historical books" and knew very well how inhumanely Ivan the Terrible had settled accounts with the Jews of Polotsk when he captured that city. He was also quite aware that the Jews could not live "peacefully" in the Russian territories because they were not permitted to set foot in them. Also not unknown to him was the decree of the pious czarina Elizabeth Petrovna that she did not wish to enjoy any "greedy profit" from the enemies of Christ.

All this, apparently, Levinsohn pretended deliberately not to know and, in this indirect and certainly very naive way, to tell the Russian government that it ought to be tolerant toward the Jews and grant them civic rights. He also knew that the "liberal" Principles of 1804 remained, in fact, on paper.[45] However, like his predecessors, the *maskilim* of Berlin, he firmly believed in the benevolence of "enlightened absolutism," and was therefore persuaded that it was not the government that was at fault but the backwardness and fanaticism of his own brethren. Levinsohn was also quite aware that among the Principles of 1804 were some extremely harsh measures, and that it was precisely these that were enforced. Indeed, on one of the most important of them—the decree expelling all Jews from the villages located within fifty versts of the border—he considered it necessary to dwell in his *Te'udah Be-Yisrael*.

Why, asks Levinsohn, was the decree issued that precisely Jews alone should be driven out from the area within fifty versts of the border? This was not done because of religious prejudice or wickedness, but only because among us Jews there are so many *Luftmenschen*, petty traders, shady dealers, and brokers. The earnings of these persons are too small for them to be able to support their families honestly and so they frequently swindle and also deal in contraband, which is strictly forbidden by the law of the land. To be sure, it is not the Jews themselves who are responsible for the fact that such a large percentage of them are engaged in petty trade, but the grievous circumstances in which we found ourselves in earlier, dark generations. Now, however, the dark times are past. Thanks to the graciousness of our kings and princes, we may engage in whatever work or enterprise we desire. We may also devote ourselves to the labor that was so favored by our people in ancient times—agriculture. Arise, then, my beloved brethren—Levinsohn exclaims—the dark times are over; a new,

---

45. An exception is provided only by one of Levinsohn's points: Jews had the right to establish factories. In order not to be dependent on foreign manufacturers, the Russian government was especially interested in increasing the number of cloth factories. Among the Russian cloth factories, there were, as we have already noted above, a certain number of Jewish ones in the 1820s.

bright era is beginning. Throw away the shady dealing and petty trade. Learn crafts, enrich yourselves with knowledge, engage in agriculture, as your fathers did in ancient days. For only agriculture provides man with true happiness and joy. Thereby you will obtain favor among the people in whose midst you live and with our lord, the czar, who greatly wishes your happiness and welfare.[46]

Levinsohn realized quite well the profound indignation that his work would provoke in Hasidic circles. In order to safeguard both himself and his book against the persecutions of his enraged opponents, he wished to take the same measure as the one Moses Mendelssohn had employed in his time in publishing his translation of the Torah and the commentary to it *(Biur)*. When Mendelssohn learned that the rabbi of Hamburg, Raphael Kohen, intended to issue forth against his work with the weapon of the ban, he managed to bring it about through his friends in Hamburg that the king of Denmark (under whose dominion the city of Hamburg at that time was) signed up as a charter subscriber to the translation. Obviously, the rabbi did not dare ban a work which the king himself had favored with his subscription.[47] Levinsohn, too, upon finally managing to conclude an agreement with the proprietor of a press in Vilna regarding the publication of his *Te'udah Be-Yisrael*, dispatched a copy of his work in December, 1827 to the minister of public instruction A. S. Shishkov and, along with it, a long explanatory letter in which he presents the content and the basic theses of the work.[48] At the end of the letter he requests two things: (1) that the minister allow him to "ornament his work with his [the minister's] name," and (2) that he grant him, the sickly author, a certain amount of financial support so that he might be able to write further works with the purpose of "improving the moral condition of the Jewish populace."

Shishkov transmitted the manuscript to the Jewish apostate Zandberg who occupied the post of expert and authority with the Committee on Jewish Affairs. Zandberg, in his written report, acknowledged Levinsohn's work as extremely useful but expressed the wish that all the passages in which attacks are made on the Hasidic movement be eliminated. It would be desirable, he added, to have the work confirmed by *haskamot*, or approbations, from Russian-Polish rabbis. Zandberg also concluded that it would serve no purpose to dedicate the book to a Christian official, because this would frighten off Jewish readers.

---

46. *Te'udah Be-Yisrael*, Chapters 56, 65-67.
47. See our *History*, volume VIII, p. 43.
48. The letter was published by J. I. Hessen in *Perezhitoye*, I.

The Effect of Te'udah Be-Yisrael

The negotiations dragged on for a whole year. In the meantime Shishkov left his ministerial post. Finally, Nicholas I confirmed with his signature the decision taken by the Committee on Jewish Affairs that Levinsohn be granted for his Hebrew work, which aims at "the moral renewal of the Jewish people," the sum of a thousand rubles. At the same time *Te'udah Be-Yisrael* came off the press, and as a "protection document" the author published in it his most humble thanks for the czar's gift.

The letter of protection was effective. *Te'udah Be-Yisrael* did, indeed, provoke a colossal storm in Hasidic circles. The czar's "reward" however, made the heretical work and its author unassailable. For generations there lay in Hasidic hearts profound wrath against the heretic of Kremenets, and the writer of these lines still remembers from his childhood the bitter anger with which old Hasidim used to mention the "Te'udke, may his name and memory be blotted out."

The attitude of the Mitnagdic circles towards Levinsohn's book was much kinder. It is even related that the rabbi of Vilna, Rabbi Abele, is supposed to have told his associates that the only fault of *Te'udah Be-Yisrael* is the fact that it was not composed by the Gaon of Vilna. It is difficult, however, for the present-day reader to conceive the enormous impression that Levinsohn's work made on the better, intellectually curious segment of the Jewish youth. For this group the book was literally a revelation, a spiritual and intellectual liberation.

Hundreds of students in *yeshivot*, who unconsciously groped in the dark, wandered about lost over the paths of life, and dreamed powerlessly of the new word which might open their eyes and show them the right path, recognized in *Te'udah Be-Yisrael* the liberator and faithful guide, the living well that refreshed their languishing lips. In attics, in the most hidden places, late at night in the dark corners of the studyhouse, with the last flickering of the tallow candle, inhabitants of prayerhouses and *yeshivah* students absorbed with trembling hearts and with utmost secrecy the pages of *Te'udah Be-Yisrael* and with bated breath accepted the challenge of the sickly *maskil* of Kremenets, who called them to knowledge, to productive labor, and to wider horizons.

In 1834 the young Mathias Strashun wrote to Levinsohn: "Only your book opened my eyes, and I became a different person. I read the book twice and thrice and still could not sate myself with it. A marvelous light suddenly drove away the shadows of darkness from my eyes. Your words kindled a holy fire in my heart, and this fire will no longer be extinguished."[49]

49. *Sefer Ha-Zichronot*, 49.

In 1841 the scholar Shneour (Senior) Sachs wrote to Levinsohn: "In my early youth, when I was void of knowledge and groped in the darkest night, your *Te'udah Be-Yisrael* suddenly shone before me like a pillar of light. It aroused my thirst for light and knowledge. It disclosed to me the way that I will travel throughout my whole life."[50]

The historian S.J. Fuenn speaks with the same enthusiasm of the impression that Levinsohn's work made on him. "Every page of *Te'udah Be-Yisrael*," he relates, "was literally a revelation for me."

The *maskilim* of Galicia greeted *Te'udah Be-Yisrael* with no lesser enthusiasm. The author of *Kinat Ha-Emet*, Jehudah Leib Miesis, warmly congratulated Levinsohn. And in 1826 Solomon Jehudah Rapoport wrote to Levinsohn: "With what great pleasure I read your work! I have long waited for such a book and hoped that the man of knowledge who would bestow it upon our people would arrive. Your work possesses the two qualities that must grace every important literary work: useful content and fine, beautiful style."[51]

Te'udah Be-Yisrael cheered the little groups of frightened *maskilim* scattered over the various provinces of eastern Europe. It became the banner, the signal, which called to unity and organized activity.

"Countless young Jews," writes Gottlober in his memoirs,

then [after the appearance of *Te'udah Be-Yisrael*] opened their eyes and began to study Hebrew and the language of the country.[52] They

50. *Be'er Yitzḥak*, 67.

51. *Sefer Ha-Zichronot*, 17. In this connection the following point is worth noting: As is to be seen from the date of the letter (1826), Rapoport became familiar with *Te'udah Be-Yisrael* while it was still in manuscript. From Jacob Lando's letter to Levinsohn (*Be'er Yitzḥak*, 12) we see that Levinsohn sent a copy of his work to Brody as early as 1822. It is virtually beyond doubt that precisely under the influence of *Te'udah Be-Yisrael* Rapoport published, in *Bikkurei Ha-Ittim*, 1828, a long letter of response to a good friend of his. To be sure, this letter is ostensibly a reply to his friend's question which was written as early as the end of 1822. However, it is easy to conjecture that this query is something that never existed. First of all, it is difficult to understand why Rapoport published his answer only five years later. And, secondly, it is generally difficult to believe that a friend of Rapoport's who is crowned with such epithets as "friend of my soul and man of my covenant, the splendid *maskil*, pure of intellect" should have to ask whether he may permit his brother to study languages, sciences, and medicine, or to learn any craft. It is easier to believe that all these questions were simply copied verbatim from the introduction to *Te'udah Be-Yisrael*.

52. Testimony to the fact that Levinsohn's propaganda to the effect that one ought to study the language of the country had a certain success (at least in his own region) may be provided by Gottlober's album of the 1830s, preserved by us, in which his friends and acquaintances wrote all kinds of inscriptions. In this album (*Stammbuch*) Russian is accorded equal rights with German and Hebrew. To six German inscriptions there are four in Russian: one in prose from Tzevi Grünbaum, the later well-known government official Fedorov, the other three in poetic lines (clumsy, grammatically incorrect). Under one poem Jacob Wekstein is signed; the other two are signed merely with initials.

undertook these things with firm courage and were not frightened by the fanatics who stood in their way. In every city and town they established societies, and the individual *maskilim* who were already scattered here and there earlier aided them in this. They separated themselves from the Hasidic community and applied themselves to education and knowledge.[53]

In Berdichev the *maskil* Israel Rothenberg organized a society called *Shoharei Or Ve-Haskalah* (Seekers of Light and Enlightenment) for the purpose of uniting all who strive after light and knowledge. In Vilna, where the strength of Hasidism was incomparably less than in Volhynia, the local *maskilim* decided shortly after the appearance of *Te'udah Be-Yisrael* to establish a yearbook that might unite all of the progressive elements around itself.[54] In 1834 the first yearbook was already prepared for the press under the title *Minhat Bikkurim*.[55] The board of editors consisted of Yitzhak-Isaac Benjacob, Mordecai Aaron Günzburg, Hayyim Katzenellenbogen, and the poet Abraham Lebensohn (Adam Ha-Kohen). In their prospectus it was noted that the yearbook, of approximately twelve to fifteen printer's sheets (usually equal to sixteen pages), would consist of the following sections: (1) poetry and rhetoric, (2) exegesis, (3) historical articles, travel accounts, natural sciences, biographies, (4) moral instruction, (5) criticism and reviews, and (6) scholarly correspondence. It is also noted that all the articles will be written "in the purity of the holy language, clearly and cleanly."[56]

M. A. Günzburg sets forth the character and goal of the work in an editorial *(kol kore)*. The article begins with a parable. A crane once flew over a forest from which no singing of birds was heard. Astonished, the crane considered the silent forest when suddenly a nightingale flew up to him and explained that there are, indeed, many songbirds in the forest but they are silent because there is no one for whom to sing. Among the inhabitants of the forest taste is so corrupted that they find it much more pleasant to listen to the chirping of a cricket. "But by the fact that the nightingales are silent," the crane exclaims, "you yourselves accustom the inhabitants of the forest to the chirping of crickets."

53. A. Fridkin, *Avrohom Ber Gottlober Un Zayn Epokhe*, 311.
54. In 1854 S. J. Fuenn wrote to Levinsohn: "The idea of establishing a newspaper has engaged us not one and not two, but all of twelve years" (see *Sefer Ha-Zichronot*, 61) M. A. Günzburg writes in 1833 that five years have passed since he undertook to publish the collection *Minhat Bikkurim* (*Devir*, II, 82).
55. "*Minhat Bikkurim* for the year 5594 from the creation of the world, and it is a new offering for the Israelites dwelling in the land of Lithuania."
56. At the end of the prospectus it is also indicated that the journal will be printed in 300 copies, which will be dispatched to various cities to certain persons who will distribute the copies among the subscribers.

After the parable comes the explicit lesson. "It is beyond doubt," declares the author,

that our land (Lithuania) is not poor in men of science, but they are compelled to hide their treasures of knowledge and not display them publicly. For the Jewish people is different from all other peoples. Among them, men of knowledge are the pride of the people; among us, they must conceal themselves like criminals. They must disguise themselves, hide under masks, occupy themselves all day with extraneous matters, and only under the cover of deep night, when no one sees, do they engage secretly in the sciences and scientific matters—so great is their fear of the fanatics and rebels against the light . . . To many of those thirsting for knowledge, this kind of disguise and play has become repulsive and so they have left the land and settled abroad, where they can engage openly and freely in the sciences. But there are also among us those who strive for knowledge but are hindered by the fact that they do not have command of any European language. Who, then, shall be concerned for these, if not men who already have open eyes and enjoy the light of *Aufklärung*? There are already among us enough enlightened men who might very successfully introduce light into the tents of Israel, and now the moment has come when all men of knowledge must come forth openly from their hidden corners, throw off their masks, and appear before the public in their true form.

Günzburg, however, was mistaken. The proper moment had not yet come. The progressive elements were still too weak and few in number, and the yearbook, despite the fact that all the material was already prepared, remained unpublished and was circulated only in a few copies.[57] The *maskil* and historian of Vilna S. J. Fuenn explains the failure of this literary enterprise as follows: "These men of knowledge . . . who devised this, nevertheless, because of many factors, did not have the courage to realize their intention. Furthermore, the right hour had not yet come."[58]

This unpublished collection of articles,[59] which was to have "spread culture and education through all the dispersions of Israel," indicates very clearly how weak and helpless the Jewish enlighteners in the social and scientific realms still were in Russia at that time. Among the founders of the yearbook were undoubtedly men of considerable literary talent. Included among them were also persons of relatively solid knowledge. Yet they were incapable of producing a more or less interesting journal even from the purely

57. We have employed the copy found in Leningrad in the library of the Society for the Promotion of Culture and Enlightenment among Jews.

58. *Safah La-Ne'emanim*, 169.

59. A certain part of the unpublished material was later printed in the collection *Pirhei Tazfon*. Günzburg's "summons" was reprinted in the second part of *Devir*, 1–5.

scholarly point of view, not to speak of the social.[60] An explanation of this may be found in the abovementioned *kol kore* by Günzburg. In it we obtain a very clear picture of how the Jewish intelligentsia of the 1820s were isolated from the masses of the people and compelled not only to conceal their views from the public but even the very fact that they occupied themselves with secular books. This itself was considered a serious crime, for which one was ruthlessly persecuted. The isolation of these enlighteners was sharpened even further by the fact that they obtained the elements of European science in the vesture of German culture. Mendelssohn's Torah translation and the literature of the Meassefim brought them into contact with the German language and German literature. They became "Berliners," i.e., representatives of a foreign culture, not the culture of the land in which they lived.

While the Meassefim mechanically copied German models, at least they remained in the sphere of the civilization in whose midst they resided. The Russian "Berliners," however, with their "Daytshmerish," their Germanism, their imitation of Teutonic models, represented rather odd, foreign-fashioned, and groundless plants. It must further be noted that our *maskilim* of the 1820s and 1830s copied the German models not of their era but of the eighteenth century, which had also served as a pattern for the Meassefim in their day. This explains the fact that the amalgam of superficial rationalism and dreamy sentimentalism, so characteristic of the end of the eighteenth century, is clearly noticeable in the Hebrew literature of the 1820s to the 1840s and gives it a very unique coloration. The isolation of the *maskilim* of that time, the hatred and contempt with which the masses of the people regarded them, contributed still more to the fact that the literature of that era bore such a schematic, abstract character. But, indeed, it only contributed to it, for there were also other factors, which we

---

60. In this connection one must naturally take into consideration the very harsh conditions of censorship prevalent at that time. The Jewish censors were even more strict than the Russian. Indeed, M. A. Günzburg complains of this in his above-quoted letter of 1833: "And I will tell you the truth that our honorable friend, the master the censor (W. Tugendhold) in his rigorous examination weakens my hands also with regard to this composition (*Minḥat Bikkurim*), as well as the book *Toledot Benei Adam* which I planned to compose, for if he will lay down a law to me to refrain from every word regarding the state, then I cannot do anything useful, and also in the introduction he declared words unfit in which no strict person will find the slightest impermissibility" (*Devir*, II, 81). Some of the curiosities of the Jewish censorship under the regime of Nicholas have been preserved for the cultural historian in *Der Orient* (1845, 158). In several editions of the *Siddur* and *Maḥzor* the words *goy* (gentile) or *goyah* (gentile woman) were exchanged for the word *Yavan* (Greek). In this way the expression "save me from the clinging mud (or place of suffering)" [*hatzileni mi-tit ha-yaven*] was exchanged for "save me from the dirt of Ishmael." There are many other such curiosities.

already noted in discussing the era of the Meassefim, involved here.

Many of the *maskilim* who battled for new forms of life were themselves still strongly permeated with the spirit of abstract rabbinism and arid scholasticism. Because they were incapable of living with the interests and life-problems of the masses of the people, they devoted all their love and attention to the language. To cultivate the language of the Bible—the language itself, independently of content—became an end in itself; and not infrequently the "beautiful language, the only remnant," became the synonym, the content and substance, of Haskalah in general. And it was precisely these "men of the previous century"—as the *maskilim* of the 1820s to the 1840s were called by Lev Levanda—these men who lived such an isolated cultural life, as if beyond time and space, without any clear notion of the actual condition of the country and the state in which they spent their whole lives, who considered it their sacred duty to be dedicated patriots, ardently loving their fatherland. The concept of fatherland and state among them, however, was peculiarly interwoven with the concept of "government power" and "enlightened absolutism."

Only in the 1830s were the *maskilim* in a position to propose a more or less concrete program, and this exclusively thanks to the author of *Te'udah Be-Yisrael*, Isaac Baer Levinsohn. It was he who set forth a program to reform Russian Jewry in five points, a program which served as a recognized manifesto of the enlighteners and progressives during the course of the reign of Nicholas I. Because this program is of cultural-historical interest, we present it here with several insignificant abbreviations:

(1) Well-organized schools should be established, and in these the children should be taught Torah, religion, commandments, virtuous qualities, and ethics, all together—everything that pertains to God and to man, to the government and to the people in whose midst they live, and all this in proper order. For this purpose, appropriate books discussing these questions in a form suited to the understanding of the children at every age should be prepared. Girls also should be familiarized with the foundations of religion, morality, and ethics according to their comprehension. Both boys and girls should be taught some trade or work, because going about idle and constant lack of income are the genesis of all crimes and transgressions. The male teachers as well as the female (for the girls) ought to be persons of knowledge, of good qualities, of reverence and integrity, competent in the field of educating children. It is not at all necessary that the entire people, great and small, be rabbis, scholars, philologists, doctors, philosophers, or

poets. Only a few selected individuals are called to this, and it is difficult to imagine the tremendous harm that the idea that all ought to be scholars may cause. It suffices for the ordinary person with limited capacities to know the Bible with a satisfactory commentary, to have some knowledge of grammar, to be acquainted with the most essential laws of the *Shulḥan Aruch*, to be more or less familiar with the language of the country in both writing and speech, to have some notion of mathematics, to be capable of reading a book of moral instruction in Hebrew, and to be able to write some Hebrew. This is in regard to small towns. But in the large cities with substantial Jewish communities, such as Warsaw, Vilna, Odessa, and Berdichev, there ought to be established, besides elementary schools, higher schools (*battei midrash gedolim*) where the *benei ha-aliyyah*, i.e., young people with fine capacities, shall study the Talmud and rabbinic codes under the supervision of great rabbis to be selected from the whole country. In these schools there ought also to be instruction, according to the taste and desire of the students, in all kinds of sciences and languages by noted scholars and specialists who shall be selected for this purpose—and all this in the best order and under the most rigorous supervision.

(2) A chief rabbi and a large court of scientifically knowledgeable men (*ḥachmei madda*) should be selected to sit with him, and the rabbis, preachers, and teachers should be chosen by these persons. In addition, honorable and understanding men of wealth should be selected from the country as general *parnassim* or officials, and these should devote their attention to communal matters. The general officials, together with the chief rabbi, and with the aid of several other wise men familiar with languages and books and expert in social questions, should have supervision, with the authorization of the government, over everything regarding the welfare of the community and the individual. It is literally impossible to calculate the good that this will bring to the poor of the people and small householders, especially in the little towns, where the poor and small householders are unfortunately at present like dumb sheep; they tremble and are afraid of their leaders and rich men who shear them like lambs, suck out their blood like hungry wolves, and do not permit them to complain to the warmhearted and sympathetic government whose entire goal is to aid the poor man and to protect him from those who plunder him.

(3) There shall be preachers and reprovers in every city, as in former times—wise men blessed with oratorical talent. They shall give addresses on specific days, especially the Sabbath and festivals, and provide moral instruction for the people in suitable

words that shall be full of grace and good sense, so that they may make an impression on the hearts of the listeners. They must call the attention of the people to all the bad qualities which have become rooted in our life in general and in every city and community, as well as in each individual. These preachers shall not speak about esoteric references and allusions in the sacred texts and about Kabbalah but arouse in the people the desire for useful work and artisanry, and explain to them the obligations of the individual both to God and to himself, as well as to his family and strangers, to the government, etc.

(4) The government should be earnestly petitioned to provide at least a third of the inhabitants of every community with fields, so that these persons may cultivate them and devote themselves to raising cattle and sheep, as did our ancestors. In these colonies also schools shall be established in which the children shall pursue, up to the age of twelve, the studies noted in the first point above.

(5) The rabbis shall strictly admonish the Jewish population not to allow itself any luxuries, not to wear expensive silk clothing or ornaments of gold and pearls, and also not to make use of expensive objects in housekeeping that can easily be dispensed with, for these luxuries cause hatred and lead to all kinds of transgressions and crimes. Especially our brethren who will devote themselves to agriculture should avoid all luxury. They should lead a plain life and dress in inexpensive, simple, but clean garments.

This program, together with detailed explanations in regard to the proposal for establishing Jewish schools and involving Jews in agriculture, was at first disseminated in numerous copies.[61] In 1839 Levinsohn published it in the second part of his *Bet Yehudah*,[62] which he had originally conceived as a continuation of his *Te'udah Be-Yisrael*.

Even before *Te'udah Yisrael* appeared in print, Levinsohn undertook another work which at first bore the title *Ma'amar Korot Ha-Dat Le-Yeshurun*. In it he attempted to give, in clear and popular form, a systematic historical-scientific overview of the history of the development of Judaism. Like *Te'udah Be-Yisrael*, this work was written in the form of a response to a certain number of questions that are posed in the introduction: on the nature of the Jewish religion, the significance of the Torah of Moses and the Babylonian Talmud, the attitude of the religious Jew to the Christian populace, etc. In 1828 this work was already completed. Levinsohn sent it to Vilna and subsequently, when an authorization had been received

---

61. See *Bet Yehudah*, 1839, 355.
62. *Ibid.*, 348-354.

from the censor in 1829, the manuscript was given over to the press that had just published *Te'udah Be-Yisrael*.

Aside from the official Russian censorship, however, there was an internal Jewish censorship—the rabbinate of Vilna. As soon as the rabbis learned of the questions posed at the beginning of Levinsohn's manuscript, they saw in it nothing but heresy. They immediately dispatched a letter to Levinsohn with the command that he not dare print this work, for such questions may bring great harm to the religion. The printer also became frightened and promptly sent the manuscript back to the author. Then Levinsohn hit upon the following scheme. He pretended to be a simpleton and declared in his reply to the rabbis that these questions were not posed by him, the author, but that a high official named Immanuel Liven had put them to him and that he had written his work, in which he defends the religion of Israel, as a reply to all the accusatory questions that had been raised. This Immanuel Liven was a fictitious character, someone who never existed, but since the minister of public instruction at that time was named Karl Liven the rabbis believed that it was he who applied to the "learned Jew" Levinsohn with these questions. Hence they no longer dared prevent Levinsohn from publishing his work. Nevertheless, the printer in Vilna withdrew from the production of the book (apparently not without the initiative of the rabbis).[63] Of the further "adventures" that the manuscript had to go through, Levinsohn himself tells in one of his letters.

"At that time," he writes,

I was very sick and the illness lasted all of two years. I was naked and bare, literally without bread to eat, without any aid whatsoever, and without the least hope. In addition, I had all these unpleasantnesses and difficult experiences. Just at that time the well-known scholar (and publisher) Moses Landau of Prague[64] proposed to me to publish my work. However, nothing came of this. Shortly afterwards my friend Berish Blumenfeld of Brody requested me to send him my manuscript, saying that he would print it in Galicia. I did not have another copy and had no alternative but to send my only manuscript across the border. There also nothing came of the matter. Thus my composition began to wander about through the world, from Brody to Hungary, from there to Prague, then to Vienna, and finally again to Brody to Blumenfeld. Just then a fire broke out in Blumenfeld's house, and several other houses were also destroyed. For a time it was believed that my manuscript had been burned, until it was accidentally discovered among Blumenfeld's possessions that had been saved. In the meantime my friends in Vilna informed me that there was

63. See *Iggerot Ribal*, 1896, 71 (Levinsohn's letter to Dr. Reuben Kulisher).
64. One of the editors of *Bikkurei Ha-Ittim*.

some hope that my work might be published in Vilna. After many difficulties the manuscript was finally (in 1835) transported from Brody to Vilna, and there again provided with a censorship authorization. But three more years elapsed before my work finally appeared in print [under the title *Bet Yehudah*].[65]

As in *Te'udah Be-Yisrael*, so also in *Bet Yehudah* Levinsohn touches with great caution upon those questions that may frighten and anger the orthodox reader.[66] He even notes in *Bet Yehudah* that "for the sake of peace, scholars and sages not infrequently silence the truth." In point of fact, however, Levinsohn does not silence what he considers to be true but gradually expresses his rationalist ideas, even though they are disguised and interwoven with quotations from the Talmudic sages. He sets forth the slogan that "nothing is true if it is not in agreement with reason."[67] What is not consistent with reason "can in no way be true." Basing himself on Maimonides and other great scholars, he gives the reader to understand that the commandment "And thou shalt love the Lord thy God" can be fulfilled only "after one has obtained clear and precise conceptions with the aid of reason"[68] and that knowledge and wisdom precede action.[69] He also points out that a "sage is superior to a prophet," and that the best legislator is common sense and the "perfect man" or "full man" is one who is "an all-rounded scholar," expert not only in the Torah but also in all the "wisdoms and sciences."[70]

Since, during the Biblical era, religious life among the Jews was intimately associated with political life, Levinsohn considers it necessary to present, in the first part, a general historical overview of the period from the patriarchs to the destruction of the Second Temple. In this connection it is worth calling attention to one characteristic feature. We have already noted that Levinsohn, like other *maskilim* of that generation, had a great fondness for "enlightened absolutism" and was enchanted by the kindness of the "gracious kings" of Europe. Nevertheless, in speaking in his historical overview of the ancient period of the patriarchs, when the Hebrew tribes were still nomads and lived mainly from pasturing and raising flocks, he repeats twice with great enthusiasm what a happy life they then led, since they lived freely and without hindrance, were not subordinate to anyone, knew of no masters

---

65. *Sefer Ha-Zichronot*, 40.
66. Only his hostility to the Hasidim does he refuse to conceal, and he declares angrily that "every criminal and person avid for plunder is today called a Hasid" (*Bet Yehudah*, 320).
67. *Ibid.*, 23.
68. *Ibid.*, 116.
69. *Ibid.*, 60.
70. *Ibid.*, 68.

over themselves, had no notion of taxes and levies, and were free of all burdens.[71]

After giving the reader to understand the difference between "natural religion" and "revealed religion," Levinsohn notes the significant cultural-historical fact that among most of the civilized peoples (the Egyptians, the Greeks, and the like) there were two laws: (1) a written law in which the fundamental rules were given to the common people briefly and without explanation, and (2) an oral law, with commentaries and reasons for every rule, bound up with ideas and theories which transcended the comprehension of the multitude. This second law was transmitted to the special caste of priests and scholars. In this, Levinsohn explains with a pious mien, they clearly imitated the chosen people of Israel which received, at Mount Sinai, the Torah wherein the laws are presented in brief without commentaries. For the Torah was given to the entire people, which consisted of ordinary farmers who were occupied with difficult work and had no time to devote themselves much to its study.[72] All the explanations and commentaries, as well as all possible doubts and questions, were transmitted by Moses to the elders and scholars of the generation as an oral Torah. These men, the court and scholars of the generation, explain the laws and commandments of the Torah according to the "principles of wisdom" that Moses handed over to the elders, or "according to logical reason," and adapt them to "the time and place."

Further relying on numerous quotations from recognized authorities, Levinsohn explains to his readers that in various generations, according to the prevalent conditions, the sages of the generation interpreted certain laws and customs differently. Thus we know that in the region where Rabbi Jose the Galilean lived the flesh of fowl cooked in milk was eaten,[73] and where Rabbi Eliezer lived wood was chopped and fire kindled on the Sabbath to prepare "an iron implement for circumcision." In general—Levinsohn notes and attempts to confirm through numerous examples—the scribes and sages of the Mishnah were lenient in regard to many laws. In so doing, he explains, they did not—God forbid—destroy a negative precept of the Torah but attempted to discover in the Torah itself a certain permission contrary to this negative precept, or to find some other means, so that the Torah should remain

71. *Ibid.*, 37, 39.
72. *Ibid.*, 57.
73. Incidentally, Levinsohn pretends to be simple-minded and notes (*ibid.*, 110-111) that in the sentence "you shall not seethe a kid in its mother's milk" the commentators—begging pardon—made a mistake in interpreting the plain meaning; it is not actually a question there of the flesh of a kid, but of ripe and unripe fruits.

unaltered. And these things were done "according to the time and the place."[74]

Levinsohn also does not tire of calling the attention of his readers to the fact that many customs, laws, notions, and conceptions (among them some foolish, superstitious ones) were taken over by Jews in their long historical sojourn from other peoples among whom they lived.[75] In this connection a characteristic feature which distinguishes him decisively not only from such *maskilim* as Frank and Hirsch Baer Hurwitz, but also from Jehudah Leib Miesis, Aaron Wolfsohn-Halle, and others, is worth noting. This is his attitude toward the Talmud. As a faithful disciple of Naḥman Krochmal, Levinsohn regards the great cultural-historical significance of this monumental work of Jewish creativity with profoundest respect. He repeats numerous times that "one ought not to judge other times and places from the perspective of present-day time and place," and that, in reading an author of earlier centuries, one must take into consideration the time and circumstances under which the author in question wrote.[76] To the extent possible under the contemporary conditions of censorship, Levinsohn proudly rejects the attacks made on the Talmud by Christian theologians and incidentally notes with caustic irony the bizarre and childishly naive interpretations that great theologians of former times gave to certain verses of the Torah.[77]

At the conclusion of his work Levinsohn, as we have already noted, sets forth his program of reform and strongly propagandizes for agriculture. He does not grow weary of noting what a great crime it is to engage in smuggling.[78] Why, he asks, do the rabbis remain silent on this matter? Did not the sages of the Talmud declare that "one who violates [the laws of] taxation is called a robber?" How much misfortune this practice has already brought us, how much hostility and hatred on the part of the government![79]

Levinsohn dwells on still another point that is of special interest. Scholars of the era note quite frequently the onesidedness of the reform program which the representatives of Haskalah set forth. The *maskilim* directed all their attention to the intellectual backwardness of the Jewish masses. They propagandized very energetically for the reform of education, for enriching Jewish

74. *Bet Yehudah*, 113, 130.
75. *Ibid.*, 121, 194, 256, 328, 330, etc.
76. *Ibid.*, 133, 334.
77. *Ibid.*, 273.
78. One must take into consideration in this connection that Levinsohn spent his whole life near the Austrian border, where the number of Jewish smugglers was certainly a rather considerable one.
79. *Bet Yehudah*, 151-152.

youth with European science, and completely ignored the civic disabilities of the Jewish populace. In this complaint there is certainly much truth, but not the whole truth. This is particularly noticeable in Levinsohn, the chief battler and standard-bearer of Haskalah.

First of all, the censorship conditions in the era of Nicholas I's reign must be taken into consideration. One must also not overlook the general disabilities and the repressive system that prevailed in czarist Russia at large, where the most numerous segment of the population, the peasant class, was in a condition of serfdom. When Levinsohn sets forth his program of reform in *Bet Yehudah*, he does, in fact, also speak of civic rights. He discusses the "Principles of 1804"[80] and notes the liberal points that are set forth in them, to the effect that "all Jewish children have the right to study, without being in any way distinguished from other children, in all Russian schools, gymnasia, and universities." There are also many other "good and useful ordinances," he adds, that endow the Jews with numerous "rights and privileges of the state" *(zechuyyot ha-medinah)*. Levinsohn surely means the provisions according to which Jewish manufacturers, artisans, and merchants are permitted to settle temporarily outside the Pale and various forms of relief are granted to Jews willing to engage in agriculture. The most piquant thing, however, is the remark that Levinsohn makes in this connection. He says:

Would that all other civilized peoples *(ha-ummot ha-metukkanot)* would follow the path of righteousness which the good Russian government walks, and grant the Jews civic rights along with all Christian citizens, making no distinctions whatever. Indeed, I am astonished at the civilized peoples who prohibit the Jew from enjoying the rights of the country simply because he is a Jew.

It is difficult to say whether this was merely pretense on Levinsohn's part and that he attempted, as he had already done in *Te'udah Be-Yisrael*, in this disguised way to put forward, under the censorship conditions which existed at that time, the demand for civic rights or, on the other hand, whether he meant it seriously and was so far removed from the actual life of Russia and the civic situation in the czarist empire that he could portray Nicholas I's regime as a model of humanitarianism and justice. An indication that the first supposition is the more correct one may be provided by another passage in *Bet Yehudah* in which he notes that after "the days of Haskalah, or enlightenment, arrived, the Jews also began to be treated as brethren and in many countries were accorded

80. *Ibid.*, 364.

freedom and civic rights; and for about fifty years now Jews have also served in the armies of European nations."[81]

Just at the time that Levinsohn wrote his *Bet Yehudah* (1827), Jews also began to serve in the Russian army. Levinsohn knew the form obtained by this "civic right" which the Jews won as a gift from Nicholas I's despotic hand so well that, three years after the decree concerning Jewish military service went into effect, he considered it necessary to write about it in a special work. Of this in the next chapter.

81. *Ibid.*, 21-22.

CHAPTER THREE

Levinsohn's Communal Activity; Max Lilienthal

[The decree of 1827 regarding Jewish military service and Levinsohn's *Hefker-Velt*—The social significance of the work—Levinsohn's relationships to the government—The *maskilim* and the Mitnagdim against the printing presses of Volhynia—Levinsohn's part in the decree of 1836 concerning Jewish presses—The "excise people"—The projected society of *maskilim* called "Tziyyon"—Levinsohn's propaganda about settling Jews on the soil—Levinsohn as an apologist—The significance of his *Efes Damim*—Levinsohn's disfavor among the high officials—Levinsohn's *Aḥiyyah Ha-Shiloni Ha-Ḥozeh*—The sad failure of Jewish colonization—The proposal for reforming the schools—The minister of education Uvarov—Max Lilienthal and his "sermons"—The reformation of the schools as a weapon against the "false religious conceptions" of the Jews deriving from the Talmud—The question of the "shameful costume"—Uvarov as "fighter" for Jewish enlightenment—The enthusiasm of the *maskilim*—Lilienthal as emissary—The dissatisfaction of the *maskilim*—Lilienthal's *Maggid Yeshuah* and M. A. Günzburg's *Maggid Emet*—The sad disillusionment—Benjacob's memorandum to Levinsohn.]

N 1827 Nicholas I endowed the Jews of Russia with the "civic right" of military service through a special ukase. The *maskilim* of the type of Frank and Hirsch Baer Hurwitz regarded this as a promise of civic equality, for, along with equal obligations, the "enlightened and gracious" government would certainly also grant equal rights. The Jewish masses, however, perceived in the decree the worst of all the afflictions which they had to endure in the course of the dark period of Nicholas' tyrannical reign. The "superstitious" masses in this connection manifested a far keener historical sense than the *maskilim* and the "enlightened." In the spirit and the text of the ukase, in the cruel and inhumane manner in which it was implemented, it was quite obvious that here was no question of "civic rights" but of a firmly established goal, namely, to coerce the Jews into throwing off their "false belief" as quickly as possible and to cease being distinguished in their conduct and way of life from the Christian populace.

According to the ukase of 1827, almost double the number of recruits were taken from the Jews as from the Christian population. The ukase permitted the conscription of twelve-year-old children as soldiers, and the Jewish recruits "who hold on to their old religion" were not permitted to have any dealings whatever with the Jewish populace. For all arrears, or taxes not paid on time,[1] the *kehillah*, or Jewish community, was punished with an increased quota of conscripts. Of the inhumane sufferings that the Jewish child-recruits, the so-called "cantonists," had to endure, of the afflictions imposed upon them because they refused to adopt the Christian faith—of these we know not only from Jewish memoirs and accounts but also from objective, documented descriptions of Russian contemporaries.[2] As a result of the ukase concerning recruits, the demoralized autonomous Jewish government, the community council office with its leaders, the whole band of "town fathers," obtained a very sharp weapon in their battle against the oppressed and impoverished masses of the people. The dark period of the "informers" and "kidnappers" (*khapers*), which constitutes one of the most shameful pages in the history of the autonomous Jewish government, began.

Isaac Baer Levinsohn lay sick in his upper room at the edge of town but had an open eye and attentive ear for everything that took place in the back alleys, in the poor little houses where the oppressed masses sighed and suffered.[3] He, the invalid who had been bed-ridden for many years, witnessed this and could not be silent about what he saw. He was the first among the *maskilim* who issued forth with a battle-document of a thoroughly social character, in which the great injustice committed against the poor and defenseless strata of the Jewish populace is disclosed with righteous wrath and vehement temper.

1. Because of the enormously burdensome levies in many communities, the tax arrears attained very large sums. For instance, in the province of Podolia the arrears reached the considerable sum of over one and a half million (see S. Borovoi in his work on Jewish colonies, 1928, p. 126).

2. E.g., Herzen in his *Biloye i dumi*, and Nikolai S. Leskov in his story *Ovtsebik*.

3. In his letter to Jacob Tugendhold of December 1833 Levinsohn complains: "I am wearied of hearing every day the cry of those who are robbed of hope and of seeing the tears of the oppressed who expect to receive any help from me, but I have no power to aid them, for a serious illness has stricken me now for many years" (*Tarbiz*, V, 203).

Di Hefker-Velt

We noted previously the contempt Levinsohn had for the "corrupted" Yiddish language. However, he had an excellent notion (after all, he was raised among the *maskilim* of Galicia) of the great importance of the jargon as a weapon. Hence he wrote his battle-document in the folk-language and, since he possessed a spark of the gifted journalist, he became, against his will, just as Aaron Wolfsohn-Halle and Isaac Euchel had in their day, one of the builders and founders of the new Yiddish literature.

Levinsohn's battle-document, *Di Hefker-Velt*, is written in the form of a conversation between a traveler who has come "from Belorussia" with two men of Volhynia, Zeraḥ and Feitel. These two residents of Kremenets familiarize the foreign traveler with what takes place in their community. Feitel complains that in his community "the monthly *parnassim* are thieves and murderers, concerned only with enriching themselves at the expense of the poor people," who are "robbed and plundered day and night." When the traveler asks in astonishment, "Why do you appoint such people community officials?", Feitel answers: "What do you mean?—They appoint themselves." The traveler does not understand and says: "How is that? They must be elected by ballot!" Feitel then gives him to understand:

Yes, they are elected, but how does the balloting take place? There are some rich men in the city, and they are in league with the community officials—to be sure, not for nothing. They are bribed: one is given a notary-fee, another a gift. Banquets are arranged for them, and they are also presented with half rubles. The rest of the common people must certainly reply "Amen" to whatever these persons say, for they are in the lowliest of conditions among us. They are Canaanite slaves to the rich, for if any one of them should open his mouth, he is at once given ten soldiers to feed, or a ruble for porridge-money for the soldiers is demanded of him (since the rich are in league with *kahal*), or his child, his only son, is taken away from him as a recruit. The common people must do everything that the rich man or *kahal* bid.

Amazed, the traveler exclaims, "What you have in your community is Sodom—God forbid!" The second resident of Vohlynia, Zeraḥ, adds his bit: "In fact, since military recruits have been taken, no rich man's child, no influential man's child, no middleman's child, no boy from the study-house has been given away, but only the children of poor people, honest artisan's children who help their parents in their work, decent servants, decent teacher's assistants." Again the traveler does not understand. "But," he asks, "what do they do with an only child, for example? Such a child cannot be given away according to the law."

"Yes," Zerah replies, "as you say, according to the law. You are quite right—in legal proceedings, that is. But, in fact, only little children who have not yet reached the age of twelve are given away, for with a child they can make all kinds of swindleries." Feitel on his part adds:

You should see, my friend, how they drag little children, like pigs, from their mother's bosoms! The pity of it breaks one's heart. The "kidnappers" seize even such small children as they know the military commission will certainly not accept, for they realize that the mothers will sell their shirts and give these to them to have their children left alone. How can one bear to see small children begging their fathers and mothers to blind them or maim them in some other way, so that they shall be free of terror?[4]

"Yes," Feitel further says, "the poor man is always the sacrificial victim. See, my friend, no matter how many forgeries and frauds *kahal* and the other influential men commit, the people must give a deposition every year that they were honest, and the poor people whose skin was flayed from them with illegal assessments and taxes must themselves sign the statement. And if it must be sworn to, they must also swear."

Zerah, in this connection, adds his words: "Oh, the robbers, in addition, play a pious role. They are always traveling to *gute Yidn* for the Sabbath, pretend to be God-fearing, and especially the *groschen* is light among them [i.e., they make and spend money easily]. They are just like the cardplayers." And when the traveler remarks: "As I see, here, unfortunately, there are many common people, poor artisans and householders, who must perish of hunger," Feitel replies:

What, then, do you think? Whoever, unfortunately, is an honest man is wretched. How many do you think there are all together of those who

4. This motif later found a resonance in the well-known folksong:

> Tears are poured out in the streets,
> One can wash in the blood of children . . .
> Little birds are torn away from school,
> Russian clothing is put on them.
> Our *parnassim*, our rabbis
> Even help to deliver them as Russians.
> Zushe Rokover has seven sons—
> And not one of them is among the Russians.
> But the widow Leah's only child
> Is a sacrificial victim for the sins of the community.
> It is a good deed to deliver up common people—
> Shoemaker, tailor—they are, after all, idlers.
> Scabby Khaytzikls from a fine family—
> Of these not a one may go away among us.

scintillate in town? Thirty or forty persons. These are the cream of the crop. The general principle is this: whoever can be something of a doer in town lives from this. The rest of the people—they toil, tear their clothing in mourning, earn their *groschen* with the bitter sweat of their brow. What use is it? They must labor for the wives and children of others. All their "good luck" goes into the overstuffed rich; these mulct them day and night with levies, with taxes, with recruit-money, with ox-money. May God have great mercy upon them.

Later Feitel adds:

If it were not for the recruiting system, once upon a time the *kahal* was very afraid to skin the poor so grossly. Indeed, they were quite fearful; the common people would actually at times pounce on and vilify them, and actually sometimes submitted a complaint to a governor. The terror was not so great. At present, since recruits are taken, the common people tremble in fear of opening their mouths. In short, they are completely sold to the rich man like Canaanite slaves. As the gentile proverb says: "They beat one and do not even allow him to cry."[5]

Levinsohn, however, recalls very well that the ukase concerning the conscription recruits was a gift of the "gracious king." He also has no doubt of the fact that his opponents, the "band of town-householders," will attempt to use his *Hefker-Velt* against him, and let it be heard in the "high windows" of the government offices that he is a "rebel against the government." Hence, he protects himself and has Feitel pose the question: "Why don't you rather ask, my dear fellow, does one need a situation better than the fact that the czar, may his days be long, was so concerned with

5. Levinsohn returns to the question of recruits in his satire *Toledot Peloni Almoni Ha-Kozevi* in which he portrays in the darkest colors the "chief of the kidnappers" and of the community council room. He describes how this community councilman "used to divide the family of the rich man into two small ones in order to exempt them from providing recruits, and would pair together poor families, making of them one large one, in order to take as many recruits as possible from it. If a rich man has several grownup sons, he lists him as another, terribly poor man who has an only son and, moreover, one still very young—the child may be eight or nine years old altogether; nevertheless, the poor little boy is surrendered for the rich man's six grownup sons." Levinsohn portrays this community councilman's house in the following fashion: "His house is wide open, buzzing with many people, men, women, and children from the poor class of the people, who wail with the wail of misfortune, and their cry reaches the heavens. Here a child shrieks bitterly, there a woman spreads out her hands [in pleading]; here an old woman faints, there an old man of eighty falls to the ground in embittered weeping. And the ear of this 'chief of the kidnappers' regards the sound of the weeping like the sound of a flute. He walks about his house hither and thither and laughs or whistles to his birds, or sits down with his children at the table to luncheon or to supper, to fulfill what is said: 'And the king and Haman sat down to drink, but the city of Shushan was perplexed.' "

conscripting recruits justly, so that everything should proceed honestly and properly?"[6]

Did Levinsohn actually believe that Nicholas I with his decree of 1827 "was concerned with conscripting recruits justly," or did he write this merely for show, taking into account the contemporary conditions of censorship? It is virtually beyond doubt that the former supposition is more correct. After all, Levinsohn like the other *maskilim* of his generation, perceived the government as his only support in his battle for Haskalah, the only power that can reconstruct and renew Jewish life. As a convinced rationalist and idealist, Levinsohn was certain that it is sufficient to give the government understanding, to explain to it the true significance of Judaism and what ought to be done to make useful and enlightened citizens out of the Jewish populace, for the "gracious government certainly to carry this through."

It is clear that the *maskilim* obviously witnessed at every step the dark injustices and deeds of violence that occurred in actual life in the cruel times of Nicholas I. However, they endeavored to convince themselves that not the czar and his associates were responsible for this, but the avaricious and ignorant petty local *tchinovniks* (officials). Typical in this respect are the following lines which Levinsohn's disciple and admirer Abraham Baer Gottlober wrote to a friend of his:

I know very well how lovingly the hearts of the gracious czar and his good counsellors are directed toward us; they are concerned only about the citizens of the land, and in everything they undertake, their only purpose is to achieve the useful and the good. But with all their goodness and honesty, they are, after all, not gods who could immediately, at first glance, firmly decide what is necessary and useful. Hence, they appoint under themselves all kinds of officials and government people. The latter again also do nothing without their collaborators and employees, and the smaller and lower the officials are, the weaker becomes the drive for truth and justice among them. Many of them do not think at all about honestly fulfilling the laws and decrees; they are concerned only with what is of use to themselves and their own benefits.

However, not a few disillusionments were to come in this connection to the patriotically-minded Levinsohn. In November

6. Also in his just-mentioned satire *Toledot Peloni Almoni Ha-Kozevi*, when Levinsohn portrays the dark deeds of the community council people, he considers it necessary to note in this connection: "And the good commands of the government they trample with their feet." *Di Hefker-Velt* could not, under the censorship conditions prevalent at that time, appear in print. It was merely circulated in handwritten copies. *Di Hefker-Velt* was first published in Sholom Aleichem's *Di Yidishe Folks-Bibliotek*, I, 1888, and later several times reprinted. We employ the edition of 1896.

1832, he addressed a long letter directly to Nicholas I about reforming the character of the Jewish school system and about facilitating the possibility of Jews engaging in agriculture.[7] He also did not consider it possible to leave undiscussed the question of the "cantonists" and points out the extremely rigorous and harsh conditions under which recruits were selected from the Jews. To this Nicholas responded with the following resolution: "Inform Levinsohn that recruiting soldiers among Jews has as its purpose to remove the idlers or parasites (*unichtozhit tuneyadtsev*) who lie like a heavy burden on their own brethren."[8]

A year earlier (in 1831), the sickly but tireless Levinsohn submitted to the minister of education, Karl Liven, a long memorandum, written in German, about reforming Jewish education and establishing Jewish schools. In 1833 he addressed the government with a project which evoked certain differences of opinion among subsequent historians of culture, some of whom saw in it a truly "fatal step" (*rokovoi shag*) that represented a "sad enigma."[9] This is the project that Levinsohn submitted to the minister of internal affairs, D.N. Bludov, on closing all the existing Jewish presses and, in their place, opening only three new ones—one in Vilna, and two in other cities where Jewish censors were located. This project is closely connected with the decree of 1836 concerning the closing of all Jewish presses and casting the strict censorship of Nicholas I on all Jewish books already in print as well—a decree of great importance for Jewish cultural history of the nineteenth century. Hence it is worth dwelling on this "misfortune-bringing step" of Levinsohn's at some length.

We observed previously how much hardship Manasseh of Ilya and Isaac Baer Levinsohn had to suffer in printing their works. The pious owners of presses, especially the Hasidim, did not wish to "desecrate" their presses with heretical volumes. At the same time the Jewish book-market was flooded with a tremendous number of Hasidic books and propaganda writings so intensely despised by the *maskilim*. These were printed in thousands of copies by the

7. In his letter to Jacob Tugendhold of the sixteenth of Kislev 5593 (December, 1832) Levinsohn writes: "I have written a letter to the noble emperor and I hope, with the help of God, to receive some answer quickly; and in it I wrote for the good of my people. I also informed my lord that a very large number of heads of households took it upon themselves to engage in agriculture, and many have already settled in villages and are working their plots of ground. And with the help of God I explained this matter, as is known, to the dear government, and according to the testimony of the letters that are in my hand from the great men among the heads of the country and from the minister. And in the letter I was privileged to write to the czar, may his glory increase, I spoke much of this, and it is now three weeks since I sent this letter" (see *Tarbiz*, 1934, V, 204)

8. Zinberg, "Isaac Baer Levinsohn" (in Russian), 1910, p. 66.

9. *Perezhitoye*, III, 2, 14.

numerous presses in Volhynia. It would, however, be erroneous to think that only the *maskilim* regarded the Volhynian presses and their productions with great hostility; these evoked no less disgust in Mitnagdic learned circles. Many rabbis and scholars began to note with great indignation that the Volhynian presses (Slavuta, Sudylkow, and others) allow themselves, in reprinting the works of acknowledged authorities, e.g., the *Responsa* of Rabbi David ben Solomon Ibn Abi Zimra and Bezalel Ashkenazi, to throw out whole paragraphs and sections. Hence, they used to admonish that it is impermissible to use the "books of the *Rishonim*" coming off the Volhynian presses until one compares them with earlier editions.[10]

Great bitterness was evoked in Lithuanian learned circles by the fact that the Slavuta printers, the well-known brothers Spira, declined to print in their edition of the Talmud (1817-1822) the notes of the Gaon of Vilna. This discontent finally led to a serious conflict which, in its time, agitated the whole rabbinic world. When the Slavuta printers, at the beginning of the 1830s, were preparing to undertake a new edition of the Talmud, they learned that the Vilna printer Romm wished to become an "intruder on their territory" and also reprint the entire Babylonian Talmud. This called forth a stubborn battle between the Slavuta and the Vilna printers in which over a hundred rabbis participated on both sides.[11] It is clear that this conflict was actually a direct consequence of the many years of dissatisfaction prevalent in the rabbinic-Mitnagdic circles toward the Hasidic printers of Volhynia.

It is beyond doubt that both sides, as was the case at the time of the religious conflict at the end of the eighteenth century, did not content themselves merely with lawsuits and warnings but also not infrequently addressed their complaints to the *nachalstvo*, or government administration. Therewith, apparently, is explicable the fact that in 1827 the czar Nicholas suddenly became interested in the Jewish presses and demanded of the minister of education that he submit to him, within two days, information regarding the number of Jewish presses with an indication by whose permission they were established. The ministry assembled the necessary information on the basis of the "memoranda" which two apostates, the previously mentioned Zandberg[12] and Podello, had submitted several years earlier. In these two reports, about twenty Jewish presses are listed. Zandberg notes in this connection that the Jewish presses constitute quite profitable businesses; some of them

10. See *Kiryat Sefer*, II, 100-101.
11. On this battle, see Hillel Maggid-Steinschneider, *Ir Vilna*, 21-26.
12. S. Borovoi, *Narisi z istorii yevreyskoi knigi na ukraini*, II, 1926.

annually print books valued at a sum of one hundred thousand rubles, others of ten thousand rubles. Others again, Zandberg adds, when occasionally they have no work, conceive books themselves or address other authors, requesting that they provide them with any works whatever for printing, be it even foolish and wildly bizarre books, as long as there is in them *halatzah*, joking, hidden ridicule and contempt of other religions. Such books arouse hatred toward the Christian fatherland and disloyalty to the government among the young.[13]

From a secret report of the minister of education Uvarov, we learn that at the beginning of 1828 the edition of *Shivhei Etz Hayyim*, which had appeared in 1826 in Ostrog, was proscribed and a roster of fifty other works which ought to be prohibited was put together. Immediately after this (in March, 1828), there appeared an imperial decree ordering the confiscation of all harmful Jewish books.[14] In 1831 the *maskil* Wolf Tugendhold, who was the Jewish censor in Vilna, submitted a report to the minister of education that, among the Jews in Russia, numerous Hasidic books that were printed without the authorization of the censorship are circulating. In this connection he issues forth with a whole act of accusation against the presses of Volhynia and Podolia. "In these presses," declares Tugendhold, "not one useful book has as yet been printed. These are true nests of Kabbalist and mystical works. Hence, the Jews who dwell in these regions are centuries behind their co-religionists living in other territories in their spiritual and intellectual development."[15]

In 1833, Levinsohn relates, the Kiev professor Savitzky addressed to him the question whether it is true that in the Jewish presses many Jewish books are printed without the authorization of the censorship, and among these are numerous pernicious works.[16] At first glance, it seems hardly comprehensible why a Russian professor should suddenly become interested in Jewish presses. The matter becomes clearer when one becomes familiar with the secret letter of January 1834 which Bludov sent to Uvarov. In it is related that Savitsky, along with two Jews named Mekel and Berenstein, have proposed to the minister for internal affairs a project on how to battle against the dissemination of nefarious Hasidic books: to examine in the strictest fashion, through special commissars, all books which are presently in the possession of Jews and have been printed until now in Russia and Poland; to separate

13. See J. I. Hessen, *Yevreyskaya Starina*, 1909, II, 251-255.
14. See *Voskhod*, 1903, VI, 136.
15. See S. Borovoi, *op. cit.*, 9-10 and *Voskhod*, 1903, VI, 131-132.
16. *Shorshei Ha-Levanon*, 295.

from them the non-Hasidic books, and to destroy all the others, without exception, and strictly punish those who will allow themselves to hide such books in their homes; to close all existing Jewish presses, open no more than three new ones, and grant certain entrepreneurs the privilege of operating these for fifteen years.[17]

These two Jews with their project simply intended "business." They hoped that the privilege of opening the three new presses would be granted to both of them, and as a monopoly, would produce a very good commercial venture.[18] To strengthen their cause, so their project might be even more favorable to the *nachalstvo*, or government administration, they attracted the learned professor, probably also not "in order not to obtain a reward," i.e., not without pay and merely for the cause itself.

Thanks to these projects, rumors spread among the Jewish intelligentsia that all the Hasidic publications would soon be proscribed. "How does it stand," Joseph Perl asks in his letter of 1833 to Levinsohn, "with the ukase about the books of the Hasidim which, according to rumor, will be burned and removed from the world?"[19] Then Levinsohn also came forward. In his letter to one of the rabbis who were empowered in 1836 to censor Jewish books,[20] he relates that

when I obtained the inquiry from Savitsky, I was afraid that—God forbid—great harm might come therefrom for all Jewish presses and Jewish books. Hence, on July 20, 1833, I proposed to the minister Bludov a project that there be no more than three Jewish presses, one in Vilna and two others in places where there is a censor. I also dispatched to the minister a list of old and new works, noting which are fitting and necessary to be reprinted: books of prayers, commentaries to the Bible or Talmud, the books of the codifiers among the *Rishonim* and *Aharonim*, books of science and grammar, books on morality and ethics, essential textbooks for children, and those works which the poor masses and women eagerly read. I explained this in full detail, indicated the great virtues of these books, their enormous value and moral significance, and the importance of their authors . . . My intention was exclusively the good of our Jewish brethren and the welfare of our government. However, there is much to speak of in this matter, and this is not the place for it. God is my witness that, since I have become a mature man, I have devoted all my energies to bringing utility to our brethren in Russia. My only goal is to raise the

17. *Voskhod*, 1903, VI, 131.
18. See *Russian-Jewish Encyclopedia*, XV, 799.
19. *Be'er Yitzhak*, 41.
20. *Shorshei Ha-Levanon*, 1842, 295. For a further discussion of this letter and Levinsohn's complaints against the rabbinic censors who, out of ignorance, spoiled many works through their clumsy censorship, see our work (in Russian) "Isaac Baer Levinsohn and his Time," in *Yevreyskaya Starina*, 1910.

honor of our people, of our sacred Torah and of the works of our sages, to protect them from every injury and to deflect all false accusations against us and against our sages, may their memory be for a blessing.

It is beyond doubt that in the roster of useful books and those that it is desirable to reprint which Levinsohn submitted to the minister, there was not one work of the Hasidic literature that he so despised. On the other hand, there were in it a considerable number of books about whose fate Levinsohn was greatly concerned and which he tried to protect with all his powers. After all, he knew very well with what contempt a certain type of *maskil*, e.g., Hirsch Baer Hurwitz and the Galician Jehudah Leib Miesis, regarded the codifiers and even the Talmud. He was also familiar with another category of "the enlightened" of whom he speaks with such bitterness in his *Bet Yehudah*[21] as of people "who are men of no repute, lacking knowledge," who consider themselves *maskilim* because they have grasped "at the point of a knife" [i.e., very superficially] a few German and French phrases, who consider themselves complete philosophers, mock the Jewish religion, declare it pure superstition, and boast of their vile deeds.

We must, in this connection, also take into consideration that in 1827, simultaneously with the recruitment decree, there appeared another decree which had a certain economic as well as cultural significance for the Jewish populace. This is the reform of concessions in regard to the right of selling liquor in the country. This reform produced among the Jews a new half-privileged category, the *otkuptshiks* and *aktzizniks* (lessees of the liquor trades and those employed by them). With quite favorable material conditions, in constant contact with the government, the *aktzizniks* occupied a rather independent position in the community. They cast off the old-fashioned costume and wore European clothing, had a greater or lesser command of the language of the country, and allowed themselves to violate certain religious customs.[22]

---

21. *Ibid.*, 320-321. Levinsohn frequently refers in his letters to the instantaneously and superficially "enlightened" and to the "counterfeit Haskalah."

22. This behavior of the "liquor excise people" found a certain resonance in the folk-creativity. The folksong about the "excise people" is well known:

> The liquor excise people
> Are very wanton;
> They shave their little beards,
> And ride on ponies,
> They parade in the streets,
> And gorge themselves without ritually washing their hands.

(See the Marek-Ginsburg anthology, 54)

These half-educated *maskilim*, quite superficially anointed with culture, would come to the government with their projects for "enlightenment"—not to speak of such "men of practical understanding" as the apostates Zandberg and Podello who used to supply the ministry of education with essential information about Jewish affairs.

We noted previously that Hasidism was so despised by Levinsohn not so much for its "superstition" and hostility toward secular knowledge as chiefly because it paralyzed the will of the people, removed them from productive labor, and strengthened in them blind trust in the aid of the *tzaddik* who bestows "life, children, and livelihood." The removal from productive work was, indeed, according to Levinsohn's firm conviction, the major factor explaining why the government and the surrounding populace regard the Jews with such suspicion and cannot recognize them as useful citizens. Especially characteristic in this respect is Levinsohn's highly interesting above-quoted letter of December 1832 to the *maskil* Jacob Tugendhold, who was the censor of Jewish books in Warsaw.[23] Just at that time *Bikkurei Ha-Ittim* succumbed. *Kerem Ḥemed* had not yet appeared. Hence, Levinsohn reports to Tugendhold about a new annual collection of articles entitled *Tziyyon*.[24]

The first volume is almost finished and ready for printing. However, he notes in this connection that something more is involved here than establishing a scholarly journal. I inform you, writes Levinsohn, that it is a question here of forming a society of *maskilim* that sets itself the task of supporting the "men of science and those who seek after it" and spreading knowledge as much as possible.

How long will we look on as the sect of the Hasidim are closely associated with each other in a firm bond? They aid each other and, in consequence thereof, achieve their foolish purpose toward which they strive and have the upper hand. And the men of our fellowship (i.e., the *maskilim*) are weak and poor. Responsible for this is, indeed, only the division of hearts, the fact that we cannot agree among ourselves and do not cling together firmly. But we should take into our society men who are not only lovers of science but also morally clean men, men of righteousness and justice. The members of this society ought to help each other and be concerned for the general welfare, in order to find grace and favor in the eyes of others, especially in the eyes of our czar with his officials, and in the eyes of the people amidst which we dwell. For all of these eagerly wish to do good for

23. This letter was first published by B. Weinryb in *Tarbiz*, V, 1934, 199-207.
24. Each collection was supposed to consist of five printer's sheets. Besides Hebrew works, there were also supposed to be printed in parts thereof articles in other languages ("the bulk of it will be in the holy tongue, and a small amount of it in German, Russian, and Polish").

our people and desire happiness for it. Only the foolish Hasidim, with their evil and false deeds, bring about the hostility of the government. For God knows and every understanding man among us knows how much we wish to obtain the czar's love and the love of the country, and that we are prepared loyally to serve the czar with all our heart and wish him and all those associated with him happiness. The government would certainly also repay us with grace and love, if not for these fools among the Hasidim who remove us [i.e., the Jewish people] so greatly with their follies.

"You must know," Levinsohn notes, "that the well-known leaders of the Galician Haskalah also support us, and if there will be true love and brotherhood among the morally clean *maskilim*, the help which the people of Israel will obtain through them will be enormous." But, Levinsohn repeats in this connection, one must be extremely careful not to receive into the society anyone who merely looks like a *maskil*, for there are those who are, indeed, very competent in speech and in science but are, nevertheless, a thousand times worse than any of the sect of the Hasidim who cannot even read plain Yiddish.

Levinsohn projected this "society of *maskilim*" as a secret order whose goals must remain concealed not merely from those who have subscribed to the annual collection *Tziyyon*, but even from a segment of their editors and collaborators. "Only the few excellent men must know about its purpose," he writes.

Nothing came of the annual *Tziyyon*[25] or of the society of *maskilim*. On the other hand, Levinsohn endeavored with inde-fatigable industry to realize the other point that is touched on in his letter to Tugendhold and that occupies such an important place in his above-mentioned reform program: involving a considerable segment of the Jewish populace in agriculture. As we know, he wrote about this in his letter to Nicholas I at the end of 1836, and a few months later circulated propaganda letters to many Jewish communities urging them to betake themselves to agriculture and to form Jewish colonies. Thanks to his propaganda, in his own native town fifty-two families of Kremenets decided to petition the government to distribute to them land to cultivate in the Kherson region. The author relates with satisfaction in *Bet Yehudah*[26] how these families authorized him, Levinsohn, to apply in their name to the appropriate offices, and how the government agreed to allow all the families to establish a colony in the province of Kherson.[27]

25. Also unrealized was a later (1843) project of Levinsohn's—the publication, along with Erter and several other Galician *maskilim*, of a monthly journal (see *Sefer Ha-Zichronot*, 70).
26. P. 353.
27. All the documents mentioned by Levinsohn are published in *He-Avar*, 1918, I, 185–190. However there is great doubt whether the project was actually fulfilled (on this see Borovoi, *op. cit.*, 133).

Levinsohn notes in this connection that he received a hand-written letter on this matter from the secretary of state Longinov that "is dearer to him than the most precious things." Whole legends circulated about Levinsohn's influence with the government. His disciple and admirer, the well-known participant in Haskalah activities, A.B. Gottlober, tells as an eyewitness of a handwritten letter that Nicholas I is supposed to have sent Levinsohn.[28] The latter himself, for exclusively strategic reasons, so that his opponents would be afraid to issue forth against him, was wont to underscore his influence among prominent officials.

To be sure, not everything was mere legend. We have already seen how, in 1828, Levinsohn was awarded, by the "supreme command," a thousand rubles for his work, which stimulates "the moral renewal of the Jewish people." It is also beyond doubt that the enlightener aroused great interest among cultured and prominent Russian officials who knew only of Jewish brokers, dealers, and barbaric fanatics and who suddenly realized that in a castaway town, in a poor hut, lives a Jew who writes and speaks fluent German and Latin and possesses extensive and many-faceted knowledge in the various realms of humanistic scholarship. When any of the prominent officials had occasion to travel through Kremenets, he used to visit Levinsohn with interest to see this extraordinary phenomenon with his own eyes. Count Dmitri Tolstoy, the later so lamentably known minister, even considered it necessary to sketch the portrait of the sickly "learned Jew" who lives in Kremenets under such grievously impoverished circumstances, and later presented this portrait to the Grand Duchess Maria Nikolaevna.[29]

However, it is not without reason that Levinsohn underscores in his above-quoted letter that his "sole aim is to raise the honor of our people, of our sacred Torah, and of the works of our sages, to protect them from every injury and to deflect all false accusations from our sages" (see above, pp. 62–63). This, in fact, he accomplished, commensurate with his powers and opportunities. Indeed, thereby Levinsohn necessarily had to arouse suspicion and a certain dissatisfaction in Nicholas and his collaborators.

We have observed previously how even such a liberal man as A. Chartoriski was firmly convinced that "no culture and education for any European people is in any way conceivable except in the spirit of Christian morality," and that "true education" can be obtained by Jews only when "they will accept the morality of the Christian religion." In the manifesto of December 24, 1827, in

28. See *Sefer Ha-Zichronot*, 143-44.
29. *Iggerot Ribal*, 8; *Sefer Ha-Zichronot*, 144.

regard to matters of the ministry of education, it is especially stressed that the foundation of true education must be "Christian piety (*Khristianskoe blagochestie*)." The minister Bludov was firmly persuaded that the Jewish faith, which is based mainly on the "wildly foolish" doctrine of the Talmud, is contrary in spirit to Christian society and, therefore, always more or less pernicious.

This expressed view obtained the "supreme" assent of Nicholas I.[30] Nicholas, in general, regarded religious questions from the purely "police" standpoint. His ideal, after all, was to make of all of mighty Russia one great barracks, in which all the inhabitants would be drilled automata. Their entire life, all their thoughts, demands and desires, should be strictly regimented, firmly determined according to the command and dictate of the government authority. Religion ought also to be a "government-ordered matter" and serve the levelling principle, so that all should believe similarly, in one and the same fashion, as the government power commands. But the Jewish populace, with its religion, with its entire way of life and external appearance, was screamingly inconsistent with the levelling system of Nicholas. In this the czar saw on audacity, a "rebelliousness," and was persuaded that responsible for it is "the false belief of the Jews," along with the "wildly foolish" Talmud.

Levinsohn, however, set himself the task of "deflecting all false accusations from our sages." He believed with iron firmness in the persuasive power of apologetic. At the same time as he propagandized among the Jews of Kremenets for the establishment of an agricultural colony in Kherson, in another community of Volhynia (Zaslav) a great misfortune occurred. The bloody ghost of the Middle Ages, the ritual-murder charge, was resurrected there. Many prominent members of the community lived in dread. In their great distress they applied to Levinsohn to intercede with the government for the innocent persons who had been arrested and to compose a special work in which he would demonstrate clearly that the ritual-murder libel has no foundation whatever. Levinsohn faithfully fulfilled their proposal. He set aside all his literary works and, with tireless industry, collected the necessary documents and decrees for a discussion of this question. In 1834 his defense document, *Efes Damim*, was already completed.

The work is written in the old-fashioned form of a debate between the patriarch of the Orthodox church in Jerusalem, Simias, and the chief rabbi there, Maimon. In Heinrich Heine's well-known *Disputation* the Capuchin monk and the rabbi greet each other with terrible curses and invectives. A quite different

30. See Borovoi, *op. cit.*, 7.

spirit dominates Levinsohn's disputants. Peaceably and calmly the debate proceeds. The patriarch regards the alien faith with respect. Not out of hatred and a sentiment of revenge does he introduce arguments which might confirm the blood libel, but because he wishes to know the truth for himself. And when his opponent demonstrates to him with solid proofs how false and ungrounded this accusation is, he thanks him heartily. At the end the patriarch and the rabbi embrace like true brothers.

Efes Damim appeared in print in 1837. Three years later, when a new ritual-murder accusation in remote Damascus agitated all of Jewry, at the initiative of Sir Moses Montefiore, his secretary Dr. Eliezer Halevi translated Levinsohn's work into English. The translation made an impression in the learned world, and the work was recognized as "a good weapon, sharpened and polished by a faithful and expert hand." *Efes Damim* was also supposed to have been published in Polish and Russian translation immediately after its publication in Hebrew.

The Russian translation was to have been provided by Osip Rabinovich,[31] the future editor of the first Russian-Jewish journal *Razsvet*. This translation, however, was not accomplished for the following reasons. As soon as Levinsohn had completed his *Efes Damim*, he immediately dispatched a special copy of the work to highly placed officials so that they, too, and the "gracious king" who, "after all, strives only for the pure truth," might be persuaded that the bloody accusation has no foundation whatever and is nothing more than a libel. The results, however, for Levinsohn were quite unanticipated.

We noted previously the grievous material distress in which the sickly author lived. Even for his *Efes Damim*, which was commissioned for the "general welfare," he did not receive any support whatever from the communities, despite the fact that the collecting of the material necessary for the work and the copying of the various historical documents involved certain expenses. Helpless and abandoned, Levinsohn, in 1836, even before his *Efes Damim* appeared in print, applied to the place whence he had once previously (in 1828) obtained material support—the government. He submitted his petition to the then minister of internal affairs Bludov, to whom all the documents in regard to his propaganda for engaging Jews in agriculture had been transmitted not long before.[32] The minister, however, did not deem it necessary to be an intercessor for the sickly Jewish scholar and to support his petition.

---

31. See *Be'er Yitzhak*, 106. Only somewhat less than fifty years later (1883) did *Efes Damim* appear in a Russian translation by Y. Sorkin.
32. *Bet Yehudah*, 353.

Bludov himself explains his reasons in his official memorandum to the minister of education Uvarov. He there calls Uvarov's particular attention to Levinsohn's last work, *Efes Damim:*

Can not the representatives of the Orthodox church especially find unreliable and literally seductive *(soblaznitelni)* such a discussion between a rabbi and the patriarch of Jerusalem, in which the former endeavors to show that in the Talmud there is nothing that is inconsistent with the Christian faith? This is especially impermissible because this view [of Levinsohn's] is absolutely false and has no foundation whatever.[33]

Uvarov agreed with Bludov's conclusion, and Levinsohn's petition regarding material support did not reach the czar. We noted previously how the high officials and the representatives of the grand nobility considered it a well-known fact that the Talmud is a "book of lies," filled with nothing but foolishness and superstition. A certain type of *maskil* of Hirsch Baer Hurwitz's character encouraged the Russian officials in this idea. Levinsohn, with his respectful attitude toward the Talmud, which he regarded as a highly important cultural-historical monument, actually discredited himself in the eyes of the Bludovs and Uvarovs. They began to look with suspicion on this unique "enlightener." The objective historian must praise Levinsohn for having had the moral courage not to be frightened by the suspicion and ill-will of the officials who were the only source from which the needy and sickly writer could hope for material aid. After all, he believed so firmly in the persuasive and enlightening power of logical ideas based on common sense and on historical facts.

Just at that time a certain apostate from Vitebsk, Asher Tiemkin, composed an anti-Talmudic tract entitled *Derech Selulah.* The attention of Nicholas I was drawn to this work and, at his command, Tiemkin's tract was published (in 1835), along with a Russian translation.[34] Levinsohn refused to take into consideration the "supreme" endorsement and composed a special counter-document entitled *Yemin Tzidki*, in which he demonstrates with great erudition that all the accusations of the author of *Derech Selulah*, a work which ostensibly aims to "enlighten the eyes of his brethren," are filled with ignorance, deceptions, and falsified quotations. Especially characteristic in this respect is another apologetic composition by Levinsohn entitled *Aḥiyyah Ha-Shiloni Ha-Ḥozeh*.

In 1839 an English missionary named McCaul published a work

33. See J. I. Hessen, *Perezhitoye*, III, 16.
34. See Elijah (Ilya) Orshanski's work, *Russkoye zakonodatelstvo o yevreyakh* (Russian Legislation Concerning the Jews), 22-23.

Old Paths (in Hebrew translation, *Netivot Olam*) which was supposed to demonstrate that the Talmud, as well as other Hebrew religious and ethical writings, are filled to overflowing with barbaric superstition and preach hostility and hatred for all other religions, especially the Christian. This missionary book was translated into several languages and obtained rather wide circulation. As a response to *Netivot Olam*, Levinsohn projected a major work in four parts, *Zerubbavel*, in which he undertook to give a historical-critical evaluation of the Talmud and thereby show how ungrounded and false the attacks on the Jewish religion and ethics made by all of the Tiemkins and McCauls are. But before he undertook this scholarly work, which he wrote in the course of more than twelve years, he composed *Aḥiyyah Ha-Shiloni Ha-Hozeh*. This work is written in such a militant and polemical tone that it could not under any circumstances be printed in czarist Russia and was published abroad only after the author's death (Leipzig, 1863).

Aḥiyyah Ha-Shiloni is, in fact, not an apologetic work but an act of accusation, a challenge to Christian society that speaks with such arrogance and contempt about the ethical demoralization and barbaric superstition of the Jewish populace which believes in the "mendacious and misanthropic" Talmud.

Like *Efes Damim*, *Aḥiyyah Ha-Shiloni* is written in the form of a "debate" between the Lutheran Don Alfonso and the Jewish scholar Zedekiah Mizraḥi of the town of Yesharim.[35] Under the latter's name the author himself speaks.

The Christian peoples, Mizraḥi argues, glory so in their tolerance. Nevertheless, they appoint missionaries to propagandize among the Jews, urging them to adopt the Christian faith. These missionaries cover our religion with mockery and shame, and we are forced to be silent. Even when you challenge us to a debate, you do not let us speak. You merely compel us to listen to your arguments and wish to persuade us by coercion, not through the word but through the power of the fist, because you are the rulers of the country and we are strangers. Can a slave dispute with his master? You blaspheme our faith. You fabricate libels against us, and our mouths are closed and we are forced to be silent.[36] You glory so in your religion, since its foundation is love of mankind. We Jews know very well what your love for mankind means. The innocently shed blood of whole generations, the thousands of our unfortunate brothers and sisters tortured to death, cries out

---

35. In *gematria*, the word *yesharim* is equivalent to Kremenets; Aḥiyyah Shiloni Ha-Hozeh, to Yitzhak Dov Levinsohn; and Zedekiah Mizraḥi, to Yitzhak Ber.
36. *Aḥiyyah Shiloni*, 7-11.

concerning this; every page of our history, every stone of your land, tells of it. And even at the present day, when the bloody sword no longer rules as before, we feel your love very well: here we are robbed of our rights of citizenship, there we are driven from the land, and elsewhere we are contemned and our life is embittered in every way possible.[37]

Pointing out that Christians violate the basic teaching of the Law of Moses as well as of the Christian faith, "And thou shalt love thy neighbor as thyself," Mizraḥi asks:

What will they answer when the day of judgment arrives, when their redeemer (as they believe) will appear again and conduct the great world-judgment? The day of judgment will be hard for you Christians. For your redeemer will ask you: If you believe in me and in my precepts, why did you not fulfill the most important of my fundamental commandments: to love every man as yourself—including even your enemy? Once you transgress the basic element of my teaching, you destroy my whole structure. And if you yourselves do not fulfill my commandments, why do you persecute those who do not believe in me?[38]

"You," Mizraḥi exclaims, "demand of us that we adopt the Christian faith—and you yourselves are not Christians!" And he points out how the Christians trample Christ's ethical teaching on love and justice with their feet.[39] If I wished to list all the ethical commandments of your gospel which you do not fulfill and of which you do just the opposite, Mizraḥi concludes, I would have to write a special thick volume. You who accuse Jews of avarice—do you yourselves fulfill the words of the gospel: "He who is greedy for money is the enemy of God?" Even your clergy will not bury a dead person until they are paid beforehand, no matter how poor and needy the deceased's relatives may be. You Christians think yourselves so great and speak with such contempt about Jewish "superstitions," when the foundations of your faith are so closely associated with fantastic miracles and legends which you took over from the ancient idolatrous peoples.[40] With your faith, which is built purely on miracles and legends that are in complete contradiction to logical ideas, it is generally wisest not to enter into inquiries regarding religious questions.[41] Your missionaries complain so about the cruelty of our rabbis who have devised so many severities, and the people, unfortunately, sob under the heavy

37. *Ibid.*, 13.
38. *Ibid.*, 14.
39. *Ibid.*, 53-54.
40. *Ibid.*, 97, 105.
41. *Ibid.*, 11.

yoke. "But how can the cruelty of our rabbis," Mizrahi asks, "be compared with the bloody deeds of the Catholic clergy?"[42]

It suffices to read through the emotive pages of *Ahiyyah Ha-Shiloni* in which Levinsohn portrays with sentimental enthusiasm the moral beauty of Jewish patriarchal life and the purity of the Jewish ethic and family life[43] to obtain a clear notion of the great distance which separates the author from such enlighteners as Jehudah Leib Miesis, Hirsch Baer Hurwitz, and others like them.

Nicholas' ministers and officials refused to forgive Levinsohn and did not consider it desirable or useful to support such a suspicious enlightener who praises the "mendacious" Talmud so greatly. It was also considered unsuitable to recommend his works for the newly established Jewish schools. The petitions for material assistance which Levinsohn submitted to the government remained unanswered, and it was only less than two years before his death, when Alexander II already sat on the Russian throne and the "period of great reforms" began, that the government purchased from him for three thousand rubles a certain number of copies of his *Te'udah Be-Yisrael* and *Bet Yehudah* which were now recognized as useful textbooks in the Jewish schools.

Levinsohn undoubtedly knew how the high officials regarded the Jewish faith in general and the Talmud in particular. But, he believed so firmly in the good will of the "gracious" government, which strives only for the truth, that he was firmly persuaded that he could manage to convince the "truth-loving" government with his logical arguments. The true reality—life in czarist Russia, over which Nicholas' knout-regime ruled with such cruel and despotic stubbornness—however, ruthlessly destroyed the utopian hopes of the naive enlightener of Kremenets.

We noted previously that in 1836 Levinsohn addressed a memorandum to Nicholas I "on the desperate needs of our brethren." This was shortly after the ukase of 1835 which included certain concessions to Jewish colonists and agriculturists. In his above-mentioned letter (see p. 65), Levinsohn relates that, "with God's help," he was honored on December 22, 1836 with a gracious reply which permits him to hope that the czar will soon come to the aid of the Jewish people. With great pleasure he reports that all the documents in regard to his propaganda about settling Jews in colonies had been transmitted to the minister Bludov (see above, p. 68). He hoped that no little salvation would result from this.

---

42. *Ibid.*, 107-108.
43. *Ibid.*, 116-128. Levinsohn, in this connection, deems it necessary to stress that Jewry is indebted for its moral power and ethical purity to the Talmud, the "great teacher of the Jews" (123).

However, he had no notion of the fact that at that very time, Bludov, together with the well-known chief of gendarmes Beckendorf, was making intercessions to nullify the decree of 1835, according to which Jews would be permitted to settle in Siberia on free, hitherto uncultivated land, in order to colonize it. Bludov was motivated by the belief that, since the Jews, "as is known, cannot glory in their morality," they might also "ruin and demoralize the local inhabitants" in Siberia.[44]

The above-mentioned project, on which Levinsohn expended so much energy—the settling of several score families of Kremenets on the soil of Kherson—was stifled in the bureaucratic chancelleries. Another attempt to establish a Jewish colony which was taken over by a friend and admirer of Levinsohn's in Dubno ended much more tragically. This ten-year, melancholy history of colonization, which so clearly reflects the horrible abyss of human rightlessness and wild police-bureaucracy maliciousness, was described years later by Michael Kulisher in his *Kto Vinovat* (Who is Guilty?).[45]

No greater success was achieved by all the colonization projects submitted to the government by the enlightened representatives of the Jewish bourgeoisie. In later years the half-assimilated Jewish bourgeoisie, in its struggle for civic rights, attempted to distinguish itself from the "superstitious" and insufficiently useful Jewish masses and demanded equality only for the "elite" who bring utility to the state. In the earlier period, however, the young, relatively small-sized Jewish bourgeoisie still felt itself too strongly linked with the collective, with "the community of Israel," and so, in their striving for equal rights, they endeavored, first of all, to refute the charge that the Jews are idlers and parasites and do not engage in productive work.

As early as the beginning of the nineteenth century, Nathan Note Notkin, the friend and fellow-battler of Nevakhovich, proposed to the government that it establish Jewish colonies in the southern steppes of Russia, so that the Jews might engage in agriculture and sheep-raising. He also proposed that Jewish textile and weaving factories be established, and that in this way Jews be drawn to productive labor. In 1820 the merchant Hillel Markewitz submitted to the minister of finance a memorandum on attracting the Jewish populace to industrial work.[46] In 1840 three enlightened Jewish merchants addressed the government with a petition that they be allowed to purchase 5000 desyatinas [a desyatina is

44. See V. Nikitin's Russian work on Jewish agriculturalists, 209, 217.
45. *Yevreyskaya Biblioteka*, IV, 217–243.
46. J. I. Hessen, *Istoria Yevreyskogo Naroda v Rossii*, 1927, II, 8.

equivalent to 2.7 acres] of ground in Bessarabia and there settle a certain number of Jewish families to cultivate the soil.[47]

However, all these proposals were drowned in the abyss of the bureaucratic chancelleries. Levinsohn also had occasion to become convinced how far the Jewish colonies that had been established in the province of Kherson through the government were from the idyll which his friend Joseph Perl portrayed in his *Boḥen Tzaddik*. Testimony to this is provided by the memorandum that Levinsohn's admirer and follower, Benjamin Mandelstamm, submitted in 1846 to Sir Moses Montefiore,[48] in which he provides such a melancholy portrait of the persecutions and troubles which the Jewish colonists had to endure.

No fewer disappointments were to come to Levinsohn in the realization of the second point of his reform program—the establishment of model academic and vocational schools. At the end of the 1830s, the enlightener of Kremenets witnessed with satisfaction how his plan for reforming the education of children obtained prospects of being realized in the near future. In 1838 the governor of Podolia, under the influence of Levinsohn's memorandum,[49] noted in his most humble report the necessity of reforming the character of the schools among the Jews. In the same year Sergei Uvarov, then minister of education, also became interested in the question of Jewish schools.

Uvarov was a talented man of broad European education but, in addition, an unprincipled careerist with enormous ambition and narcissism. This European who, in his whole life, had never read a single Russian poet and regarded Russian literature with contempt, himself an atheist who did not believe either in God or the devil, as soon as he obtained the position of minister of education in 1833, declared, in order to find favor with Nicholas I: "Our duty consists mainly in seeing to it that the education of the people should be carried through in the unified spirit of orthodoxy, autocracy, and nationality."

The memorandum that Levinsohn and his followers in Vilna, the communal leader Nissan Rosenthal and the poet Solomon Salkind, submitted to the ministry of education aroused in Uvarov an interest in the question of "improving" the Jews and making "useful citizens" out of them through a reform of education. In 1838, travelling through Vilna, he invited the representatives of the local Jewish intelligentsia, Nissan Rosenthal and Hirsch Katzenel-

---

47. S. Borovoi's abovementioned work on agricultural colonization, 187-189.
48. *Hazon La-Mo'ed*, 58-59.
49. See S. J. Fuenn, *Safah La-Ne'emanim*, 170.

lenbogen, to visit him and carried on a rather long discussion with them about the reform of schools among the Jews.[50]

In the same year, when Uvarov visited Riga, the Jewish community there submitted a petition to him regarding permission for the opening of a school for children with two classes, with a program very similar to that of the Berlin *Hinnuch Ne'arim*.[51] Since Riga, as well as the other cities in Kurland, were under the strong influence of German culture, it is not surprising that the spirit of the Berlin Haskalah dominated the representatives of its Jewish community. According to the program that was put together by the leaders of Riga Jewry, the Pentateuch was to be studied in the school "according to Mendelssohn's German translation" and the Jewish religion was to be studied on the basis of Holy Scripture, "in the pure spirit of the prophets." This was an indication that religious questions would be explained exclusively according to the Bible, not taking into consideration the Talmud and its commentators. A point to the effect that the chief teacher ought to be a foreign Jew (i.e., a German) "who was raised in the spirit of pure enlightenment" was also set forth.

Uvarov, who like all the high Russian officials, saw in the Talmud the source of Jewish "superstition" and had also had occasion in the course of the years that he spent abroad to become acquainted with certain representatives of the "Frenchmen and Germans of the Mosaic faith," eagerly assented to the request of the community of Riga. In 1839, the law regarding the school in Riga was already promulgated and a young doctor of philosophy from Munich, Max Lilienthal, whom the well-known editor of the *Allegemeine Zeitung des Judenthums*, Ludwig Philippson, had recommended, was appointed its director. More important for Uvarov was the fact that the young foreign doctor brought with him letters of recommendation from the king of Bavaria to Maximilian Lichtenbergsky and to other highplaced officials.

Lilienthal was a capable and energetic man and managed in a short time[52] to bring the new school to such a flourishing condition that several months later the professor of Dorpat, Rozberg, who formally reviewed the school in July, 1840, reported to Uvarov enthusiastically that "the success surpassed the most brilliant expectations." Uvarov became interested in the energetic foreign teacher and apparently had personal conversations with him about the projected reform of the schools. Testimony to this is provided by the following fact: Lilienthal was not content merely with the

---

50. See S. Ginsburg, in *Minuvsheye*, 126.
51. See our *History*, Volume VIII, p. 59.
52. The school was opened on January 15, 1840.

position of director of the newly established school; he was also a preacher in the Riga community and, as early as September, 1840, undertook to print a collection of his *Predigten in der Synagoge zu Riga* with a dedication "to his high excellency, Sergius Uvarov."

In a special address to "his excellency," Lilienthal praises to the skies the "boundless sympathy" with which the minister "endeavors to obtain a better future for the Jewish populace through schooling and instruction." He asserts in this connection that "all Jewry of the civilized world knows to whom it is obliged to give gratitude." The sermons themselves—some of them highly patriotic, the rest religious-ethical—are of little interest. They are typical emotive, phraseological pulpit oratory of an average level. However, the "foreword" which precedes the volume provides a certain interest, for from it we can clearly learn how Lilienthal, who played such an active role in the first years of the school-reform, regarded Russian-Polish Jewry and its culture.

After the author notes the great progress that the Jews in Western Europe have made in the realm of enlightenment, he dwells on the cultural conditions of the Jews in Russia. "Here," he declares "the Jew remains on the very low level on which the immortal Mendelssohn in his day found him. In political life despised or pitied, in religious life barbarized, he still completely represents the melancholy, fearful picture that reminds us of the ruins of the Middle Ages." Lilienthal considers it necessary to point out in this connection that all this is not a result of "malice" but of the terrible persecutions which Jewry had to endure in previous benighted generations. "How could they learn ethics and life-wisdom?" he asks emotively. And he answers: "No, every feeling had to die in him [the Jew], every spark had to be extinguished. Unfortunately, he had to become what he became."

Lilienthal is firmly convinced that Russian-Polish Jewry is not only spiritually, but also ethically and morally, inferior. Every sentiment, after all, has died out in the Russian-Polish Jew, every spark has been extinguished. The Jew, however, must not "remain behind the times." His "spiritual and moral infirmities" must be healed. "He must first be educated for the new era." "But who will provide this education?," Lilienthal asks. The sick man, he answers, cannot heal himself; the captive is incapable of freeing himself from his chains. Who, then, will help, who will be the educator? "O," Lilienthal feelingly exclaims, "this education is the duty of the rulers and princes established by God." No other government, he affirms, has so earnestly and energetically undertaken to regenerate Judaism and to organize it as "Russia's great monarch" and his ministers. And he notes in this connection with great complacency that "the schools that have been established and are to be established are, or will be placed, under the strict supervision of the supreme authority," and consequently will not be subject to the caprices and religious moods of the various representatives of the community.

The newly established Jewish schools, Lilienthal emphasizes, must be subject to "the one exalted plan of a religious and ethical enlightenment" which "the crown," i.e., the czar Nicholas and his collaborators, have devised. And joyfully he points out that "in the whole empire committees are organized" which are to "take counsel on and discuss" the "improvement of the cult of the Jews, the raising of their political life, the possibility of a better instruction."

In fact, soon, on December 19, 1840, at the command of Nicholas I, a special committee, which was to consider by what means the way of life of the Jews is to be thoroughly reformed in order to adapt them better to the "wishes and views of the government" and engage them in useful work, was established. The chairman of the committee, the minister Kiselev, circulated to all the members a special memorandum which found great favor with Nicholas. In fact, on the basis of this memorandum, the czar gave his assent to the formation of the committee. Since this memorandum "on setting the Jewish people in order" best explains the covert aims which motivated Nicholas and his collaborators to come forth in the extraordinary role of persons concerned for education and battlers for Jewish "enlightenment," it is worth dwelling on its basic thesis.

In the memorandum it is noted that all the measures which the government has hitherto taken in regard to the Jews have been unsuccessful and the Jews are still, as before, in a condition that is injurious to the order of the state. "We must therefore investigate the basic reasons why Jews remove themselves with such stubbornness from the general way of life and, on the basis of this investigation, create a system of thoroughly changing this people in consonance with the wishes of the government." The author of the memorandum wishes to see the fundamental reason for this "stubborn removal" not in the civic disabilities of the Jewish populace but chiefly in its "false religious notions."

In the memorandum it is also stressed that the "isolation of the Jews and their ethical demoralization is, in general, not a partial or accidental defect of their character but has made itself at home in the people through the fault of the crude teachings of the Talmud." The author was apparently well acquainted with the letters frequently submitted to the government by the representatives of Haskalah in which they used to deplore the defective order of education prevalent among the Jews, an order that required radical reform. Every little boy, it is noted in the memorandum, "as soon as he becomes four years old, is given over into the hands of teachers who are sunk in the deepest ignorance and superstition. Under the influence of these fanatics, the children obtain all the pernicious and destructive notions of intolerance towards other peoples." Hence, the author comes to the conclusion that, in regard to the Jewish question, the most radical and best method is "the moral-religious education of the Jewish people."

In conformity with this memorandum, seven points were placed before the committee according to the "supreme decree." Of these the most important are: (1) to work through newly established schools on the moral training of the Jewish youth in a spirit that must be in full opposition to the hitherto dominant Talmudic teachings; (2) to make an end to the independent administration of the *kahal* and to subject the Jewish populace to the general administration; (3) to appoint official district rabbis who would receive their salaries from the government and, with their authority, carry through its requirements; (4) to forbid the Jews to dress in the special Jewish costume; and (5) to make agriculture available to the Jews.

It is easy to recognize that virtually all the points listed used to be constantly set forth in their memoranda by the *maskilim* themselves, even if in a somewhat different fashion. Points three and five are included in Levinsohn's program mentioned above. For point four many of the *maskilim* fought ardently. We have already observed that as early as 1810, when Prince Dolgoruki asked the young Hirsch Baer Hurwitz what he lacked to feel happy, the latter pointed that he would wish above all that "we Jews be forbidden to wear our shameful dress." The previously mentioned *maskil* Benjamin Mandelstamm pointed, in the memorandum which he submitted to Lilienthal, among the basic causes of the melancholy Jewish situation, to the unique costume which distinguishes the Jews from the rest of the population. The well-known *maskil* Mordecai Aaron Günzburg wrote a special article "Al Ha-Begadim" (On Clothing).[53] The historian S. J. Fuenn was also firmly persuaded that the major reason for the hostility and isolation that prevail between the Jews and the Christian populace is the "distinction in dress." He therefore concludes that "before the government takes any step for our benefit, we must make it realize that it should, first of all, issue a decree to set aside this obstacle."[54] And, indeed, three years later, in 1843, a group of

53. See *Leket Amarim*, 90-92,
54. See Fuenn's letter to Stern (of 1840), printed in *Pardes*, III, 152.

Vilna *maskilim* and wealthy merchants submitted to the aide of the minister of education, S.A. Shirinsky-Shikhmatov, a petition in which they endeavored to show that with the reform of clothing is linked "the happiness·of the whole people" (*schaste tselomu narodu*), because the old-fashioned costume is the greatest obstacle to education, and all measures that are undertaken to train the Jewish people may remain fruitless as long as the Jew will not be dressed like all his cultured fellow-citizens.[55]

The *maskilim* of Volhynia also did not wish to remain backward in this respect. One of their chief representatives, A. B. Gottlober, also submitted a memorandum regarding the reform of dress.[56] When in 1845 the decree was issued that five years hence (in 1850) "it will be strictly forbidden to wear the presently customary Jewish dress," a group of Volhynian *maskilim* led by Gottlober made a written agreement according to which they obliged themselves not to wait the entire five years but, indeed, soon, on a specific day, they would all, without exception, cast off the old-fashioned garments and put on European clothing. This day will be for them "for happiness and rejoicing," and they will offer praise and thanks to the czar for the graciousness which he has done with them.[57]

In both memoranda one and the same characteristic feature is noticeable. Both the *maskilim* of Vilna and of Volhynia identified their own wishes with the demands of the whole people. Because the rich merchants, who carried on extensive business with the external world, and the "secular" and "contemporary" enlighteners were ashamed to wear the old-fashioned garments that distinguished them from the European world, they honestly believed that in the reform of clothing consisted "the happiness of the entire people." Only after numerous disappointments did Gottlober understand many years later the bitter truth that he expressed in a private letter: "Let us not deceive ourselves and think that we are the people. We are the isolated ones, the exceptions . . . "[58]

The task of realizing the first of the above-noted points—through newly established schools to free the Jewish youth from the Talmud's corrupting influence" (*tletvornoe vliyanie*) and to train the

---

55. *Perezhitoye*, I, "Documents and Reports," 11-14. Among the signers of the memorandum are the names of the well-known *maskilim* Solomon Salkind, Mordecai Aaron Günzburg, Mathias Strashun, and Isaac Benjacob.

56. We discovered the rough copy of this memorandum in Gottlober's archive.

57. At the same time (on the tenth of Elul 1845) Gottlober also composed his satirical poem *Di Gzeyre Daytshn*. Only the first seven stanzas of this long poem, which Gottlober quotes in an article of his in *Ha-Melitz*, (1869, No. 29, p. 224) have been preserved.

58. See *Reshumot*, II, 421: "Why should we speak falsely within ourselves to say that we are the people? We are the exceptions to the rule."

young generation morally "in consonance with the wishes of the government"—was placed on the minister of education Uvarov. This crafty courtier knew very well the motives for which Nicholas I agreed to come forth in the role of an "enlightener" and one concerned for Jewish education. Indeed, as early as January 1841, a memorandum about the reform of Jewish education was already prepared in the hands of the minister of education. In it is noted how "the better among the Jews" themselves already understand quite well "that the Talmud has morally corrupted, and to this day corrupts (*razvrastchal i razvrastchaet*), their brethren" and "that to reform the nature of the schools among the Jews also means to purify their religious notions."

"The teaching of the newly established schools," it is further pointed out, "ought gradually to destroy in the Jews their fanaticism and isolation and unite them with the general foundations of citizenship (*grazhdanstvennosti*)." The fanatical adherents of Jewish superstition and fanaticism, Uvarov notes, are becoming frightened and assert that this leads to apostasy. A certain truth, the minister concludes with a pious mien, does, indeed, inhere in this, for "is not the religion of the cross the purest symbol of universal citizenship?" However, in order not to frighten the Jews away, it is further noted in the memorandum, the anti-Talmudic tendency of the new schools must, for the time being, remain secret.

Immediately after this, Uvarov summoned Lilienthal from Riga and assigned to him, as an expert pedagogue, the task of working out a systematic plan for the Jewish schools and also of corresponding with Jewish educators in Germany to discover which of them are inclined to occupy a teaching position in the new schools.

The report that the government had taken the firm decision to carry through, in a short time, the reform of the Jewish schools made an enormous impression in the Haskalah circles. Weak and small in numbers, surrounded by a hostile environment that perceived in them heretics and breakers of restraints and therefore persecuted them ruthlessly,[59] they suddenly saw such an omnipo-

---

59. The battlers for light, Gottlober relates in his memoirs, had to suffer a great many troubles from the wrath of the benighted people that burned like a hellish fire. They did everything they could to torment them and destroy their hopes and their efforts. They drove them out of town, took away their means of earning a living, ruined them, made them an object of shame and ridicule, and kindled the fire of controversy between sons-in-law and their fathers-in-law, who were benighted people without knowledge. They told these men that their sons-in-law had rid themselves of their Jewishness and devoted themselves to licentiousness; they told lies to the young women to the effect that their husbands had ceased to believe in God and would soon commit apostasy. In this way they dug out an abyss between them and their wives and forced them to be divorced, so that they would be driven out of their father-in-law's house and have nothing to eat and, naturally, they would then

tent collaborator who desires, with a mighty hand, to actualize their loveliest ideal. Their hearts were filled to overflowing with patriotic gratitude to the "gracious" and "enlightened" government.

However, objectively to evaluate the hurrah-patriotism of the representatives of Haskalah, one must take into consideration the bizarre contradictions which manifested themselves in the realm of popular education under Nicholas' regime. The same government which closed the doors of educational institutions to the broad strata of the people and set forth as a motto that "to give elementary education to the whole people, or to a large part of the people, may bring more harm than utility"[60] forcibly dragged the Jewish children to the schools. The same Uvarov who, as Nicholas' humble servant, saw in education a great demoralizing danger for the Russian people and declared "when I manage to push Russia back fifty years, I will know that I have fulfilled my duty," became, in regard to the Jews, a bearer of culture and was certain that, with the aid of education, he would succeed in liberating the Jews from their "fanaticism" and isolation" and "bring them close to the basic foundation of general civic conceptions (*obstchee nachalo grazhdanstvennosti*)." Rightfully a Russian scholar, A. Beletsky, marvels: "For the Jews, who were considered harmful citizens, an enormous privilege was created and, in regard to school education, they were placed in more favorable conditions than tens of millions of other Russian subjects who were not considered harmful."

Hence, it is quite comprehensible that the *maskilim*, who had obtained as a legacy from the Berlin Haskalah the firm belief in the benefits of "enlightened absolutism," perceived in Nicholas the "kind ruler" and gracious supporter of education and enlightenment. "From the deep swamp in which our people are so terribly sunken," writes the above-mentioned *maskil* of Vilna Benjamin Mandelstamm, "only the czar with his kindnesses can help us out."[61]

However, the *maskilim*, along with this, still had great fear lest the orthodox would stand in the way and take steps in hidden byways to hinder the plan of school-reform. Hence, the Vilna *maskilim* wrote to their fellow-battlers in Dubno:

Among you[62] lives the well-known man who thinks constantly about the welfare of his people, Isaac Baer Levinsohn. Beg of him, then, that in such

knock education and enlightenment out of their minds. These persons depressed many people permanently because they could not stand up against them (A. Fridkin, *Gottlober Un Zayn Epokhe*, 85).

60. Quoted by S. Ginsburg, *Minuvsheye*, 1923, 109.
61. *Ḥazon La-Mo'ed*, II, 18.
62. In all, forty *versts* separate Dubno from Kremenets.

a moment he not stand at a distance, but rather come forward as quickly as possible with his influential word. We are certain that he will undoubtedly address the government and petition for his people that our condition be improved. Perhaps God will be gracious to us, and then we and our children will owe the deepest gratitude to this precious man, and his name and deeds will be inscribed for generations on the pages of our history.[63]

The *maskilim* of Dubno, in transmitting this letter to Levinsohn, added for their part:

We consider it superfluous to beg you to be diligent in this important matter. We know very well that you yourself will not rest until you realize the great ideas which you have expressed in your precious works and which, indeed, have aroused among the high officials the wish to remember us for good, as we, in fact, know from their words, which are based on your theses and conclusions.[64]

However, in this particular the *maskilim* were in error. Levinsohn was, indeed, enchanted by Uvarov, in whom he saw the "selfless helper" who decided to drive away the deep darkness which prevailed over the Jewish quarter through light and enlightenment. He even celebrated the Russian minister in special poems of praise.[65] Uvarov, however, had a quite different attitude toward Levinsohn. We already know of the suspicion with which Nicholas and his ministers regarded Levinsohn because of the fact that the latter battled so energetically for the "mendacious book," the Talmud. It is, therefore, understandable that this suspicion had to be sharpened at the time of the school-reform that had been undertaken and that had, after all, been devised with the definite purpose of freeing the Jewish youth from the Talmud's "corrupting influence."

Hence, it is beyond doubt that the cold attitude toward Levinsohn on the part of the minister of education was one of the major reasons (the rest will be mentioned later) that Lilienthal avoided meeting with the battler for Haskalah who lived in the town of Kremenets. It ought, therefore, to occasion no surprise that when Lilienthal considered it necessary to make a special visit to the

63. *Sefer Ha-Zichronot*, 56.
64. *Ibid.*
65. Well known is his memorial poem:

> A terrible cloud covered the sun of wisdom,
> But God commanded, and a savior and teacher arose.
> Hardly had his spirit taken breath and there was light,
> And the people called: The cloud has passed, the cloud has passed! . . .

spiritual leaders of the orthodox Jews and the Hasidim, Itzikl Volozhiner and Mendele Lubavitcher, he did not find time, in complete contradiction with his numerous epistolary assurances, to become acquainted with the recognized leader of the Russian *maskilim*.[66]

The *maskilim*, however, did not rely on the sickly Levinsohn alone. Furthermore, not all of them agreed with him that one ought to battle only with the weaponry of persuasion, solely with the power of the word. "Our only hope remaining to us," writes the above-mentioned Benjamin Mandelstamm, "is that the czar should give us guides endowed with full authority to lead our blind and deaf *with a mighty hand* [italicized by Mandelstamm] over the way of life."[67] At his first meeting with Max Lilienthal, Benjamin Mandelstamm declared that with the aid of a bridle and whip alone can success be achieved in conducting the orthodox masses in the desired directions, for "only through the rod can fools be led to follow the right way."

It lies beyond the scope of our task to dwell at length on the singular epic of the schools, to describe the committees established for the sake of the projected school-reform, Max Lilienthal's tours through the region, and how the reorganization of the schools was carried through.[68] We shall merely touch on those details that obtained an echo in literature and characterize the tendencies of the contemporary Jewish intelligentsia.

When Lilienthal, as Uvarov's fully authorized deputy, toured the major Jewish communities, the local *maskilim* welcomed him with enormous enthusiasm.[69] He was crowned with the title "angel of God" and perceived as the liberator and redeemer. Benjamin Mandelstamm tells with enchantment of Lilienthal: "He was in my eyes virtually like a new Moses through whom God had chosen to aid his people."[70] Soon, however, the disenchantment began, and the same Mandelstamm writes shortly thereafter:

Many of the *maskilim* are indignant with Doctor Lilienthal because he keeps aloof from those who battle for science and knowledge. He carries

66. We have written at length about the relationships between Lilienthal and Levinsohn and between Lilienthal and the Russian *maskilim* in our work (in Russian) "Isaac Baer Levinsohn and His Time" (*Yevreyskaya Starina*, 1910).

67. *Ḥazon La-Mo'ed*, II, 17.

68. On this, see M. Margolis' work in *Yevreyskaya Biblioteka*, I; P. Marek's *Ocherki po istorii prosvestscheniya*, 1909; S. Ginsburg's work in *Minuvsheye*, 1923, 89–157; and also in *Kazyönnoye yevreyskiye uchilistcha*, I, 1920.

69. Very characteristic in this respect is a copy of a document deriving from a circle of the *maskilim* which is preserved in Gottlober's archive.

70. *Ḥazon La-Mo'ed*, II, 20.

on conversations and negotiations only with the orthodox and Hasidic Jews and also himself plays at being a deeply pious man who must recite his prayers twice a day with the congregation. The enlightened, therefore, consider him a hypocrite and regard with suspicion everything he says.[71]

The causes of the disappointment and dissatisfaction evoked by Lilienthal with his tactics in the camp of the progressives are quite understandable. The enthusiasm that the report of the school-reform projected by the government had called forth in the camp of the *maskilim* was not associated merely with unadulterated, ideal motives. The economic condition of a considerable segment of the *maskilim* was quite deplorable. The milieu that was so hostile to them made their material situation even more difficult, and the way of life of many representatives of Haskalah who actually perished of hunger is well known.[72] The news concerning the Jewish government schools which would soon be established in the Jewish pale of settlement aroused among many *maskilim* the hope of obtaining a teaching position in these schools and thus being freed from worries about earning a living.[73]

Isaac Baer Levinsohn received heaps of letters from *maskilim* with one and the same petition: that he intercede with Max Lilienthal and the government and recommend them as suitable candidates for the teaching positions that were open. "I beg once more," writes the well-known scholar Jacob Reifmann to Levinsohn, "that you remember me for good to Lilienthal. I shall soon write at length and will add a letter to Lilienthal."[74] Jacob Eichenbaum writes to Levinsohn:

Your sister's son has told me you have informed him that Max Lilienthal will soon visit you. We know how respected he is among the officials of the state and that the government takes great account of him in all questions regarding the condition of our people. Therefore, I strongly beg you that you mention me for good to him so that he may remember my name, and when our czar, with God's help, will accomplish his will and Jewish schools will be established in the whole country, he may think of me, to give me a teaching position. Until now I have not yet managed to obtain an assured source of livelihood . . . I am never certain how I shall feed my family the next day . . . and God has blessed me with six daughters and one son . . .[75]

71. *Ibid.* See also *ibid.*, 36, 37.
72. It suffices to mention the sad story that Gottlober relates in his memoirs about the tragic life of the *maskil* of Dubno (a disciple of Manasseh of Ilya), Wolf Adelson.
73. This hope also finds a sharp echo in the just mentioned document deriving from the circle of the *maskilim*.
74. *Yalkut Ribal*, 96.
75. *Be'er Yitzḥak*, 93.

A. B. Gottlober,[76] who later applied directly to Lilienthal after becoming acquainted with him when the latter visited Moghilev near the Dniester, addressed the same request to Levinsohn.[77] Tzevi Grünbaum (the latter Vladimir Fedorov)[78] and many other *maskilim* applied to Lilienthal directly about teaching positions.

Also characteristic in this particular is the "summons" which the *maskilim* of Vilna issued at that time in a separate copy specially dispatched to Levinsohn.[79] Among the four points listed as radically necessary reforms, one figures under the title "lack of livelihood in general and among the *maskilim* in particular." It is there noted:

The *maskilim* who, with great self-sacrifice, knock on the doors of knowledge and science go about bowed under the yoke of fools who ruthlessly persecute them. Their condition is very lowly; they live in extreme poverty and want. Aside from the great sympathy that every understanding person feels when he sees how these ideal men are so degraded and have not the wherewithal to live, this situation has an even more frightening effect on the common people; the slightest desire to seek after knowledge and education is lost, for why—each one thinks—occupy oneself with the sciences when it is obvious, after all, that one will thereby not only obtain hatred and persecutions on the part of the fools but also will receive support from no one and be compelled to wander about for the sake of a piece of bread?

Precisely in this respect Max Lilienthal disappointed the hopes of the *maskilim* most grievously. At the beginning the government did intend, following Lilienthal's proposal, to invite teachers from abroad for the newly founded schools. Lilienthal carried on epistolary negotiations regarding this matter in Uvarov's name with numerous Jewish scholars in Germany.[80] Over two hundred men abroad waited impatiently for the time when the new schools would at last be opened. Jewish newspapers abroad even reproached Lilienthal for postponing his invitation so long. It is clear that, under these circumstances, he could take the local *maskilim* into very little account as teacher candidates.

In addition to this, two purely personal motives were operative. First, the diplomated doctor from Bavaria looked on the *Ostjuden* in general with a certain contempt, and he regarded their enlightened men similarly. "The dirty, bearded Jews who are barely touched

76. His letter has still not been published.
77. *Ha-Boker Or*, 1879, 919.
78. *Yevreyskaya Starina*, 1910, 415.
79. *Sefer Ha-Zichronot*, 53-55.
80. About Lilienthal's negotiations with Abraham Geiger, we know from Geiger's reply (see his *Nachgelassene Schriften*, V).

by the rays of enlightenment"—so Lilienthal describes the Russian *maskilim* in a letter of his to an official of the ministry of education.[81] Beyond this, the young, twenty-six-year-old Lilienthal was intoxicated with the important role that fate had bestowed upon him so unexpectedly: to tour the pale as emissary and plenipotentiary of the Russian minister of education. He wished by himself, without any collaborators, to link his name with the reform of education in Russian Jewry. He, the foreigner who was so slightly acquainted with local conditions and the way of life of Russian-Polish Jewry, attempted to play the diplomat who understands, with his ingenious trickery, how to deceive both hostile sides. However, Lilienthal was very little suited to the role of diplomat, and his double-dealing merely brought it about that both parties regarded him with strong suspicion.

We noted how disappointed many of the *maskilim* of Vilna were at Lilienthal's behavior. The same thing was repeated in certain circles of *maskilim* in the southwestern region. When, on his second tour through the pale, Lilienthal visited Odessa, he stopped at the house of a respected *maskil*, Moses Friedberg. An ardent admirer of Levinsohn, Friedberg refused to conceal his indignation that Lilienthal did not deem it necessary to visit Isaac Baer Levinsohn and listen to his views regarding school reform. Friedberg declared to his guest:

There is no other man who is so familiar with the needs of our people as Levinsohn. We do not have any other doctor so expert, who knows and understands as well as he wherein the illnesses of the people of Israel consist and wherewith these can be healed. And if the committee that needs to devise the reform of the schools requires the counsel of an expert physician, it is most essential to invite Levinsohn. For if even the most competent doctor from abroad is invited,[82] as long as he is not familiar with the conditions of our country and will wish to cure in his way, as he has become accustomed in his country, there is a strong apprehension that he will not only be of no help but will even aggravate the situation. Hence, the best thing, indeed, is to consult with the local doctor, who knows the local circumstances, the character and way of life of the inhabitants, well. He will best understand what can do harm and wherewith help can be brought.[83]

The dissatisfaction in the camp of the *maskilim* was strengthened still more when Max Lilienthal, at the end of the summer of 1842,

---

81. Quoted by J. I. Hessen in *Perezhitoye*, III, 22.
82. An allusion to Dr. Lilienthal.
83. *Be'er Yitzhak*, 101.

published in Vilna his manifesto *Maggid Yeshuah*,[84] which is written in the typical emotive style of a German preacher. Benjamin Mandelstamm sent this brochure to a friend of his and wrote with bitter sarcasm:

Familiarize yourself with all the "salvations and consolations" with which Lilienthal comforts us. There, among the German Jews, in all the newspapers a sound of jubilation and salvation is heard. All tell of the doctor's greatness and the wondrous deeds that he has accomplished for our benefit. There the Jews already rejoice in our happiness, and we know of nothing. We have still not been helped at all.[85]

Indignantly Mandelstamm mentions Lilienthal's story of how he complained, before Uvarov and other high officials, about the welcome he received from the Jews of Minsk and glories in the fact that he took no revenge on them for it. "The people," Mandelstamm exclaims, "live in poverty and distress, are oppressed and miserable, and God has sent us the doctor who has found nothing better to do than to complain of us before the high officials and to remind them that we are a 'stiff-necked people.' "[86] He was particularly incensed by Lilienthal's report that a special commission of rabbis which would consider the reform of schools among the Jews of Russia would be convened. Lilienthal, Mandelstamm notes, declares with such pride: "I will tell you great things about salvations shortly to come that our fathers have not seen and our grandfathers have not heard of." Are these the salvations? Wherewith can the rabbis—these "mute idols" void of every knowledge and science—help us? Perhaps they will endow us with a seventh order to the six orders of the Mishnah, or add a fifth fringe to the four fringes on the garment now ritually prescribed?[87]

The well-known *maskil* Mordecai Aaron Günzburg attacked Lilienthal even more sharply. To the latter's *Maggid Yeshuah*, Günzburg promptly responded with a brochure entitled *Maggid Emet*, which was published in Leipzig under the pseudonym Jonah ben Ammittai.

Maggid Emet begins immediately with an address to the Jews of Russia: Listen, you Russian citizens! The Germans make them-

---

84. Reprinted in Letteris' *Michtevei Kedem*, 1863, and in Gottlober's *Ha-Boker Or*, 1879, 912-918. Lilienthal wrote his brochure in German, and it was translated into Hebrew by the young S. J. Fuenn who, at the end of the translation, wove his initials into an anagram as a memorial.

85. *Hazon La-Mo'ed*, II, 38.

86. *Ibid.*, 41.

87. *Ibid.*, 40. Nissan Rosenthal also expressed himself decisively in opposition to the commission of rabbis in his memorandum that he submitted to Uvarov (see *Kazyönnoye yevreyskiye uchilistcha*).

selves great and reproach us that "among hundreds of thousands of Russian Jews, there was not a single one to be found on whom the government could rely, until a German doctor from a distant land appeared and the government empowered him to fulfill its will." This judgment, so degrading to us, Günzburg asserts, is not correct. He points out that in Vilna there are already many cultured men "who send their children to the gymnasia and universities." Like Mandelstamm,[88] Günzburg also asserts that among the Russian *maskilim* there is a more suitable candidate than Max Lilienthal to serve as a mediator between the government and the Jewish people, and this candidate is the director of the model school of Odessa, Bezalel (Basilius) Stern.[89] Günzburg cannot forgive Lilienthal for the fact that the latter, on his second visit to Vilna, always associated with the rich men and the orthodox Jews and regarded the *maskilim* who "possess only knowledge but not sacks of gold" with contempt.[90]

However, Günzburg refused to be content merely with this brochure. He pretended to be a non-partisan on the sidelines and wrote a review[91] of *Maggid Emet*, the work by the obstensibly unknown to him Jonah ben Ammittai, in which he once again settles accounts with Max Lilienthal. Ironically he tells of the enthusiasm and reverence with which the *maskilim* waited on the "doctor of philosophy" Lilienthal, and how great their disappointment was when they perceived in this diplomated doctor the complete antithesis of what "the Queen of Sheba saw in King Solomon." Once more Günzburg returns to the problem that was

---

88. *Ḥazon La-Mo'ed*, II, 42: "Our only hope is still on Dr. Stern of Odessa . . ." Concerning the great respect that the *maskilim* of Vilna had for Stern, see the letter addressed to him by S. J. Fuenn *(Ha-Pardes*, III, 149-156).

89. Stern, however, was also actually not a Russian Jew but of the *maskilim* of Galicia (see our *History*, Vol. IX). Despite the fact that he had lived for a considerable number of years in Odessa and was the "learned Jew" on the staff of Prince Vorontsov, he considered himself a "German" and looked with a certain contempt on the Russian-Polish Jews with their "jargon" and "fanaticism." Characteristic in this respect is the memorandum that he submitted to Vorontsov regarding the colonists of Kurland who settled in the government, or province, of Kherson. He requests that every Kurland colonist be granted aid not of 600 rubles, like the Polish-Russian Jews, but of 800 rubles, because the Kurland Jews are distinguished from their Russian-Polish coreligionists by their higher culture and lesser degree of superstition. In consonance with this, Stern also requests that to the Kurland colonists better and more convenient parcels of land, which should be separated from the other Jewish colonists, be distributed, in order to avoid all the unpleasantnesses and controversies that may arise because of the fanaticism and quite different world-view of the Polish Jews who settled there earlier (see S. Borovoi, *Yevreyskaya Zemledeltscheskaya Kolonizatsiye*, 158-159).

90. For a further discussion of Günzburg's *Maggid Emet*, see our above-quoted work on Levinsohn in *Yevreyskaya Starina*, 1910.

91. *Ha-Moriyyah*, 1878, 38-48.

particularly painful to him: the arrogant attitude of the German Jews toward Russian Jewry and its scholars. "Like clay in the potter's hand," he laments, are we in the hands of our learned German brethren. They edit journals in quite considerable number, and whoever holds pen in hand and can write a letter to a newspaper considers himself an omnipotent judge, capable of judging the whole world. I do not—God forbid—complain of the journals in general. They definitely bring great utility to our people. However, they ought certainly to take account of the fact that also "we have a mouth to answer," that we are not speechless and can give a response. "Let these scholars be more cautious in the future, for they will know that they will have to give reckoning and account for their words."[92] And Günzburg stresses once more the conclusion that is so important to him: "The government has no need to summon men of knowledge from a distant land. It ought only to issue a call to the learned of its own country, and they will immediately assemble."[93]

From an objective point of view, Max Lilienthal did not deserve all the attacks of the "enlighteners." He was by no means so unjustified in associating with the orthodox and Hasidic Jews, for he realized that they were incomparably more powerful in numbers and influence than the *maskilim* and that without their assent it would be extremely difficult to carry through the reform of the schools. And when he had no success among the orthodox, it was not merely because he was too unskilled a diplomat and an insufficiently significant personality, but mainly because Nicholas and his collaborators, in fact, intended, through their reform of the schools, not enlightenment, but making the Jews useful citizens for the government through apostasy and assimilation.

It must also be conceded that Lilienthal was more far-sighted

92. *Ibid.*, 43.
93. The wealthy battler for culture Nissan Rosenthal also expressed his categorical opposition to inviting teachers from Germany in the memorandum that he submitted to Uvarov. Incidentally, he did this in a very ingenious way. Just at that time the battle for religious reform again waxed in Germany and, in the leadership of the reformers, were such radical free-thinkers as Abraham Geiger and Samuel Holdheim. Hence, Rosenthal indicates to Uvarov, one must fear lest the foreign teachers bring to us with them the contagious disease of rationalism, whose propaganda has now grown so strong in western Europe. This had its effect, and Uvarov rejected the plan of importing foreign teachers. Characteristic of the relationships between the majority of the *maskilim* of Vilna and Lilienthal is also the following fact: S. J. Fuenn, in the second part of *Pirḥei Tzafon*, which was published at the beginning of 1844, printed an article in which he marvels in an exalted, rhetorical style at Uvarov's graciousness to Jews. In this connection he especially emphasizes the role that Nissan Rosenthal, with whom Uvarov carried on long conversations, played in the projected reform of the schools. However, he does not mention the emissary Lilienthal by so much as a word.

than all the *maskilim* who attacked him so wrathfully. The statement with which the orthodox Jews of Minsk greeted Lilienthal is well known: "As long as the state will not grant the Jews full rights of citizenship, education will be only a misfortune for them." The *maskilim* who were so dissatisfied with Lilienthal, e.g., M.A. Günzburg, would not, and could not, grasp this. Torn away from actual life, having little familiarity with the social conditions of the country, the sad truth remained unknown to them that in Nicholas' Russia, with its old-fashioned knout-order, the Jew without rights had not the means to utilize European education. They naively believed that enlightenment and European clothing would automatically bring complete salvation. Lilienthal, however, realized that the orthodox Jews of Minsk were right. Hence, in his conversations with Uvarov, when the latter complained of the "barbaric fanaticism and moral corruption" of the Jews, he always pointed out that the best means of eliminating all this is complete emancipation.

We know of this interesting point not only from Lilienthal's memoirs, which he published many years later (in 1855) in the *Allgemeine Zeitung des Judenthums*, but also from documents preserved in the archives of the ministry of education. In one of the memoranda that he submitted to the government in 1842 after his tour through the pale, Lilienthal notes that, for the newly founded schools actually to attain their goal, it is necessary, first of all, to free the Jews from their condition of civic disability. The incarceration of the Jews in the narrow pale and the numerous other restrictions had brought the Jewish populace to terrible impoverishment, and the only solution is to grant the Jews full rights, to distribute land to them for colonization, to establish factories for Jewish workers, and to give the Jews free access to the universities.[94]

In his *Maggid Yeshuah* also Lilienthal notes that he considered it important to transmit to Uvarov the justified complaints of the orthodox: For us it is better that our children grow up without education, because then they will not be ashamed to occupy themselves with humble, beggarly means of earning a living, such as being brokers and the like; but what will happen if they obtain education and no new sources of livelihood will be opened for

---

94. *Kazyönnoye yevreyskiye uchilistcha*, 1920, 111-112. It is interesting that another German Jew, a former ritual slaughterer in Weimar and in Russia and a professor in the academy for the clergy after he adopted the Christian faith, came to the identical conclusions in the memorandum that he submitted at the same time. "Not the offended man," he writes, "but the offender must first stretch out the hand of peace. Give the Jew a fatherland and he will cease to dream of Palestine. Give him equal rights with the Christians and he will become a good citizen. Only on the ground of complete civic equality between Jews and Christians in the spirit of Christian love is the (Jewish) assimilation possible" (*ibid.*, 80-81).

them? In the previous modes of earning a living, at which they will look with animosity and contempt, they will now consider it impossible to engage, and so they will find no solution except to abandon the faith of their fathers.

Apparently the crafty Uvarov gave Max Lilienthal certain assurances. Thereby is explicable the fact that several days after Nicholas signed the decree concerning the reform of the schools and establishing the commission of rabbis, Lilienthal wrote in a letter to one of the prominent *maskilim* of Vilna at that time, Tzevi Hirsch Katzenellenbogen:

And if you say: this ukase will, after all, not give us any bread or clothing; what use to us are our science and knowledge if there is no piece of bread and no garment on the body?—then, know and understand that this is only the first; before the end of the year three or four others will appear, and only from them will you see that the government means well for the Jews, and the days to come will be much better than the earlier ones when we were a mockery and an object of derision.[95]

In his *Maggid Yeshuah* Lilienthal also notes that one should hope for decrees regarding the amelioration of the material situation of the Jews.[96] For this reason (as we shall see later), Mordecai Aaron Günzburg even attacked him: How, then?—Lilienthal wishes to coax us like small children with nuts and sweetmeats, so that we should obtain a desire for the reform of the schools.

Not all the *maskilim*, however, were in agreement with Günzburg. First of all, a distinction must be drawn among the *maskilim* between those who were literati and those who were wealthy merchants and businessmen. For reasons to which we have alluded previously (see above, p. 73) the rich, enlightened merchants desired greatly that the Jewish masses not only free themselves from fanaticism and superstition but move as quickly as possible to productive labor and become "useful fellow-citizens." And it must be conceded that, in the memoranda they used to submit to the government, they would even at times cast off the stock, servile-subordinate style and permit themselves to speak openly and courageously.

Typical in this respect is the memorandum that the businessman and communal leader Litman Feigin, well known at that time, submitted in 1833 to Nicholas. He deems it superfluous to mention the "favors" which the Jewish people enjoys in the

---

95. We found a copy of this interesting letter in Gottlober's archive and published it in Russian translation in *Perezhitoye*, III, 380-382.

96. "And by our giving a good education to our children—only by this will the exalted government be entreated to open to us new doors to earning a living."

Russian land. He speaks in open statements and points out "how frightfully degraded the Jewish people is through the steps that the government has taken against it." "The cry of woe of the Jewish people over its miserable condition," the memorandum begins, "is heard over the whole world. With full right has it awaited an amelioration of its condition. Finally, the situation becomes ever more intolerable hour by hour. Not only have all rights of citizenship been taken away from the Jew, but even all sources of livelihood."[97]

Also the above-mentioned communal leader Nissan Rosenthal, who in 1841 established the first Jewish model school in Vilna and, as a personal acquaintance of Uvarov's, took a large part in the reform of the schools,[98] considered it necessary to submit to Uvarov a special memorandum in which he indicates that measures must be taken, first of all, to combat the terrible impoverishment of the Jews, and for this purpose agricultural colonies and factories must be established. Rosenthal even worked out in this connection a special "plan concerning agriculture and factories and technical institutes."[99]

On Rosenthal's memorandum Uvarov wrote with his own hand the following comment:

Rosenthal's view is a result of Jewish subtlety that wishes to discover the government's concealed intention in order to exploit this betimes and to know how to adapt it to its purpose. Rosenthal is not capable of grasping the whole matter. The Jewish question will not be solved through agriculture and factories; its essence lies much higher.[100]

Rosenthal and the other *maskilim*, indeed, did not "grasp the whole matter." With all their "Jewish subtlety" they naively believed that it was a question of "enlightening" and educating the Jewish youth, whereas the minister of education intended to fulfill the goal of his despotic master, who endeavored to bring it about that "all Russians [literally, Greeks] should have one face" and that all his subjects, without exception, should live and think only according to his "supreme" will. Hence, the schools needed to eradicate the "fanaticism and the pernicious superstition that is rooted in the teaching of the Talmud" and gradually persuade the newly rising Jewish generation of the truth of the religion of the

97. Feigin's memorandum was published by J. I. Hessen in *Yevreyskaya Starina*, 1911, 394-402.
98. On this, see Günzburg's *Maggid Emet*, S. J. Fuenn's *Safah La-Ne'emanim*, 164, and our work on Isaac Baer Levinsohn, *Yevreyskaya Starina*, 1910, 524-26.
99. *Kazyönnoye yevreyskiye uchilistcha*, 114-115.
100. *Ibid.*, 114.

cross, which is, after all, as is known, "the purest symbol of universal citizenship."

Lilienthal finally realized wherein the real goal of the reform of the schools consisted (it is possible that it was proposed to him that he himself adopt the Christian faith). In 1844 he secretly fled from Russia.[101] Isaac Baer Levinsohn's favorite idea—reforming the education of the Jewish youth—was also transformed into the same crude caricature as the other basic foundation of his program, namely, granting the Jewish populace the opportunity to engage in productive labor. Instead of courses in artisanry which would, according to the first plan devised, constitute the basis of the Jewish schools, the government was concerned mainly that, in these schools, there be a battle against the "corrupting" influence of the Talmud. Benjamin Mandelstamm's younger brother, Leon Mandelstamm,[102] whom Uvarov, following Lilienthal's departure, empowered to realize the reform of the schools, published one catechism after another. With these textbooks the government hoped to supplant the Talmud and its pernicious effect. The catechisms, on which so much money from the Jewish candle-tax was expended, rotted in many thousands of copies in the warehouses and aroused just indignation and dissatisfaction among the Jewish masses.

In vain did Levinsohn point out in a special letter to Uvarov that it would be much better "to place more weight on European education" than to carry on a battle against the Talmud.[103] Uvarov, after all, had long looked with suspicion on the strange "enlightener" who defends such a "noxious" book as the Talmud. In vain did Levinsohn note that not "with compulsion and force" ought the people to be led on the new way but "with love and with much patience."[104] He witnessed what became of his favorite ideal. In 1845 the well-known *maskil* and bibliographer of Vilna, Isaac Benjacob, dispatched to Levinsohn a rather long memorandum[105] in which he gives a full picture of the Vilna rabbinical school with the melancholy conclusion: "For it is a contaminated house and its corruption stems from its origin, and not in this way will the light of wisdom and enlightenment rest on the people of Israel in our land." He begs Levinsohn to address himself to the government and relate

---

101. In the series of articles that Lilienthal later published in the *Allgemeine Zeitung des Judenthums* he, in fact, emphasizes that Nicholas' policy in regard to the Jews consisted in one definite goal: that all Jews should assume the Russian Orthodox faith (1848, No. 15).
102. The first Jew who obtained higher education in a Russian university.
103. The letter was published by S. Ginsburg in *Perezhitoye*, I, Part Two, 35.
104. *Sefer Ha-Zichronot*, 119.
105. Published in *Ha-Kerem*, 1887, 42-62.

to it the whole truth of "how it goes with the institute which was supposed to give the people educated spiritual leaders."

Levinsohn was already too aged and physically and mentally broken to carry the battle further. However, the old idealist in him had not yet expired. All his sad experiences still had not extinguished in him the belief in the progressive power of "enlightened absolutism." "You must not forget," he writes to his admirers in 1857, "that the Jewish schools were established when there were in the land great obstacles [a reference to Nicholas' despotic police-regime]. But see how there now stands at the head of the state the man on whom the spirit of knowledge and science rests. This is our Alexander II, who goes before the people with the torch of enlightenment."[106]

On his sick-bed Levinsohn had no notion of the new powers fermenting in the land. He did not know and understand that a new era was beginning.

106. *Sefer Ha-Zichronot*, 119.

CHAPTER FOUR

M. A. Günzburg, Adam Ha-Kohen and Micah Joseph Lebensohn, Abraham Mapu

[The "fathers of Haskalah" in Galicia and Lithuania—New Zagare as a center of Haskalah—Abraham Isaac Landa and his *Sefer Ha-Kundes*—The *maskilim* of Vilna—Tzevi Hirsch Katzenellenbogen and Mordecai Aaron Günzburg—From *Tzofnas Pane'akh* to *Gelot Ha-Aretz Ha-Hadashah*—Günzburg's *Aviezer*—Jacob Eichenbaum and his work—Adam Ha-Kohen Lebensohn—Lebensohn the grammarian and battler for Haskalah—His allegorical drama *Emet Ve-Emunah*—Lebensohn as an occasional poet—Language as an end in itself—The significance of Lebensohn's *Shirei Sefat Kodesh*—The problem of death in Lebensohn's work—His poems "Ha-Da'at Vaha-Mavet," "Ha-Hemlah," and "Ha-Mitonen"—Kalman Schulman as Günzburg's successor—Micah Joseph Lebensohn and his tragic life—The significance of his *Shirei Bat Tziyyon* and *Kinnor Bat Tziyyon*—Mordecai Hochmann's poem of Zion—Abraham Mapu, the romantic author of *Ahavat Tziyyon*—The significance of the first Hebrew novel.]

HE WELL-KNOWN publicist of the later era of Haskalah, Moses Leib Lilienblum, draws, in his article "Avot Ha-Haskalah Ha-Ivrit Be-Lita Uve-Galitziah"[1] a comparison between the men who laid the foundation of the Galician Haskalah and the leaders of Haskalah in Lithuania. The former, the author maintains, set as their goal, each in his own fashion, to exercise an influence on the people, to provide them with a response to the demands of the new times. Jehudah Leib Miesis and

1. *Ahiasaf*, X, 354–360.

Isaac Erter strove to free the people from the pernicious notions and ideas which they had received as a legacy from the previous benighted times.

The same thing was done by Solomon Jehudah Rapoport. As a journalist and scholar, he created the critical study of history in Jewry. The profound Naḥman Krochmal assumed the responsible task of becoming a "guide to the perplexed of the time," familiarizing them with the course of history, with the spirit of the Jewish past, in order to understand the present more clearly and better to grasp the tasks of national consciousness. This path was also followed by their disciple, the Volhynian Isaac Baer Levinsohn.

Of a quite different character, Lilienblum notes, were the Haskalah leaders of Lithuania. They created a "rhetorical Haskalah" *(haskalah melitzit)*, a "flat, superficial Haskalah" which hovers beyond space and time and, therefore, also beyond life and beyond scientific knowledge. For the beginning of knowledge is knowledge of our life—knowing and understanding life, whether it be the life of the present or that of past generations, insofar as this life is still linked with our present.

There is a certain truth in Lilienblum's overly harsh characterization. "The effect of the literature of one country on the literature of another," writes N. V. Plekhanov, "is proportional to the similarity of the social relationships prevalent in these countries." This fundamentally more or less justified thesis, however, requires certain corrections. The effect of one literature on another is experienced most strongly when the second country is on a lower economic level and must still attain the social conditions in which the first land, whose literature serves it as a model, already finds itself. The influence that the literature of a certain country has on other literatures assumes, among the latter, quite unique forms, in consonance with the local environment and the specific local conditions.

In the first chapter, when we described the tragic fate of the youngest disciple of the Gaon of Vilna, Manesseh of Ilya, we pointed out how at the beginning of the nineteenth century in Lithuania the reactionary tendency was strengthened in Jewish learned circles. We observed the reasons for which the "external wisdoms," or secular sciences, were again declared pure heresy. These reactionary tendencies, however, were not capable of long separating the Jewish community in Lithuania from the outside world of ideas. The conceptions of the Berlin Haskalah gradually penetrated into the circles of the learned youth, in part directly as a result of business relationships with Prussia, and in part indirectly through the communities located on the boundary of Kurland, where German culture was dominant. Especially typical in this respect is the little town of New Zagare which then still belonged to the province of Vilna. Leon Mandelstamm, a native of Zagare, writes in his autobiography:[2] "Despite the fact that physically my native town belonged to the province of Vilna, spiritually and intellectually it was distinguished by its Kurland culture and I am, therefore, accustomed to consider myself a Kurlander."

"Zagare," enthusiastically relates A. S. Sachs in his description of the youthful years of the bibliographer Solomon Abraham Freidus,[3]

was the cradle of the Haskalah . . . The little town of Zagare was a habitation of scholars and scribes. It was the center of Torah and wisdom. The greatest leaders and setters of tone in Jewish intellectual life were either themselves from Zagare or obtained their influence in Zagare . . . A small town not far from the Prussian-German border, especially from Ginshperk (Koenigsberg) and quite close to the Kurland and Livonia "localities," e.g., Lepai (Libau), Letave (Mitau), and Riga, Zagare was the midpoint, the trading center to which "foreign merchandise" used to be imported and whence exports would be distributed to the "places," the larger sales-localities. The "Leipzig head-kerchiefs," which were regarded as a kind of talisman in the Lithuanian and Kurland cities and towns (every respectable mother-in-law had to present a "Leipzig kerchief" as a present, on the occasion of her son's lecture in the synagogue, to the latter's bride, her future daughter-in-law, as soon as the marriage ceremony was over) came in large packs to Zagare. Here they were unpacked and distributed. Not a little "ritually forbidden" *(terefah)* merchandise was imported from Leipzig and Koenigsberg, that is to say, smuggled in, to avoid the payment of duties. The young matrons of Zagare were "women of valor," competent housekeepers, and apparently not ugly. Hence, they themselves would frequently travel to Prussia for merchandise and make acquaintance with the border officials who "looked between their fingers"—naturally, with the help of bribery—on the lovely young carriers of contraband . . . On certain trips the women would take along their husbands, young householders, who used to sit, some over the Talmud and rabbinic codifiers, some over books of Haskalah, and study. The young men would also smuggle—not merchandise, however, but the ideas of the Berlin Haskalah of Moses Mendelssohn and his disciples, as well as German philosophical works and ordinary books.

It is, naturally, a considerable exaggeration when A. S. Sachs affirms with his small-town patriotism that in his town of Zagare "the Haskalah was born and there acquired the life-energy through which it spread its wings over all of Russia." Nevertheless, it is

2. Published in the first volume of *Perezhitoye* (1908).
3. In *Studies in Jewish Bibliography . . . in Memory of Solomon Abraham Freidus* (1929).

beyond doubt that the "sages of Zagare" had a substantial influence on the Haskalah movement in Lithuania. These men of Zagare, who considered themselves Kurlander, contributed not a little to the fact that the Berlin Haskalah penetrated into the "Jerusalem of Lithuania," the old scholarly city of Vilna. Here, under very different social conditions, however, the Berlin Haskalah assumed quite singular forms.

In Prussia the Haskalah movement, as we noted in our discussion of it at length in the eighth volume of our work, was a result of a rather complex set of intellectual and social factors. In the major city of Prussia the leaders and battlers of the Haskalah movement found themselves in a certain contact with the progressive elements of the French colony resident there and the German intelligentsia. In the chief city of Lithuania, however, the representatives of Haskalah were surrounded by the compact mass of orthodox Jews, distinguished and isolated from the outside intellectual world. In Galicia the protagonists of Haskalah were at least in close association with the local group of German officials, who perceived in the German enlighteners in Polish Galicia the only representatives of their own German culture. It was quite different, however, in Lithuania.

Among all the representatives of Haskalah in the latter country, Mendelssohn's German translation of the Bible was the only bridge which led them to European, i.e., German, culture.[4] "They were not Russians but Germans," points out old Gottlober.[5] Moreover, the alien German culture with which the Lithuanian *maskilim* became familiar was not a living growth, as it had been among the creators of the Berlin Haskalah, but a preserved one, a product of the archives of the bygone eighteenth century. This foreign culture, naturally, could not serve as a connecting link with the external world. Already on the threshold of the new era, in 1856, Benjacob complains in his above-mentioned memorandum sent to Isaac Baer Levinsohn: "We are, after all, like dumb men" and cannot even make ourselves understood among the Russian officials.[6]

This isolation naturally added even greater intensity to the feeling of despair and powerlessness among the small circles of *maskilim* in Vilna, magnified their fear of the compact orthodox milieu, of the wrath of the rabbis and officials of the *kahal*. It is

---

4. It is worth noting that already at the end of the 1840s the *maskilim* of Vilna, led by Adam Ha-Kohen Lebensohn and Isaac Benjacob, undertook to reprint the Bible anew in a German translation with a new commentary (seventeen volumes, 1848–1853).

5. *Ha-Boker Or*, VII, 1879.

6. *Ha-Kerem*, 1887.

worthwhile, from the cultural-historical point of view, to point out the following characteristic feature. In Galicia the *maskilim*, in their battle against Hasidism, produced such master-works as *Megalleh Temirin* and *Gilgul Nefesh*, and the impetuous Jehudah Leib Miesis issued forth with his anti-rabbinic *Kinat Ha-Emet*. At the same time, in the Vilna literary world the following happened. The rabbi of Podkamen (near Brody), Rabbi Ḥayyim Landa, married his daughter in Vilna to a very rich man and a great scholar, Rabbi Leibele the son of Rabbi Baer. This couple raised a daughter, and Rabbi Leibele took, as his son-in-law, his wife's younger brother Abraham Isaac Landa. This son of a rabbi was a good student but already infected with the ideas of the Galician Haskalah and, furthermore, a wit and a joker. The young son-in-law was apparently bored with the deadly serious pietists of the Vilna synagogue courtyard. He conceived a desire to pluck their beards, to remind them what a marvelously beautiful thing exists in the world—healthy, joyous laughter.

The son-in-law's jester's tricks were extremely repugnant to the pious, arid, Mitnagdic scholar Rabbi Leibele. Despite the fact that the young couple lived together amicably and well, he forced Abraham Isaac Landa into divorcing his daughter and shortly thereafter married her to the intensely pious scholar Ḥayyim Naḥman Parnas.[7] Abraham Isaac Landa was extremely enraged at his erstwhile father-in-law who separated him from his beloved wife. Hence, he wished to pour out his wrath and feeling of contempt for the arid, melancholy scholars with their "pomp," their conceit and power, and he composed his *Sefer Ha-Kundes*,[8] a work sparkling with wit and love of life.

Landa was undoubtedly a talented literary man. His work is composed in the parody-style of Kalonymos bar Kalonymos' *Masechat Purim*.[9] *Sefer Ha-Kundes*, however, is written not in Talmudic fashion but in the codifier's style of the *Shulḥan Aruch*. The work is divided into chapters, and every chapter into paragraphs which explain and define how a true prankster ought to conduct himself. This work, written in ingenious parody-style, grows gradually into a colorful satire of the petty, comical, old-fashioned way of life in which people were not permitted to know of youth and the joy of youth. Six-year-old children had to think seriously

7 On Ḥayyim Naḥman Parnas, see Hillel Maggid-Steinschneider, *Ir Vilna*, 187. Parnas was the spokesman of the orthodox Jews of Vilna who attacked Max Lilienthal and the reform of the schools.
8. The full title is: *Sefer Ha-Kundes, Bo Yesuppar Maaseh Ha-Kundes Ve-Taḥbulotav U-Pe'ulotav Ve-Chol Asiyyotav Mi-Reshit Ha-Shanah Ad Aḥarit Ha-Shanah.*
9. See our *History*, Vol. II, p. 223.

only about serving God and fulfilling commandments, and a talented man with healthy senses and with joy in his blood had to become the "member of a gang of urchins," the prankster, whom the "important men," the pietistic Rabbi Leibeles and Rabbi Baers, regarded as a "wretch" desecrating, with his "profligate" behavior, the respectable family.

In 1824 Landa obtained the permission of the censorship and, in fact, soon afterwards published his *Kundes* in Vilna. The leaders of the community with the whole band of town fathers, however, quickly became aware of the "wanton" booklet. They promptly confiscated it, and even before it left the printery burned the entire edition. This was accomplished so thoroughly that only in the hands of the old resident of Vilna, Hillel Maggid- Steinschneider, was there a copy of the confiscated *Kundes*. His son, Professor David Maggid, published it with a Russian translation and with some biographical details about the author in *Yevreyskaya Starina* (1913, pp. 493-521).[10] Only in recent times did the scholar P. Kon manage to find a single printed copy of *Sefer Ha-Kundes* in the library of the University of Vilna.[11]

It should occasion no surprise that the lust for battle, the life-nerve of the Berlin and Galician Haskalah, virtually died out among the Lithuanian representatives of Haskalah. We have already pointed out how the *maskilim* of Vilna, encouraged by Levinsohn's *Te'udah Be-Yisrael*, decided to organize themselves around their own journal. However, it took all of twelve years before they finally summoned up their courage and in 1841 issued forth publicly with the anonymous, bloodless, and temperament-less *Pirhei Tzafon*. Not a single comtemporary issue is discussed there. It is, indeed, as Moses Lilienblum writes, "beyond time and place."

To be sure, in the second (which was also the last) volume of *Pirhei Tzafon*, published in 1844, when the government placed on the agenda the reform of the schools, A. Kaufmann's long article on the question of education appeared. Characteristic, however, is the following point. The young author dwells on the education of women. He projects the following: the establishment in various

---

10. Apparently later the author himself circulated his work in copies in his native town and in the region of Kremenets, because Isaac Baer Levinsohn was familiar with *Sefer Ha-Kundes* and in his double pamphlet *Oto Ve-Et Beno* and *Toledot Menahem Ha-Kozevi* his "hero," in whom there was a spark of Khlestakov, boasts that he is the author of *Sefer Ha-Kundes*. Abraham Isaac Landa later returned to Galicia and settled in Brody. In 1841, when a group of *maskilim* of Brody decided to cast off the traditional fur hat and to put an ordinary man's hat on their heads on the Sabbath, the author of *Sefer Ha-Kundes* cooperated with them in this (see Gottlober, *Ha-Melitz*, No. 19, p. 224).

11. See *Kiryat Sefer*, VIII, 129–133.

cities of special institutes of study, with a six-year program, for girls who are to obtain a strict moral education in these schools. The teachers and educators ought to be females only. In the entire course of the years of study and education, *the girls must be strictly forbidden to see men and, especially, to speak with them* [italics ours—I.Z.]. Even the parents must be forbidden to pass over the threshold of the institute without special permission from the female supervisors.

It is also interesting that the editor of *Pirḥei Tzafon*, S. J. Fuenn, when setting forth in his above-mentioned letter to B. Stern (p. 88) his reform program, in fact paraphrases the items of Levinsohn's program dealing with the question of education and the institute for rabbis and preachers. However, he says not even a word about the points in Levinsohn's program that touch on the question of engaging the Jewish masses in productive labor.

The same thing is repeated in the other leader of the Vilna *maskilim*, Mordecai Aaron Günzburg, in his *Maggid Emet*. We quoted above the passage of *Maggid Yeshuah* in which Max Lilienthal stresses that, as soon as the Jewish populace will amicably accept the school reforms planned by the government, decrees on ameliorating the material situation of the Jews are to be hoped for speedily. This incenses Günzburg. "Lilienthal," he complains,

tries to persuade us to fulfill the will of the government in precisely the same fashion as a father does with his little boy: "Go, my child, to school; I will give you nuts and sweetmeats." He promises us that the czar will endow us with new sources of earning a living. Are there not among us intelligent men in the thousands and tens of thousands who strive after knowledge and science not because of the use it can bring, but because science itself is precious to them? He regards the whole congregation of Israel as merely children.[12]

The Lithuanian *maskilim*, these battlers or—more correctly— dreamers of new forms of life, were, in fact, themselves imbued to a considerable degree with the spirit of arid rabbinism and overly subtle casuistry. For them, too, the actual interests and needs of the people remained foreign and incomprehensible. While Levinsohn deemed it necessary to stress that Hebrew is called the holy language not because the language itself is holy—(it was first hallowed through the content, the immortal works produced in it),[13] among the *maskilim* in Lithuania the tongue of the Bible was transformed into a kind of cult. The language itself, separated from

12. *Maggid Emet*, 13.
13. See above, p. 34.

any content whatever, was set forth as the supreme ideal. To it, the "beauteous language, the sole remnant," the most inspired songs of praise were chanted. Very frequently it was transformed among the *maskilim* into the substance and content of the entire Haskalah. They regarded themselves as priests whose task it is to serve this "sanctuary."

One of the recognized standard bearers of the Haskalah in Lithuania was Tzevi Hirsh Katzenellenbogen (born in 1797, died in 1868). Max Lilienthal considered it essential to correspond with him on the subject of the reform of the schools. For many years he was inspector of the rabbinical seminary in Vilna.[14] How poor, however, his literary legacy seems to be. He wrote poems of all kinds—paeans, elegies, and ordinary poems. One can find in them cleverness, flowery rhetoric, everything in the world. Only one small thing is lacking—poetry. He also wrote notes, commentaries, and explanations to various passages in the Bible.[15] And with this his literary activity is exhausted.

Considerably more productive than Katzenellenbogen was Mordecai Aaron Günzburg, frequently quoted above. Günzburg was born at the end of 1795 in Salant, which is located quite close to New Zagare. His father Jehudah Asher was already a bit infected by Haskalah. Articles in manuscript on grammar and mathematics have even come down from him, and his death in 1823 was lamented in elegies by the *maskilim* of Vilna, Mordecai Nathanson and Nissan Rosenthal.[16] Thanks to his father, young Mordecai Aaron devoted himself greatly even in his childhood years to the Bible and the Hebrew language. The historical works *Tzemaḥ David, She'erit Yisrael*, and others, which Günzburg read quite early in his youth, aroused his interest in history. He also studied German thoroughly, but his only love throughout his life remained the language of the Bible.

In the foreword to his first work *Gelot Ha-Aretz Ha-Ḥadashah* (Vilna, 1823), Günzburg points out that he wishes to achieve a double goal with his book: "to acquaint the reader both with historical events and with the beauty of the Hebrew language, the only ornament surviving from our erstwhile splendor." But precisely this first work demonstrates most clearly that the chief thing for Günzburg was, in fact, the second goal—demonstrating the beauty of Hebrew. On the title-page of *Gelot Ha-Aretz Ha-Ḥadashah* it is noted that the book is adapted from Campe's *Entdeckung von Amerika*. This, however, is not correct. Not Campe

14. On his activity as an inspector, see Benjacob's above-mentioned memorandum to Levinsohn in *Ha-Kerem* (1887).

15. *Naḥal Adanim* in 1821 and *Netivot Olam* in 1882 (reprinted in 1858).

16. These poems were published in Günzburg's *Gelot Ha-Aretz Ha-Hadashah*.

was his guide, but old Chaim Ḥaykl Hurwitz of Uman. Günzburg's *Gelot Ha-Aretz Ha-Ḥadashah* was, in fact, a Hebrew reworking of *Tzofnas Pane'akh*, already well known to us.[17] Even Hurwitz's epilogue, in which he points out the utility we Europeans enjoy from America, is found again in Günzburg, albeit in somewhat condensed form. Günzburg is merely angered—and he actually notes this in the foreword—that "we become familiar with such interesting events in the filthy clothing in which the printer of Volhynia has dressed them, [i.e., the Yiddish edition *Tzofnas Pane'akh*], when we possess the elegant clothes that have come down to us as a legacy from our fathers."

These "elegant clothes," i.e., the Hebrew edition of Campe's work, were, however, bound up with certain large expenditures that actually impoverished the author. To cover his debts, Günzburg decided immediately to issue the same work in Yiddish also.[18] But he refuses to dress such interesting accounts in "dirty clothes," as Ḥaykl Hurwitz had done. He notes this at once in the foreword:

This translation of *Entdeckung von Amerika* I rewrote from my Hebrew translation into a pure, fresh Judeo-German without the potpourri of Hebrew, Polish, Russian, and Turkish words which are elsewhere mingled together in the Yiddish language. I hope that those who can make no use of the lovely Hebrew translation will certainly buy this book and find in it more instruction, use, and pleasure than in the silly, false stories of *A Thousand and One Nights*.

Günzburg, indeed, was faithful to his word, and wrote his translation not in the pithy folk-language in which *Tzofnas Pane'akh* is written but in a Kurland *Daytshmerish*.[19]

In the prefaces to almost all his historical works,[20] as well as in the introduction to his guide for letterwriting *Kiryat Sefer* (Vilna, 1835) and the collection *Devir* (Vilna, 1844) Günzburg deems it necessary to emphasize that "I will not be parsimonious with my time on

17. See our *History*, Vol. IX, pp. 225ff.

18. Indeed Rabbi Abraham Abele points this out in his *haskamah* to *Gelot Ha-Aretz Ha-Ḥadashah*: "And in order that there might be a reward for his work, he also translated into Yiddish, which is customary among our people, so that ordinary persons and women might enjoy it."

19. A rather lengthy extract from Günzburg's *Die Entdeckung von Amerika* (Vilna, 1824), which is now a rarity, is presented by Zalman Rejzen in his *Fun Mendelssohn Biz Mendele*, 225-232.

20. Popular compilations or translations. The more important of them are: (1) *Toledot Benei Ha-Adam*, (1835), a universal history adapted from Politz's *Weltgeschichte*; (2) *Malachut Filoni Ha-Yehudi* (adapted from Eckhard's German translation of Philo's embassy to Caligula; (3) *Ittotei Russiya* (a short history of Russia, 1839; (4) *Ha-Tzarefatim Be-Russiya* (on the French invasion of Russia in 1812–1813); (5) *Yemei Ha-Dor* (on the more recent history of Europe, from 1770 to 1812).

behalf of the Hebrew language." And because the chief thing was the language, not the content, he was not fastidious in seeking out the material for his numerous translations. It is, after all, not so important whether one translates a work of art or a pallid account of the voluminous writer Czacki (*Leil Shimmurim*); the main thing is the language, "the only remnant."

Günzburg, however, paid his beloved much more than he himself calculated—not only with time and trouble, but also with a considerable part of his literary talent. As early as 1828 he pointed out in a letter of his[21] that he is writing his autobiography (*Aviezer*) and several printer's sheets are already finished. Nevertheless, in the course of the subsequent eighteen years that he was destined to live, he did not manage to complete the only work with which he, with his keen eye and power of portrayal, would have been able to produce a lasting monument in neo-Hebrew literature. His *Aviezer* remained a fragment. Nevertheless, it is the only work of all of Günzburg's numerous writings that arouses interest in the historian of culture.

It must, however, be acknowledged in this connection that the author who was so celebrated in his time certainly has great merits in Hebrew literature as a reformer of style and one of the chief creators of modern neo-Hebrew prose. Günzburg was a sharp opponent of the inflated rhetorical style that is filled with quotations of Biblical verses and fragments of verses. Like Mendel Levin, he also makes use of the treasury of words collected in the Mishnah and Midrashim, and he writes in a simple, flowing style, even if it is not one that is rich in imagery and color.

The lion of the group, the most important figure in the Haskalah circle of Vilna at that time, was Abraham Dov Mikhailishker, better known by the name Adam Ha-Kohen Lebensohn, the first significant poet Russian Jewry contributed to neo-Hebrew literature. To be sure, simultaneously with Lebensohn there lived another poet who came forward with a collection of poems prior to him. The latter, however, was merely a harbinger, a promise of a creative poet—a promise that was not realized. His name was Jacob Eichenbaum.

Born in 1796 in the small Galician town of Krystianopol, Eichenbaum displayed phenomenal capacities when still a child. At the age of two he already read passages from the prayerbook fluently. At the age of four he knew all of the Pentateuch. This bizarre education, however, did not permit his extraordinary abilities to develop normally. At the age of eight the young prodigy became, to his good fortune, a bridegroom, and his father handed

21. *Devir*, II, 72.

him over to be educated by his future father-in-law, a lessee of an estate in a village not far from the Volhynian village of Arkhov. After the wedding the young groom became familiar, through some itinerant Kabbalist, with the fundamentals of mathematics. In the young Eichenbaum thirst for secular knowledge was aroused, and this brought about a conflict with his wife's family—pious and ignorant village Jews. After long arguments, Eichenbaum parted from his wife, and years of wandering began for him.

In 1815 he was already in Zamosc, where he again married. There Eichenbaum became familiar, through the local *maskilim*, with the Berlin Haskalah. He learned to speak German fluently but devoted himself with special love to mathematics. By 1819 he had completed a Hebrew translation of Euclid's *Elements*. For lack of funds,[22] however, this translation remained in manuscript. A genuine sensation was evoked by the controversy that Eichenbaum had with the French mathematician Franker regarding an error which the former pointed out in one of the latter's calculations. The debate ended with the triumph of the Jewish auto-didact. Eichenbaum also translated Franker's textbook of mathematics into Hebrew, but this translation, too, remained in manuscript.[23]

This thorough Talmudist and excellent mathematician, however, was also endowed with the spark of an authentic poet. In 1833, when he was living in Moghilev, he sent his friend Benjamin Hirsch Wolfsohn, as a gift, a very successful poem called "Arba Ittot Ha-Shanah"[24] in which lovely portraits of nature are harmoniously interwoven with the love story of two young hearts and the wintry chords are mingled with the elegiac tones of the tragically concluded love. Eichenbaum's translations of Schiller also show that he possessed the spark of an epic poet. However, this Talmudist and mathematician, who was pleased only by the sharp,

---

22. We have already quoted above (p. 84) Eichenbaum's letter to Levinsohn in which he complains about his difficult material situation and how hard it is for him to support his wife and seven children. In 1844 his situation improved after he obtained a teaching position in the newly established school in Kishinev. From 1850 until his death (1861) Eichenbaum was inspector in the rabbinical seminary of Zhitomir.

23. In 1857 Eichenbaum published a textbook (following the pattern of a French work) on mathematics, entitled *Hochmat Ha-Shi'urim*. The manuscript of Eichenbaum's other textbook, *Techunat Ha-Misparim*, is in our possession.

24. The poem was sent by Eichenbaum to his friend with the following inscription added:
Take now, my brother, this poem of mine and keep it.
Let it be a sign of love between you and me
During the time that we are separated from one another.
It will remind you of the name of your friend Eichenbaum.
(We quote this inscription from a manuscript).

mentally acute, in fact saw in poetry only play and light pastimes. Even in this realm, he was also interested above all by the brainstorm, the ingenious discovery. He wrote, for instance, in 1819 a *teḥinnah* with nothing but traditional date-abbreviations, i.e., every verse amounts in *gematria* to 5579, the Hebrew equivalent to 1819.[25] And two years later, when Bloch's *Shevilei Olam* appeared, Eichenbaum wrote a poem of praise also consisting of pure date-abbreviations, and this time every line amounts in *gematria* to the number 5581.[26]

But the goddess of poetry is very jealous. She demands of her standard-bearers that they serve her with extreme seriousness and turns her back on anyone who regards her art merely as frivolous play, no matter how talented he may be. Such a poet's creativity remains dead, unilluminated by the radiance and life-splendor of the goddess.

A special place is occupied in Eichenbaum's creativity by his well-known poem "Ha-Kerav" (The Battle).[27]

Already since the early Middle Ages, chess (*shokh-tzobil* as it is called in Old-Yiddish) was greatly loved among Jews. The game finds an echo in numerous Jewish legends and poems. Eichenbaum was a fervent chess-player. He was so infatuated with chess that he celebrated the game in a special poem. He brings together at the chess board two ingenious players and relates how the battle-game proceeded. It is astonishing to see the mastery with which the poet renders, in the language of the Bible and in flowing six-line stanzas, all the details of the battle. Every chess figure is transformed into a courageous warrior who carries on an obdurate, life-and-death struggle. And every warrior fights in his own fashion, as he ought to according to the rules of the marvelous game. But in the end, even in this masterpiece, there is more ingenuity than true art.[28]

Of a quite different character was Adam Ha-Kohen Lebensohn. The future poet had a sad childhood in his native city of Vilna.[29] His father Ḥayyim was an extremely poor man. Lebensohn was

25. *Kol Zimrah*, 99–100.

26. *Ibid.*, 50–53.

27. First published in 1840. In 1847 Osip (Joseph) Rabinovich (the later publisher of *Razsvet*) translated Eichenbaum's poem into Russian and published it along with the original.

28. The long poem in four cantos "Ha-Kosem" which Eichenbaum reworked from German in the last year of his life (published in the first year's issue of *Ha-Melitz* and later reprinted separately) has a very limited importance.

29. Lebensohn's year of birth has not been determined. Some biographers give the year as 1787, others as 1794. Kalman Schulman asserts that Lebensohn lived over a hundred years. This, however, is certainly an exaggeration. He died in 1878, close to ninety years of age.

still a small child when his mother died, and he was raised in the
house of his grandfather Jonah Domiansky. At the age of seven the
young Abraham Baer was dispatched to a *yeshivah* where he studied
the assigned Talmud lesson along with the grownup young men.
At the age of eleven he was already famed in scholarly Vilna as a
prodigy, an extraordinary swimmer over the sea of the Talmud.
His grandfather sent the young prodigy to study in the large
yeshivah of Mikhailishk. In Mikhailishk he was promptly betrothed,
and at the age of thirteen married. For all of eight years he received
maintenance in his father-in-law's house, and these years were also
years of study for him.

The young groom of Mikhailishk, with his thirst for knowledge,
refused to be content merely with Talmudic literature. He
immersed himself in the medieval books of philosophy and
occupied himself for a time with Kabbalah. The latter, however,
did not satisfy his acute and sober scientific thinking. He was far
more impressed by the keenly logical author of *A Guide for the
Perplexed* and became throughout his life Maimonides' enthusiastic
admirer.[30]

The young man also became familiar with the Berlin Haskalah
and came to be a convinced rationalist, occupying in this respect, as
we shall see later on, a much more radical position than his
contemporaries and fellow-battlers, Tzevi Hirsh Katzenellenbogen and Mordecai Aaron Günzburg, who really belonged more to
the right wing of the Haskalah movement.[31] Lebensohn also

30. When Lebensohn mentions Maimonides he accompanies his name with such emotive
lines as the following: "For whom is all the desire of Israel? To whom does all the seed of
Jacob give thanks? Who was it who split the rock of the Torah with the staff of divine wisdom
that was in his hand and the living waters, the life of the spirit, flowed to all the congregation
of the children of Israel? Was it not our lord, the teacher, the author of the *Guide for the
Perplexed (Moreh Nevuchim)* who guided us in the path with a strong hand (*Yad Ḥazakah*) and
with great awe? This, Moses ben Maimon did in the sight of all the sages of Israel—he whom
God sent in the place of Moses ben Amram. And who knows what would have happened to
the religion of Moses the man of God in this generation if it were not for Moses Maimuni?
From the aspect of faith and from the aspect of reason?" (*Kinat Soferim*, 56–57).

31. Characteristic of Mordecai Aaron Günzburg is the following point. In his above-quoted
article against Max Lilienthal he addresses the German rabbis: "I turn to you, my dear
doctors. If the government or the communities invite you to come to us, we beg you, indeed,
not to refuse. You will be very welcome among us, for you will undoubtedly be able to bring
much use. You must, however, know beforehand whither and with what task you come
here. If you come to us as preachers and teachers, you will find attentive listeners who will
eagerly receive your sermons and lectures in the pure German language and diligent pupils
who, with great avidity, will study with you the secular sciences which are so necessary to
us. But if you intend to become rabbis among us, my only advice is that you should bring
with you Torah, Torah, and Torah . . . If Aristotle himself should arise from the grave, he
also would not be privileged to occupy a rabbinic position among the holy people. We will,
indeed, receive him with great reverence, as he deserves, but we will not make him a rabbi"
(*Ha-Moriyyah*, 43–45).

attempted to study the German language. This, however, came hard to him, and even in his later years he was unable to read the German classics without outside help.[32] His only cultural language was and remained Hebrew, but he had a command of this language such as very few in his time did.

Lebensohn was not only the great master of Hebrew. The language of the Bible was his sole love, and his love bordered on idolization, on true, self-sacrificial devotion. His ideal was Naftali Herz Wessely, whom he celebrates with great emotiveness in a special poem.[33] But this was not merely because he considered the author of *Shirei Tiferet* a great poet. He was enchanted chiefly by Wessely's enormous love for the Hebrew language, the devotion with which the latter investigated the word-treasury and principles of the biblical language and commented on the books of the Bible.[34] Indeed, Lebensohn followed in Wessely's footsteps. With great love he explored all the singularities and finest nuances of biblical speech.[35] He accompanied the new Bible edition and a German translation, which he prepared together with Isaac Benjacob (1848-1853), with *Torat Ha-Adam*, a new commentary on a part of the books of the prophets. The last lines that he wrote in his life were a commentary on a verse in Psalms.

To be sure, Lebensohn lacked the requisite scientific knowledge in the realm of philology and exegesis; furthermore, he did not possess the necessary competence in other Semitic languages. But his vast love for the biblical language and the intuitive sensitivity of a poet contributed to the fact that he made quite valuable comments regarding the structure and uniqueness of the Hebrew language and its treasury of words.

Adam Ha-Kohen Lebensohn, the most devoted knight of the language of the Bible, however, had a rather cold attitude toward the Talmud and a definite hostility to the later rabbinic literature. Even in his prayer-poem "Kol Na'akat Battei Yehudah" which is written in the God-fearing, pious style of the medieval *selihot*, the poet complains before God: You, O God, have abandoned us and locked us up in darkness. Because of much suffering and distress, we have forgotten what right is, and our guides grope about like blind men; none of them grasps the needs of the people, none of them understands how to support the people. Instead of providing

32. This is noted by such a reliable witness as Lebensohn's disciple and admirer, the poet J. L. Gordon (*Yevreyskaya Biblioteka*, VIII, 164). See also *Hazon La-Mo'ed*, II, 81.
33. "Halom Erev" (*Shirei Sefat Kodesh*, I, 201–205).
34. But he said to the Hebrew language: Reveal thyself!
    And he disclosed in it mysteries not yet known.
    And in it he sang his songs that reached to the heavens.
    Wessely was his family name, and his first name Naftali.
35. *Mehkerei Lashon*, 1849.

true support, they are always building new restraints and do not see the real disaster.[36] The poet hurls wrathful stanzas against the benighted "rebels against the light"[37] and the "contemners of the Torah"[38] and the "contemners of wisdom"[39] who ruthlessly persecute the seekers after knowledge and among whom every fool and idiot is called rabbi. He cannot forgive the fact that the hypocritical pietists make the name "Berliner" a shame and a mockery, and he is firmly persuaded that "the name Berliner will yet become an ornament."

Also in the letter he handed to Sir Moses Montefiore when the latter visited Vilna in 1846, Lebensohn points out that one of the "four major damages," the four chief factors which bring about the grievous condition in which Russian Jewry finds itself, is the fact that the leaders and rabbis do not understand the needs and requirements of the people. They know only "to increase innumerably the customs and prohibitions, to collect whole mountains of new severities that ruin the people." And these severities, Lebensohn argues, have no foundation in the Written Torah or in the tradition of ancient times. They are taken exclusively from the "foolish superstitions imported from abroad, or wild customs that old women and ignorant men have fabricated."[40]

Especially characteristic in this respect is Lebensohn's allegorical drama *Emet Ve-Emunah*.[41] We pointed out in the previous chapter how, in 1841, when the orthodox Jews battled against the new schools and against Uvarov's emissary Max Lilienthal, the *maskilim* were greatly incensed by the report that a special commission of rabbis to consider the reform of the schools would be convened. The *maskilim* perceived in this a great danger for the whole enterprise. At that time the irascible Lebensohn poured out all his wrath in his comprehensive allegorical drama which he completed in the course of several months.

Emet Ve-Emunah is written following the pattern of Moses Ḥayyim Luzzatto's *La-Yesharim Tehillah*. The style, however, is quite different. In Luzzatto's work, gentle, philosophical, humanistic tones are heard. Lebensohn's *Emet Ve-Emunah*, however, is a militant document that breathes hatred and indignation. In the subtitle it is stressed: "to purify the faith from every false

36. *Shirei Sefat Kodesh*, I, 1861, 155–156.
37. *Ibid.*, II, 1856, 69–70.
38. *Ibid.*, 150–153.
39. *Ibid.*, 154–161.
40. *Yeter Shirei Adam*, 70.
41. Of the battle that arose around this work from the purely aesthetic point of view, we shall speak in the following volume.

thing and to consecrate it exclusively to the truth." In general, the work does not mention the religion acquired through divine revelation. The faith of Lebensohn's allegorical drama is a primitive, human one, the naive daughter of Hamon (the Multitude) and Peti'ut (Folly)—the ignorant, superstitious stupidity that allows itself to be led astray by every swindler. For it, crude old wives' tales are a credible Torah. It nods its head in simplicity and repeats always one and the same song: "So it is."

The central figure in the entire drama is Tzivon (Hypocrite)—the swindler and Tartuffe who is no longer an abstract allegory in general. He is the prototype of the false, base, hypocritical pietist who is portrayed in the most extreme variations in the later tendentious *belles-lettres* of the Haskalah literature. Lebensohn gathers in this negative figure all the typical features of the characters clinging to the old way of life so despised by the *maskilim*. Tzivon is a Kabbalist, a wonder-worker who has to do with the *sefirot*, with demons, and with all kinds of *baal-shem* amulets. He is always running to the ritual bath and, at the same time, he is a Tartuffe, makes pretense of sitting whole nights over the sacred Torah and simultaneously commits the vilest deeds and in contemptible fashion violates the seventh commandment. When, through his initiative and that of Mirmah (Deceit), falsehood appears in the garments of faith, declares itself the true viceroy, associates itself with religion, and becomes Hamon's son-in-law, difficult times begin for Hamon.

Tzivon and Shakran (Liar) do not tire of producing ever new religious laws. They write innumerable books, always with new decrees and severities that have no sense or foundation and are nothing but foolishness and gross superstition. People are simply unable to endure all these severities and are ruined under their heavy burden.[42]

Lebensohn, however, did not have the courage to publish his militant work. He recalled the sad fate of the work of Manasseh of Ilya and of Abraham Isaac Landa's *Sefer Ha-Kundes*. Moreover, his material situation was greatly dependent on the "men of the mansions," the plutocrats and leaders of the community. After Lebensohn stopped receiving maintenance from his father-in-law, he took up trade but lost his money. Then he settled with his family

---

42. *Emet Ve-Emunah*, 89:
> They have new things every morning; to give birth to a law takes only a moment.
> Of the making of many books there is no end; religious writings immeasurable . . .
> Every hand is tied down, so as not to be able to seek sustenance.
> Their steps they have tethered with an excess of pathological restraints . . .
> All are only misleading follies, vanities, vanities of vanity.
> Mockery and nonsense—O, nothing but wailing and mourning.

and betook himself to teaching. After ten years of teaching, symptoms of tuberculosis appeared. Hence, he had to seek a new source of earning a living and became a broker, a middleman in loans—a livelihood hanging in the air that was associated with much distraction and many degradations. Hence, it is easily comprehensible that the middlemen had to be humble and subordinate before the "sacks of gold" and was afraid to issue forth publicly with his battle document.

To be sure, five years later, Lebensohn was so enraged by the "benighted ones"[43] that he openly declared his determination soon to publish his *Emet Ve-Emunah*. This was shortly after Mordecai Aaron Günzburg's death (at the end of 1846). Lebensohn, as well as the other *maskilim* of Vilna, saw in Günzburg's death an enormous loss for the Hebrew language. "Our holy tongue," Lebensohn laments, "has become like a widow; she has no redeemer and helper." The pious preacher of the city, however, perceived in Günzburg only the heretic; hence, agreeing with the orthodox, he deemed it inappropriate to present a special eulogy and contented himself merely with mentioning incidentally at the end of his rather lengthy homily that "Mordecai Aaron Günzburg has also died." This greatly incensed the circle of *maskilim* in Vilna. They decided to convene a prayer quorum for themselves, and on the next Sabbath recited a long eulogy over the deceased writer. Lebensohn, in fact, was the orator on the occasion. His eulogy was very favorably received by the group and was promptly printed in a separate pamphlet.[44]

Lebensohn, however, was still unwilling to forgive the fact that his deceased friend "was not eulogized according to the law." He wished to settle accounts with the "hypocrites" and "rebels against the light." So, he declares at the end of his *Kinat Soferim* (71–72) that he is undertaking to publish his drama.

Nevertheless, fear of the "men of the mansions" won out. Just at that time Lebensohn was appointed a senior assistant master in Hebrew and Aramaic in the Vilna rabbinical seminary; hence, he let his battle document lie in manuscript. Only twenty years later when, as an eighty-year-old man, he retired from his teaching position and spent the last years of his life without worrying about a livelihood, was his *Emet Ve-Emunah* finally published (1867).

In fact, it was not *Emet Ve-Emunah*, which appeared so late, that made Lebensohn's name famous in the circles of the *maskilim*, but his *Shirei Sefat Kodesh*. Like Wessely in his time, Lebensohn also, until his old age, published only "occasional" poems. The main thing, after all, for him was the language, "the beauteous tongue,

43. *Kinat Soferim*, 25.
44. *Kinat Soferim*, Vilna, 1847.

the only remnant;" the content was a secondary matter. One must serve the holy language faithfully, with self-sacrifice, and he who writes Hebrew is a priest of God who offers service in the sanctuary.

Characteristic is the innocent simplicity with which Adam Ha-Kohen Lebensohn reports to the reader:

> At the table of God I sat constantly,
> And in my hand I conducted the scribe's pen to Him,
> And my hand wrote His language in holiness,
> And the language of His Torah and the language of His people.
>   Selah.

The table at which he holds "the author's pen in hand" is already *ipso facto* a "godly table," for he composes in the holy tongue, the language of God's Torah and God's people. The subject on which he writes makes no difference. The language is the principal thing. Lebensohn, in fact, made his debut in Hebrew literature with a "Carmen-poem" for the wedding of Count Tyzkiewicz.[45] Three years later Alexander I died. The Jewish poet thereupon broke out with a "voice of weeping" and wrote a rather long elegy. But since Russia did not remain without a czar and, after Alexander, Nicholas fortunately ascended the throne, Lebensohn concludes the elegy with a joyous song of praise. A year later Nicholas' coronation took place, and Lebensohn again sang a paean. Afterwards, Nicholas had a son, and once more, on this happy occasion, the Jewish poet chanted a patriotic ode. And when the successor to the throne came of age, he proclaimed the joyous tidings to the whole world:

> Listen to this, all peoples,
> Give ear, all inhabitants of the world!

In his anthology of poems *Shirei Sefat Kodesh*[46] the author reprinted not only all the patriotic poems he had written but even the *avnei bachut*, the rhymed tombstone inscriptions with tremendous praises and laudations that Vilna householders used to order for a certain price from the "linguist" Lebensohn for their deceased relatives. Everything for the poet was worthy and important, for everything, after all, was written at the "table of God," composed in the holy tongue. To the language of the Bible, which Lebensohn crowns with such titles as "the habitation of the house of God," "the chosen of the God of Israel and the preciousness of his prophets,"

---

45. *Shir Ḥavivim*, Vilna, 1822.
46. The first part appeared in 1842, and the second in 1856.

"the mistress of languages," *Shirei Sefat Kodesh* is dedicated. On more than two pages of print the poet pours our his ardent love and feeling of reverence for his "mistress." Enthusiastically he exclaims: "You know my heart. You know that, out of all the joys in the world, out of all human desires and longings, I have chosen you alone. For you do I yearn all my days. For you does my soul languish. Those who love you are also dear to me, and my heart is firmly bound up with those who seek and long for you."[47]

And Lebensohn is right when he introduces as a motto for his *Shirei Sefat Kodesh* a saying from the *Yalkut Tehillim* which suggests that this collection represents a "new song" in neo-Hebrew literature. For the erstwhile *yeshivah* student, the *maskil* and rigorous grammarian Lebensohn, with all his old-fashioned simplicity and a certain dose of study-house impracticality, was, after all, a genuine poet with a sharply developed individuality, with his own style, his own world-view.

It has already been pointed out in a previous volume[48] how the rationalist ideas of the eighteenth century, which helped the human personality liberate itself from the intellectual enslavement surviving as a heritage from the old way of life, at the same time also strongly undermined the traditional religious world-view with its firm belief in reward and punishment and the immortality of the soul. This fact was, to a certain extent, inconsistent with the optimistic world-view of the *Aufklärer*; man, after all, was born to enjoy life in the best of all worlds, which is ruled by the "pre-established harmony"—and man's life is so brief, so filled with pain and sorrow. Death soon lies in wait for him, and man disappears like a shadow, disintegrates into ashes and dust. For this reason, indeed, so much attention was paid in the era of the *Aufklärer* to the problem of death, and men engaged with such painful interest in the question of the immortality of the human soul. In this also lay the major cause of the enormous success that Mendelssohn's *Phaedon* enjoyed in its time.

The problem of death was also the focal point of Lebensohn's poetic creativity. Rationalist ideas destroyed in the poet the old, simple belief. Skeptical, critical thought undermined the foundations of the traditional religious structure. Urgently and painfully "the agonizing, ancient enigma" of which Heine speaks with such bitter sarcasm—"What does man signify, whence has he come, where does he go?"—drilled into the poet. The old, agonized questions that occupy such a central place in Hebrew

---

47. *Shirei Sefat Kodesh*, I, 9.
48. Vol. VIII, pp. 18ff.

literature[49]—the questions: To what end does man live? Wherein does the goal consist? How can man's great pain, his endless sufferings, be justified? How can one explain, how grasp the tragic enigma of the world? How can one justify the great confusion, the deep contradiction: the Creator a God full of compassion, and the world steeped in wickedness and corruption?—do not let Lebensohn's poetic conscience rest.

Tragic personal experiences sharpened these problems even more agonizingly for Lebensohn. Seven of the poet's children died. In his elegy "Misped Mar" he portrays in powerful stanzas how before his very eyes two ardently loved children, a four-year-old little girl and a boy of six, wrestled with death. The poet cannot forget the suffering-filled, childish eyes with the silent question: Why? And filled with anguish, the poet exclaims, "I will cry out: Why is this? Speak! And wherefore?"[50]

Lebensohn had a son who was a poet—a tender, lovely flower who should have become the pride and glory of neo-Hebrew poetry. And this loveliest hope for years withered, flickered, and before his eyes took its last breath. Profoundly shattered, the wretched father mourns:

> My weeping will end only when my life ends,
> And my sorrow will be silenced when my days cease,
> And this son of mine I will forget when I forget the world.[51]

And despairingly he hurls his agonized questions:

> Who has driven away my bird from my nest?
> Who has made me forget my song from my house?
> Who has shattered my harp and summoned lamentation?[52]

These personal experiences intensified the problem of death in Lebensohn's creativity. Even in his portrayals of nature, when the poet celebrates spring,[53] he sees among the flower-blossoms the withered leaves, and in the spring-song he hears the mourning-cries of decay. This spring-poem concludes with the melancholy chord:

> Wrath are we in our lifetime,
> We are children of sorrow.

49. See our *History*, Vol. I.
50. *Shirei Sefat Kodesh*, I, 231.
51. *Ibid.*, II, 200.
52. *Ibid.*, 193.
53. *Ibid.*, 23–29.

How shall we look upon our dead,
And not see death?

Even the summer evening casts dread on the poet. The shadows
of night, which already lie in wait at twilight, frighten him:

Even now the skirts of her robe appear to us,
And darkness came flying and rose from her lurking place,
Awakened swiftly to go out like the wolves of night
From the abyss of Abaddon, the depths of destruction.

Darkness for the poet is the symbol of terror and holocaust:

This darkness has no glory, no grace, no beauty;
It is all horrors, only destruction and evil.

In the poet's consciousness darkness is the primal source of chaos
and non-being.[54] Hence, he sings a song of praise to the longest day
of the year, for it drives the dark shadows of night farthest away.[55]
The shadows of night bring terrible dreams. Now the poet
dreams that he stands leaning close to a wide gate, and he sees
how thickly packed hosts of men hasten through it with great
speed. The stream of humanity has no beginning and no end. He
looks through the other side of the gate from which the stream of
men flows and a horror falls upon him: "There is nothing there.
Woe! Only silence, only chaos!" He throws himself to the other
side—and there also it is waste and void. "Only graves of
darkness." Overcome by terror, the poet cries out: "Who are you,
O children of non-being, you dead wanderers? What means the
deadly darkness of both sides of the gate?" "The events under the
sun"—so resounds the answer. What is on this side of the
gate?—"Everything that will be." And what on the other
side?—"Everything that has been." And what does the gate
signify? "It is the present moment of being." Further questions die
away from his lips, because the wanderers through the gate do not
stop their swift course: "Lo, we are pursued up to our necks."[56]
Terror falls upon the poet, a deep melancholy clamps his heart,
and he awakens from his grievous dream. "Ḥalom Over" (A
Passing Dream) is the title of this poem.[57] All of life is a swiftly
passing dream. And hard by "the passing dream" death lies in wait.
The "passing dream" itself is filled with the terror of death, the

---

54. *Ibid.*, 11–16.
55. *Ibid.*, 30–34.
56. *Hen nirdafim naḥnu al tzavarenu*.
57. *Shirei Sefat Kodesh*, 58–61.

consciousness that death lurks at every step. To this awareness of death the poet dedicates one of his major creations, his long poem "Ha-Da'at Veha-Mavet" (Knowledge and Death).[58]

Lebensohn was, after all, a rationalist, and, along with other *maskilim*, fought for knowledge and science. Knowledge *(ha-da'at)* is the divine light that illuminates human life. So, indeed, the poem begins with proud chords portraying how, in the miserable universe, man alone is endowed with the marvelous gift of knowledge:

> He alone among all the creatures
> Knows them, and none besides.

Only man thinks and remembers:

> He feels and imagines, he also remembers and knows,
> He thinks and perceives everything that has meaning.

Man has explored everything. He has even penetrated into the mystery of eternity. However, he has paid too dearly for this knowledge. Man is the only being in the entire universe who also embraces with his thought death, "the source of every plague."

"O accursed knowledge!"—the poet exclaims—"the knowledge of him who exists that he will be transformed into non-existence." In powerful stanzas the poet portrays how the consciousness of the inevitability of death poisons the source of life. Not death itself, but merely the knowledge of its existence, kills. For death does not exist for those who do not know it:

> Every day he will die — for he knows his mortality.
> He will not die in death, but in life!
> He will not die through death, but through knowledge . . .
> He knows that the knowledge of his death is his slayer,
> For there is no death for him who knows it not.
> No other living being is aware of its end.

It is literally amazing that the same poet who composed so many petty, hurrah-patriotic odes and occasional poems also produced such splendid verses as the following:

> For what is this death? — only the end of life.
> A man sees all the moments of his life vanishing;
> Hence, every moment of his death is before his eyes.
> For his life and his moments fly away together.

58. *Ibid.*, 9–31.

And in his beginning man knows his end,
In his life — his death, and in his house — the grave.

It is not, however, merely in this that the tragedy of man's life consists. The poet actually denies the fundamental motto of the enlighteners to the effect that man is born for happiness. Everything, after all, is nothing but mirage and deception. The only reality is death. Unreal even is that wherein man so exults—knowledge.

Apparently the poet's friends, who were better acquainted with the German language than he, familiarized him with Kant's critical philosophy, with its conclusion that man is incapable, with the aid of reason alone, of knowing the true essence of what is outside himself, inasmuch as all the concepts that man obtains from the external world are, first of all, formed through his own receptive apparatus and are a definite consequence of the specific forms that man's reason has by its nature. This train of ideas was best suited to the poet's mood. He sees that everything is pure deception. "Ha-Kol Hevel" (All Is Vanity) is the title of one of his misanthropic poems.[59] "See," the poet exclaims, "that all of life is nothing but falsehood!"

"Behold, O man, everything is merely a dream!" "They have deceived man, they have only deceived him; all of them have deceived me." With this the dying man in the poem "Ha-Gove'a"[60] summarizes his life's way. And he concludes with the skeptical line: "Now my soul will rise to see what there is on high."

In a poem entitled "Halom Ḥezyon La'ilah" (A Dream of a Night Vision)[61] the poet portrays the multicolored world of splendor and beauty as merely a mirage, a deceptive specter of man's perceptions and feelings. The unattainable and incomprehensible "daughter of almighty God," creation (*ha-beriah*), is totally a question mark:

There is neither beauty nor pleasure nor any loveliness;
There is neither sweetness nor delight nor any goodness of taste;
There is neither hearing nor seeing nor delight to the eye;
There is neither form nor image, neither inquiry nor reason;
For there is even no error and foolishness and stupidity,
No enigma and mystery, nor any thought.

Lebensohn, the rationalist, denies the fundamental belief of the *Aufklärer* that reason, man's common sense, is the ruler of the

59. *Ibid.*, II, 41–51.
60. *Ibid.*, II, 58–61.
61. *Ibid.*, I, 62–68.

universe.[62] "Understanding and knowledge—in these, too, there is defect." Man's knowledge consists only in the fact that he becomes convinced that neither creation nor the Creator are comprehensible. After all, as a follower of Maimonides, the poet knows that divinity can be vested only with negative attributes,[63] with that which is not. God Himself is incomprehensible and unattainable. "For know that God is higher than we." Man cannot grasp what is above him. We know only that everything is a unity. "But what is unity? Search this out, you great men!" (I, 68). And the poet comes to the following conclusion in his poem "Mehallel El" (Adorer of God):[64] "My spirit has sought everything and returned empty. Before the God who hides Himself, my soul also hides itself. When to praise means to desecrate, the best thing is silence."

In "Emet Ve-Emunah" the *maskil* Lebensohn battles for the "truth," which lights up the whole world and is the only reliable guide. But in the peom "Mevakkesh Emet" (The Seeker of Truth; I, 131–132) the "truth-seeker" stands filled with despair and doubts. Who sees the truth? Its face, after all, is hidden under a veil. "Also I—want am I? Woe, who has deceived me?" "Our understanding is powerless to reveal the secret of the Father-God." Over all the corners of the universe one cry only is heard: "Where have we a Father, where is the Creator of these things?"[65] And because reason is incapable of providing an answer, faith comes and takes the place of reason.[66] The poet, however, finds that faith also cannot give a satisfying solution. Faith asserts that the Lord is "a merciful and gracious God." But is He really a gracious and compassionate Father? To this question the poet devotes a long poem of all of a hundred six-line stanzas, "Ha-Hemlah" (Compassion).[67]

Hemlah (Compassion) wandered over the whole world and, broken, filled with despair, returned from its wanderings. In four chapters it reports all the terrors that it saw in the world. In the first chapter it tells of the robbery and bloodshed that prevail among all creatures that lurk in the forests, burrow in the ground, fly in the air, and swarm in the flood. Everywhere it saw how "the mortally

---

62. Even in his militant *Emet Ve-Emunah* the poet stresses the limitations of reason and that one cannot always rely on it as the correct guide (*ibid.*, 86–98).
63. See our *History*, Vol. I, pp. 143–44.
64. *Shirei Sefat Kodesh*, II, 6–7.
65. *Ibid.*, 15.
66. Characteristic in this connection is the following passage in *Ha-Da'at Veha-Mavet:*
    For if the eye of man could see
    Into the depth of the knowledge of the Almighty, the wisdom of his Maker,
    Then even without religion he would know salvation.
67. *Shirei Sefat Kodesh*, II, 165–200.
68. *Ibid.*, 200.

wounded shriek between the teeth of the carnivores." In the second chapter the injustice and cruelty that men commit in regard to God's creations are portrayed. In the third chapter only the great social injustice in human communities—how men sell their own brethren like cattle and sheep—is set forth in powerful verses:

Shall a man be sold there like the cattle of the field?
Shall he be displayed on the marketplace and gate like a sheep?
Shall he be examined like an ox to determine if there is a wound
   in him?
Shall he be placed there naked like the beast of the forest?

How steeped in blood and wickedness is the world! The most comprehensive chapter of the poem is the fourth. Here the poet returns to his agonized theme: the tragedy of man's life, the terror before fearful death with its numerous eyes, the cruelty of the fate that ceaselessly pursues men. And Compassion pours out its deep sorrow in mournful lines:

Woe, O world, house of mourning! Woe, O vale of weeping!
Your rivers are tears, and your dust ashes.

As in the closing section of the Book of Job, so also in the concluding chapter of Lebensohn's poem God's voice resounds from on high and replies to the charges of Compassion. But on hearing the response, one is involuntarily reminded of Heine's well-known concluding line: "But is this an answer?" Bowed low, Compassion humbly responds: "Surely I know now that You are a God of justice, and my mouth must be silent." And filled with sadness, it cries out: "How terrible is your affliction, you who dwell below! So has the Supreme One who dwells in the clouds determined!" The poet, however, refuses to be satisfied with this conclusion and is unwilling to be silent, like humble Compassion. He hurls his stormy protest in the angry verses of his "Ha-Mitonen" (The Protester)[69] which is the crown of all of his creativity.

Even Lebensohn's best poetic works suffer not a little from the fact that their author does not know the "secret of brevity." In his "Ha-Hemlah," "Ha-Da' at Veha-Mavet," and especially in his long elegiac poem "Michal Dimah," powerful, splendid verses are not infrequently watered down with flowery rhetoric. "Ha-Mitonen" is free of this defect. All the verses are as if poured from one steel mold. The reader is torn along with the stormy, wrathful lines that

69. *Ibid.*, I, 45–50.

breathe so much hopeless misery. A prose translation is incapable of providing any notion of the tremendous power of such stanzas as the following:

> Would that I knew that my voice could destroy with power
> The world and the fulness thereof, and the hosts of heaven.
> Then would I give a great cry: Let me be!
> And I would return to chaos with all living beings.

> For the living know that the grave will swallow them up
> After they are sated with toil and bitter grief;
> And while they are still in being they see that the life of man
> Flees like lightning before the thunder of death.

> . . . If you would count your days, you will count your
>   calamities,
> For at every moment you are thrust from calamity to calamity;
> So is the day of your birth, so also your whole lifetime.
> So you will grow old, so you will perish, alas! So you are
>   pursued.

This melancholy poet, who was so frightened of death, was spared for a very long time by the grim reaper. Sated with years, the aged Lebensohn departed from the world (at the end of 1878). Different was the fate of his son Micah Joseph. Like a brilliant meteor, he lit up in neo-Hebrew poetry and quickly disappeared. Death trampled the tender blossom.

Two female figures stood at the poet's cradle—the bright goddess of song and the sorrowful daughter of suffering and care. Firmly linked arm in arm, they accompanied the unfortunate man on his brief life's way and covered him with marvelous grace and beauty.

As early as his childhood years the future poet celebrated the radiant stars in verse and, indeed, even then the first symptoms of his incurable consumption appeared. However, in the sickly body lived an enormous thirst for knowledge. Micah Joseph Lebensohn's father could give him thorough instruction only in Hebrew literature and language. But by himself, as a result of his own diligence, the young man learned German, as well as French, Polish, and Russian. Raised in the house of one of the "fathers of Haskalah," the youthful poet had no occasion to battle for "enlightenment" and to be fearful of persecutions on the part of the "rebels against the light."

In the previous part of our work we spoke of the passively meditative natures to be found among the Galician *maskilim*, in whom the partisan, militant drive was lacking and who were dominated by sentimentally romantic moods. This mood was also discernible in arid, scholarly Vilna. Erstwhile *yeshivah*-students, ardent followers of the "heavenly daughter, Haskalah," walked with dreamy eyes over the forest-covered mountains around Vilna and with sentimental, sorrowful eyes sang Meir Letteris' "Yonah Homiyyah" and Adam Ha-Kohen's "Ha-Temurah," "Ha-Ḥemlah," and other poems.

The most honored place among them was occupied by Micah Joseph Lebensohn's beloved friend Kalman Schulman,[70] in whom the circle of *maskilim* in Vilna saw the successor and spiritual heir of Mordecai Aaron Günzburg.[71] Schulman was, indeed, the continuer of Günzburg's literary work. He compiled and translated numerous historical works "in the purity of the holy tongue."[72] His language is strongly distinguished from Günzburg's. The latter attempted to produce a modern prose style, whereas Schulman wrote in a rhetorical, biblical fashion, strongly spiced with Oriental metaphors.

The friendship that prevailed in this circle of youths bore an especially romantic, sentimental character, which found a certain resonance in the correspondence that has been preserved.[73] Not a little was contributed to this by the marvelous, gentle figure of the young, sickly poet whose first poem was dedicated to "friendship." Even quite slightly romantically-minded natures used to mention, scores of years later, their acquaintance with the deceased Micah Joseph Lebensohn as a lovely poetic dream of youth, lit up by tender, silvery rays. Among all his acquaintances, he remained inscribed in memory as one of those phenomena of which the Russian poet has sung:

> They were not made for the world
> And the world was not made for them.

The bond of friendship between Micah Joseph Lebensohn and Kalman Schulman was especially strong. Characteristic is the

70. Born in 1826, died in 1899.
71. *Kinnor Bat Tziyyon*, 70: "And Schulman will be for you in the place of Günzburg."
72. Among them, Weber's *Weltgeschichte* in nine volumes (*Divrei Yemei Olam*, 1867–1884); *Toledot Hachmei Yisrael*, in four parts (following Graetz); and *Milḥamot Ha-Yehudim* (following Flavius Josephus) in two parts.
73. Characteristic, for instance, is Schulman's letter to S. Sachs (in J. Lepin's *Keset Ha-Sofer*, 81–82): "Let the scoffers scoff at me with grimacing mockery, but I will maintain in my simplicity that the noble souls of persons come from one holy place and one source of life, even if they be separated on this earth at its two extremes. If paths are constructed for them, they will fly on the wings of the wind until they return and are forged together. Their sentiments will flow toward each other and they will become one soul."

following point. Promenading in the beautiful forest surrounding Vilna, the two young friends once agreed that whoever of them first departed from the world would, on the closest Sabbath thereafter, appear before his left-behind friend at the same place, to demonstrate that friendship is stronger than death and that even in the other world the deceased has not forgotten his friendship. Shortly thereafter Micah Joseph died, and Kalman Schulman asserted that several days later, at the appointed place, the figure of the deceased appeared before him.

At the age of nineteen the sickly poet wrote his friend Schulman a letter which carries as its motto Heine's well-known lines:

> The gift of life is sweet,
> But underneath it is terrible,
> In the dark, cold grave.

"It is midnight," writes the poet;

all sleep by now, but I alone cannot sleep. My disease does not let me rest . . . I know that my illness is incurable. Death lies in wait for me . . . I already see myself lying on the death-bed. I hear the weeping of my parents, my brothers, sisters, and friends. I already see myself lying in the grave, and over me the bitter lamentation is heard. I see before me the last glances with which my parents part with me forever. I see how the hand that now writes is consumed by the worm, and the heart and brain rot and disintegrate . . . O, how terrible is death, and how sweet is life . . . I have always thought that I am prepared for death . . . but to die so young, to leave the world at the age of nineteen! . . . And my heart is still so filled with love of life; the light of the sun is still so dear and precious to me. I thirst to satiate myself with all the joys of life; I wish to embrace the whole world, to see and enjoy everything. I wish to live, to live! But my hands are limp. The fever burns in all my limbs; my breath fails. Now I see death lying in wait for me. He approaches ever closer. Yet a few days, and he comes. How terrible![74]

In such an agonized struggle did the sick poet dream and produce his work. In the same year that he wrote the letter just quoted, he translated into Hebrew, from Schiller's German translation, the third and fourth books of Virgil's epic *Aeneid*, under the title *Harisut Troya*. In this translation (published in 1849) the masterful hand of an authentic poet is already felt, and the description of Troy's destruction is considerably more powerful in Lebensohn's translation than in Schiller's. *Harisut Troya* evoked astonishment not only in the circles of the *maskilim* but also among foreign scholars.

---

74. *Shirei Sefat Kodesh*, II, 248–255.

In 1849 the poet travelled to Berlin to seek help from the professors there. The latter sent him for a cure to Salzbrunn. After this he passed a winter in Berlin, and the summer thereafter at a spa. The year and a half that he spent abroad did not bring healing to his body, and his illness progressed even further. On the other hand, mentally and spiritually the poet grew significantly. He listened to philosophical lectures by the aged philosopher Schelling, became acquainted with Zunz, and made friends with the able scholar Senior (Shneour) Sachs. These men, who were familiar with his *Harisut Troya*, advised him to abandon the "alien Muses" and sing national poems. The same counsel was also given him by Samuel David Luzzatto in his letters. The young poet was literally overwhelmed by the plethora of new ideas with which he became familiar in the Prussian capital. With youthful enthusiasm he states in one of his letters: "I have no religion! My brother is mankind! The world is my fatherland! My religion is virtue!"[75] At the very time, however, that Micah Joseph Lebensohn was overwhelmed by the consciousness that the whole world was his fatherland, he produced his marvelous national poems in the national language, Hebrew—the poems entitled *Shirei Bat Tziyyon*.[76]

This work consists of six lyric poems ("Shelomoh," "Kohelet," "Nikmat Simshon," "Ya'el Ve-Sisera," "Mosheh Al Har Ha-Avarim," "Rabbi Yehudah Halevi") and all of them breathe romantic love for the historic land of the Bible—the land which, according to the poet's portrayal, is "the pearly crown of creation, the symbol of beauty and song, where every stone is a book and every crag a tablet of history."

We noted in the first volume[77] how, in the eyes of the foremost Jewish poet of the Middle Ages, Jehudah Halevi, "Zion" was not merely the historic land of his ancestors. For Halevi's poetic spirit, which was wont to incorporate the purely ideal and abstract in plastic and concrete forms, the mountains of Judea became the symbol, the emblem, of the most beautiful and exalted, "the heart of the world," for which he yearned and about which his soul dreamed.

Also in our young poet, who was born in the narrow, dirty alleys of Vilna, Zion became the tower of light, the dazzling symbol of his poetic dreams, and it is by no means an accident that the loveliest poem in *Shirei Bat Tziyyon*, the crown of his creativity, is "Rabbi

---

75. *Yevreyskaya Starina*, 1914, 269.
76. In 1859 Joshua Steinberg translated all of the poems of *Shirei Bat Tziyyon* into German. The poems "Shelomoh" and "Kohelet" were translated into French, and the poem "Rabbi Yehudah Halevi" was translated into Russian.
77. Pp. 95ff.

Yehudah Halevi." Lebensohn is not an epic poet but a splendid
lyricist. In the sorrow and yearning of the great Castilian, he
celebrates the dreams of his own soul, the emotive prayer-mood of
the pilgrim-poet when he reaches the goal of his dreams:

> Every stone of the land—an altar to the living God,
> Every crag a platform for the prophet of the exalted God.

The deep woe that grips the poet when he sees the melancholy
ruins represented by the actuality of the loveliest ideal of his
dreams; the marvelous musicality of the stanza-construction; the
elegiac, lyric chords that resound in every line—all these are
merged in a harmonious totality of high poetic art.

Saturated with intense longing for Zion as the supreme goal and
ideal is also the poem entitled "Mosheh Al Har Ha-Avarim." In
tender, elegiac stanzas the poet portrays the profound life-drama of
the great leader of the people who buried all of his generation in the
sands of the deserts until he finally attained the goal of his
sorrow-filled life. From the peak of Mount Nebo Moses sees the
land of his most beautiful dreams. But God's proscription is strict:
"You shall not come there—the land of your dreams is not to be
trodden by your foot." And the mighty leader collapses. There,
on the peak of the mountain, he lies in eternal rest, "and his eye is
still directed toward Jerusalem."

Like the poem "Rabbi Yehudah Halevi," so also Lebensohn's
famous "Shelomoh" is permeated with personal experiences. In the
latter work Micah Joseph portrays on the splendid banner of
colorful, Oriental nature the love of the young prince and poet for
the shepherdess Shulamith. "This is a song of songs for Solomon
the son of David"—with this line the poem ends. In fact, however,
it is not the love-poem of Solomon the son of David. Here the
young poet celebrates his own youth, his own spring and
enchantment with love, and does so in images, in stanzas dipped in
fragrance and dew, such as had not been heard for many
generations in Hebrew poetry.

The other poem "Kohelet," in which the sick poet who already
hears behind his back the swift steps of approaching death portrays
Solomon in his old age in the form of the skeptical Ecclesiastes with
his despair-filled maxim "Vanity of vanities, all is vanity," was to
serve as the antithesis to the poem "Shelomoh." This poem,
however, was less successful. The influence of Lebensohn *père* and
his poem "Ha-Da'at Veha-Mavet" is felt. "Kohelet" is more
thought through than lived through by the poet.

What Micah Joseph Lebensohn did not completely succeed in
doing in his "Kohelet" he brilliantly achieved in his later cycle of

poems. After completing his *Shirei Bat Tziyyon*, he wrote to his friend Senior Sachs: "I hope this coming winter to accomplish a great deal. I cannot tell you what endless poetic plans fill my brain, and if I now wished to, I could fill volumes—but it would take time."[78]

Unfortunately, however, very little time remained. The disease progressed rapidly. Nevertheless, Lebensohn managed to write a whole series of splendid lyric poems "Ahuvah Azuvah," "Yom Hulledet Ahuvati," "Aḥiot Lanu," "Ha-Ohev Ha-Nishba," "Ha-Ḥoli-Ra Be-Ir Berlin," "Ḥag Ha-Aviv," and others.[79] All these separate poems together form a unitary work in which the profound lifedrama of the twenty-two-year-old poet, over whom the shadow of death already hovered while his heart was still overflowing with thirst for life, light, happiness and joyous laughter, are rendered with great poetic power. His ardent love for the young, beautiful Hannah, the colorful portrayals of nature, are interwoven with the anguished consciousness that the play is over and that death already stretches out its frosty embrace to him.

An especially strong impression is made by his marvelous poem "Ḥag Ha-Aviv" (The Festival of Spring). On the bright spring holiday, the sick poet strides about the noisy streets of Berlin. Everywhere joy and laughter is heard, but he—the deathly sick writer—walks with despair in his heart, where everything has died away—as in a forest after a storm, as a broken ship which the sea-storm has shattered. "O, how terrible it is to creep to the grave when the heart is filled to overflowing with love for life!," the poet exclaims. And the poem concludes with the despair-filled cry: "Cursed be death! Cursed be life!"[80]

A broken, dying man, Micah Joseph Lebensohn returned to Vilna. He knew that his days were numbered, and humbly he wrote his swan-song "Ha-Tefillah" (The Prayer):[81] "Be blessed, O prayer, O daughter of hearts." This lovely poem concludes: "On your wings you bring healing for every affliction; like the dew that descends from the celestial heights you quiet man's heart and bring healing to the sick soul."

These were the poet's last stanzas. On the twenty-seventh of Shevat 1852, Micah Joseph died, not all of twenty-four years old.

That of which the Meassefim dreamed—creating "beauties in the

78. *Yevreyskaya Starina*, 1914, 269.
79. These poems were supposed to be issued by the poet in a special anthology, *Shoshanim Ve-Ḥoḥim* (see *Yevreyskaya Starina*, 1914, 273). However, because of the poet's premature death, this anthology was not published. Micah Joseph's unpublished poems were later issued by his father in a special collection entitled *Kinnor Bat Tziyyon* (1870).
80. *Kinnor Bat Tziyyon*, 30.
81. *Ibid.*, 1–6.

language of the Bible"—was at last fulfilled. A richly talented lyricist of European standards appeared in the Hebrew temple of poetry. Unfortunately his song did not resound long; at the first chords, it was choked by death.

Nevertheless, the young poet had an enduring influence on later neo-Hebrew poetry. Echoes of *Shirei Bat Tziyyon* resounded. Romantic love for the land of Zion is also heard in the lovely popular song which Mordecai Hochmann of Kletsk composed at that time:

> Zion, Zion, city of our God,
> How great is your ruin. Who will bring healing to you?

Like Letteris' "Yonah Homiyyah," Hochmann's poem was also sung with a special melody. But Zion was celebrated not only in songs and poems. At the same time that Micah Joseph Lebensohn published his *Shirei Bat Tziyyon*, the first Hebrew novel was produced—and it, too, celebrated "love of Zion," *Ahavat Tziyyon* (Love of Zion) was the title of this first neo-Hebrew novel (published in 1852). It was written by Abraham ben Yekutiel Mapu.

Abraham Mapu was born in 1807 in Slobodka (a suburb of Kovno) in the family of a poor teacher of *Gemara*. The future author spent his childhood years in dire poverty and want. Even before he had the opportunity to become properly familiar with the plain meaning of the Pentateuchal text, the father personally took charge of him in the schoolroom and stuffed his mind with difficult sections of the Talmud. Little Abraham was a gentle, yielding child; he studied with great diligence and, to his father's joy, soon became the best pupil in the school. At the age of twelve he was well acquainted with many tractates of the Talmud and his father permitted him to study "by himself" in the studyhouse along with the grownup young men. Soon "Yekutiel's little Abraham" became renowned as a "prodigy." He learned everything and eagerly hungered after it. His heart yearned and dreamed of something, but he himself did not know what it was. His only joy and pleasure in his years of childhood were music and song. The sad prayer-motifs, the tender melody with which the verses of Psalms used to be recited in the studyhouse, would call forth tears of enthusiasm from him.

When Abraham was fifteen years old his scholarly father concluded that he was already suited to gain familiarity with the elements of Kabbalah. Suddenly new worlds were opened before the dreamy boy. In the place of arid *pilpul* and subtle mental acuities, he saw all at once a fantastic world of communion with God and religious fervor. The space within the melancholy walls in the Slobodka studyhouse became narrow for him. In the airy spaciousness of the Aleksot mountain, encircled by two twin rivers (from the one side the Niemen, from the other the Vilie[82]) the young Kabbalist used to surrender himself without restraint to his dreams. Instinctively and unconsciously, the artist-observer awoke in him. He wished to be "one who sees but is not seen" in order to be able to wander over the regions of life, to observe the conduct of men, to see how they really are, without pose and all kinds of pretense. With a sarcastic smile he used to tell in his later years how he immersed himself in the stories of the Kabbalah and, on the Aleksot mountain, went through all the formulas and incantations required to attain the level of "one who sees and is not seen," and how he did not reach this level.

At the age of seventeen the dreamer was married and, while being supported in the home of his father-in-law, experienced for the first time the taste of eating bread to satiation. The young groom, becoming a frequent visitor in the home of the rabbi of Slobodka, Elijah Ragoler, once accidentally noticed in the rabbi's bookcase a book of Psalms with a Latin translation. With extraordinary diligence the young Mapu, who did not even know the Latin alphabet, studied this translation. He attempted to learn Latin with the aid of the Hebrew text. In this connection he made a sad discovery; he became convinced that his knowledge of the language of the Bible was insufficient. Hence, he betook himself to the commentators, mainly those who concern themselves with the plain meaning, the significance of the individual words. The most powerful impression was made upon him by the Sephardic scholar Abraham Ibn Ezra. It was in this odd way that Mapu became acquainted with the classic biblical text and also became familiar with the language of the ancient Romans.

At this time his father-in-law lost his fortune. Mapu therefore had no alternative other than to betake himself to teaching. Serving as a tutor in the home of a tavern-owner in a village, he became acquainted with a Catholic priest who was overwhelmed to see in the young village-teacher a person who knew Latin. The priest

---

82. A. S. Friedberg, in his recollections of Mapu, gives the following description of the Aleksot mountain: "Here is something truly to be marveled at. It is especially beautiful to see the town with both large rivers, the Niemen and the Vilie, which embrace them from both sides and unite them with both their suburbs—from one side, the little town of Aleksot, and from the other, Slobodka, which is a large part of the town itself. Every street lies before the eyes. One can see and count the people who go and drive about there" (*Hoyzfraynd*, I, 1908, 28).

gave him various Latin classics to read, among them Virgil and Horace. He also presented him with some French books.

Thanks to his knowledge of Latin, it was relatively easy for Abraham Mapu, given his enormous diligence, to learn the cognate French language. He even composed a special textbook entitled *Der Hausfranzose*. As we see, he was the first *maskil* who was not a "Berliner," for he began to study German with the aid of Mendelssohn's translation of the Pentateuch only after he had already assiduously studied Horace and Virgil and read the French romanticists with great delight. After Mendelssohn's translation of the Pentateuch, Mapu took up Kant. He also attempted to study Hegel but without the least success.

Thus, gradually the prodigy and constant student "was spoiled" and transformed into a *maskil*. The first time he returned to Kovno he took pains to keep this secret. Finally people in town became aware that "Yekutiel's little Abraham" had become "heretical" and began to persecute him. Again his favorite place became the beautifully grown-over Aleksot mountain. Now, however, it was not with the tales of the Kabbalah, not with formulas intended to make him "one who sees and is not seen," that the *maskil* Mapu occupied himself. He wished to become a Jewish writer and began to compose a novel in the language of the Bible.

Mapu's biographers[83] point out that already at that time, in 1830, the twenty-two-year-old Mapu, on the Aleksot mountain in the summer arbor from which Napoleon watched his legions crossing the Niemen, wrote the largest part of the novel *Ahavat Tziyyon* in its first draft. It is beyond doubt, however, that this "first draft" has very little affinity with Mapu's novel that was first published only twenty-two years later. From a letter of the author to Senior Sachs,[84] we learn that as late as 1843 Mapu's still unfinished work carried the title *Shulamit*, not *Ahavat Tziyyon*. Mapu himself also points out[85] that in the construction of his novel with its complex intrigues, with its extraordinary, thrilling episodes, Eugéne Suë, the French novelist, with his novels *The Mysteries of Paris* and *The Wandering Jew*, which at that time were so celebrated and translated into all European languages, served him as a model. Suë's popular adventure novels, however, appeared only in the 1840s.

In 1832 Mapu moved to a teaching position in Georgenberg near the Prussian border. From there he went to Rossyieny which, like New Zagare, was renowned for its *maskilim*. "A city of men wise in heart and lovers of their people and its holy tongue"—so Mapu

83. See A. S. Friedberg, *Hoyzfraynd*, I, 27; Reuben Brainin, *Avraham Mapu*.
84. J. Lepin, *Keset Ha-Sofer*, 103.
85. Brainin, *op. cit.*, 49.

characterizes this town. There he became friends with Senior Sachs who had a great influence on him. Mapu spent seven years in Rossyieny and thereafter a short time in Vilna where he was employed as a tutor in the home of the well-known man of wealth Yudel Opatov.

From 1848 on he was a teacher in the Jewish government school established in Kovno. In his later years he also received regular support from his younger brother who managed the business affairs of the wealthy Günzburg family of Petersburg. Mapu now had the opportunity to devote himself extensively to literary work, and in 1852 his first novel *Ahavat Tziyyon*, which represents a definite stage in Hebrew literature, appeared.

The author of the novel was a quite singular personality. "He was a simpleton in matters of the world," writes of him his biographer Reuben Brainin.[86] The people of the town used to call him "simple little Abraham." In daily matters and situations he was as awkward as a small child. Mapu was a typical dreamer, one of those dreamers in whom the tapestry of their rich imagination envelopes reality in the shimmering veil of a golden wonderland. Around him swarmed the petty, drab life of poor shopkeepers, moneylenders, artisans, *Luftmenschen*, and plain beggars, but he soared in a fantastic, imaginative world of extraordinary splendor and moral beauty. He sat on the Aleksot mountain and dreamed that he was sitting on the Mount of Olives, and Slobodka with its dirty alleys and tattered beggars was transformed in his imagination into the magnificent city of Zion in the time of the prophet Isaiah, with its palaces and towers, with its beautiful streets over which roamed the God-inspired prophets preaching righteousness and justice.

Precisely in the 1840s the tendency of the so-called "village poetry" grew especially strong in European literature. George Sand and other writers in France wrote village novels. Gotthelf and Auerbach in Germany produced village stories. The basic motifs of these works was agriculture; their favorite heroes, laborers on the soil, keepers of vineyards. This tendency was reflected in a quite unique way in the creative process of Abraham Mapu. Romantic love for the idyllic life of the farmer was, after all, highly popular in the literature of Haskalah. Given Mapu's extremely rich, Oriental imagination, the ancient personalities of the Bible were in fact closer and more comprehensible to him than the men among whom he lived. And the most extraordinary thing happened—the dreamer of Slobodka was the first person in Europe

---

86. *Ibid.*, 87.

to write a historical novel about an era separated from us by twenty-five hundred years.[87]

With the power of his marvelous intuition, the poet shows us the singular beauty of the zenith of Biblical times and provides splendid portrayals of nature on the mountains and valleys of Judea. The beautiful daughters of Zion, with their simple faith and ardent love that is "stronger than death," come to life before us. We marvel at the lovely village—portraits of harvest time, of grape gathering, when the young people work, rejoice, express their love of life and happiness in tumultuous dancing and singing. And there, from the heights of the city of Zion, the fiery words of the prophets thunder. In their ardent pathos the old Biblical language is revived and bubbles with vitality and youth.

However, it is extremely difficult to produce finely planned and harmoniously complete works of art through intuition alone, and Mapu, after all, was an auto-didact who grew up on arid *pilpul* and fantastic Kabbalah. His taste remained undeveloped and the highest artistic ideals for him were Eugéne Suë and Dumas *pére*. Hence, it is not to be wondered at that his *Ahavat Tziyyon*, with all its marvelously beautiful language and numerous splendid details, is quite weak in construction and awkward in portrayal of character. The theme, following the French models, is overburdened with many unnecessary, sensational details in order to make the novel more "thrilling" and "interesting."

For the contemporary reader it is difficult to imagine the tremendous impression this first Hebrew novel made on the reading public of that time.[88] *Ahavat Tziyyon* was literally a revelation. For the young men raised on arid *pilpul* in the narrow study-house, Mapu's novel was like a fresh, reviving spring to the languishing wanderer. Amnon and Tamar, the heroic couple of *Ahavat Tziyyon*, became the most popular personalities in the melancholy alleys of the Jewish ghetto. The colorful portraits, filled with sunbeams and love for life, of ancient existence in the land of Zion demonstrated to the young people much more clearly than all the Haskalah propaganda writings the contemptibility, the weekday drabness of the ascetic, shopkeeping, trading ghetto-life, sunk in rigorous *Shulḥan Aruch* severities, and aroused in them the thirst and drive for newer, more beautiful forms of life.

In the second half of the decade of the 1850s, in connection with

---

87. Flaubert's historical novel *Salammbo* was published ten years later (1862). The historical novels of Georg Ebers appeared even later.
88. Mapu's *Ahavat Tziyyon* was translated into Yiddish (1874), twice into English (in London in 1887 and in New York in 1903), into German under the title *Tamar* (1885) and into Arabic (1908).

the political and social changes in the country, new tendencies appeared in the Jewish quarter. These also obtained a resonance in the subsequent stage of Mapu's creativity. This, however, already belongs to the later era which we shall discuss in the next chapter of our work.

CHAPTER FIVE

Israel Aksenfeld and A. B. Gottlober

[On logical consequences that are beyond man's will and desire—
Forced and willing Yiddishists—Israel Aksenfeld—His years of wandering; the Galician influence—Aksenfeld as Levinsohn's follower—
Aksenfeld's battle against Hasidism and the *rebbes*—Aksenfeld's naively
primitive realism—The significance of Aksenfeld's work—Aksenfeld's
achievement in his *Der Ershter Yidisher Rekrut*—Haskalah literature and
folk-literature—Aksenfeld's life-drama—The battler for Haskalah Abraham Baer Gottlober—The *maskil* and "rhetorician," and the scion of the
"jesters"—Gottlober as popular poet and satirist—Gottlober's satires *Di
Deputatn*, *Der Seim Oder Di Groyse Aseyfe*, and his comedy *Dos Dektukh*.]

E POINTED
out in the pre-
vious chapter
how, among
the *maskilim* of
Vilna, the lan-
guage of the
Bible was
transformed
into a kind of
cult. The lan-
guage in and of
itself, apart
from any con-
tent, was set
forth as the
highest
achievement,
as a deified
"sanctity." Hence, it is not surprising that the *maskilim* had an
attitude of special contempt for the folk-language, the "jargon."
M. Ben-Ammi relates in his memoirs[1] the terror with which the
"rhetorician" Kalman Schulman cried out: "Shall I write jargon?
May God keep me from such a thing. I have even forbidden others
to translate my words into jargon." We know, however, that not all
the *maskilim*, even those who had an attitude of such hatred toward

1. *Ha-Tekufah*, XXV, 598.

the folk-language, were as consistent as Schulman. It suffices to mention Aaron Wolfsohn-Halle, Isaac Euchel, and Isaac Baer Levinsohn.

"In world history," Hegel points out in the masterly introduction to his *Philosophie der Geschichte*,[2]

there is generally born from the actions that men carry out something completely different from what they intended and wished, of which they had an immediate consciousness and for which they strove. Men intend only their interests. In this connection, however, something is produced that is, in its essence, a natural consequence of these achievements, but was beyond the consciousness of these men and beyond their wish . . . One must understand and remember that in the immediate act can be hidden what is outside the consciousness and will of the achieving personality.

The *maskilim* whom we have just mentioned, indeed, wished merely to struggle against the phenomena of life that they despised, "to open the eyes of the masses of the people." However, because they discovered that this can be achieved most expediently with the aid of the folk-language, they used this language as a weapon, even though they regarded it with hatred and contempt. With the cultural growth of the masses, however, the cultural value of the language the masses speak also grows. And because these *maskilim* were talented men and their work in the folk-language had a definite cultural-literary value, these battlers against the jargon, contrary to their own will and consciousness, laid the foundation stones of neo-Yiddish literature with their battle-writings.

At the same time as Isaac Baer Levinsohn, however, there also appeared battlers for Haskalah for whom the feeling of contempt toward the language of the masses of the people was already absolutely alien and who considered it obvious that whoever wishes to have an effect on the people must write in the language which the people speak and in which they think. The oldest of these writers—and, in fact, Isaac Baer Levinsohn's good friend—was Israel ben Jacob Aksenfeld.

Israel Aksenfeld was born in 1787 in Nemirov into a prestigious family. His youthful years were spent in a strictly orthodox environment and he studied the *Gemara* and the rabbinic codifiers. According to the fashion of those times, his parents married him off when he was very young. After the wedding, the young groom became an ardent disciple of the Bratzlaver Hasidim and an intimate of Rabbi Nahman of Bratzlav's secretary, Nathan of

2. Second edition, Berlin, 1840, 35.

Nemirov.[3] Family life, however, was not successful for the young Aksenfeld; he lived very unhappily with his wife, and after many difficulties he finally managed to separate from her. Gradually the Bratzlaver Hasid was "infected with heresy." With great diligence he began to study German, Polish, and Russian. He became a businessman and, when the Napoleonic wars broke out, he obtained government contracts for merchandise, gained favor among the Russian military commanders, and wandered with the Russian army through Poland to Germany and there spent some time in Breslau. "Through his journeys in various regions and through the fact that he came into business relationships and thus into contact with many different people," Aksenfeld's friend of many years Zederbaum relates, "he obtained much experience and knowledge of men. In addition, he had a remarkable memory, enabling him to recall things in detail, so that throughout his life he had material with which to entertain companies through interesting stories."[4]

The nine years from 1815, when the Napoleonic wars ended, until 1824, when Aksenfeld settled in Odessa, constitute a blank in his biography. However, we believe that precisely these years were of great importance for the author's intellectual development. Just at that time he found himself in the kind of social environment and cultural circle which undoubtedly had a definite influence on his later literary activity.

In the second volume of Bloch's *Shevilei Olam* the list of the "subscribers" who obligated themselves to purchase the first volume of the work (published in 1821) is printed. The subscribers are listed according to the towns in which they lived, and among the residents of Brody who ordered *Shevilei Olam* Israel Aksenfeld is included. Presumably, at that time (in the years 1820–1821) he lived in Brody. It appears that Aksenfeld married for a second time in Brody. Zederbaum points out in his abovementioned article that Aksenfeld wedded "the clever, truly religious, very cultured, refined, sensitive Rekheli, the daughter of the renowned Reb Abele Horwitz of Brody."

However, the marriage undoubtedly took place before Aksenfeld settled in Odessa (in 1824), because his son Auguste Alexander, who was later to become a physician, was born in 1825. But Auguste was the second son; the author had an older son, the painter Henri. From this one can assuredly conjecture that Aksenfeld spent a rather long time in Brody, there also married the daughter of a local *maskil*, and in this way had opportunity to

3. See our *History*, Vol. IX, pp. 143ff.
4. *Kol Mevasser*, 1866, No. 26.

become acquainted with the most important representatives of the Galician Haskalah. It is also highly probable that it was precisely there that Aksenfeld made the acquaintance of Isaac Baer Levinsohn,[5] to whom he related himself, as M. Wiener rightly points out,[6] "like a disciple to the acknowledged and undoubted authority of a teacher and leader." Later he was in frequent correspondence with Levinsohn, and the latter's influence is, in fact, very strongly discernible in Aksenfeld's work.

Aksenfeld's literary activity first began approximately ten years after he settled in 1824 in Odessa where he worked as a licensed attorney and notary. One may, with a certain degree of assuredness, express the conjecture that the definitive stimulus for his appearance on the literary arena was Levinsohn's anti-Hasidic satires and *Di Hefker-Velt*, with its wrathful protest against the injustices that were committed in the Jewish community in connection with the fulfillment of the ukase regarding military recruits. In any case, it is beyond doubt that Aksenfeld's first works were *Seyfer Khasidim* and *Der Ershter Yidisher Rekrut*.

In the "Roster" of Aksenfeld's manuscripts[7] that we discovered in Gottlober's archives, a roster compiled in 1862, the author points out that "all these books" he made in the plain Yiddish language from *thirty years previously* on. Presumably, his literary activity commenced only in the 1830s. From the petition Aksenfeld submitted in October, 1841 to the Russian minister of education Uvarov, we know that at that time he had finished, in all, the novel *Seyfer Khasidim*, which is, as he notes in this connection, "the first that he wrote," and also several "dramas and comedies."[8] Three of these plays are well known to us, and it is not difficult to determine the dates when they were composed.

The first was *Der Ershter Yidisher Rekrut*, in 1834–35.[9] After this came *Di Kabtzen-Oysher Shpil*, in which the young Aharon

---

5. M. Wiener (see *I. Aksenfelds Verk* I, 354) has shown that Aksenfeld was also acquainted with the grammarian and poet Tobias Feder. But we believe there was a misunderstanding regarding the letter from Aksenfeld to Feder published by Wiener. The style of the letter testifies that it was written not by Aksenfeld but, in fact, by Feder himself. Apparently the copyist here made a mistake, and the superscription of the letter ought to be "Reply of the author to Israel Aksenfeld." On the basis of a phrase in this letter, Wiener comes to the conclusion "that the writer in jargon, Aksenfeld, is consoled by the erstwhile bitter opponent of Yiddish, the well-known Hebrew *maskil* Tobias Feder that by writing in Yiddish he is not lowlier than anyone else" in the literary fraternity. This conclusion, however, is absolutely incorrect, even if the letter was actually written by Feder and not by Aksenfeld. It suffices to note that Feder died in 1817, many years before Aksenfeld became a "writer in jargon."

6. *Aksenfelds Verk*, I, 238.

7. See *Perezhitoye*, IV, 328–329; *Aksenfelds Verk*, I, 353.

8. S. Ginsburg in *Filologishe Shriftn*, II, 47.

9. See M. Wiener in *Aksenfelds Verk*, I, 329–331.

Baal-Makhshove and his bride Perele, who play a prominent role in the first play, also figure. *Di Kabtzen-Oysher Shpil* was composed after 1837 because on page 62 Mottl of Chernobyl is mentioned as deceased, and Mottl died in 1837. The date when the melodrama *Man Un Vayb, Shvester Un Bruder* was written is also not difficult to determine. In the preface Aksenfeld points out that the story "happened fifty years ago." One of the characters in the play, while reading aloud a letter dated 1765 comments: "So, that is, twenty-five years ago." It is clear from this that the play was composed in 1840. In his dramatic scenes *Di Genarte Velt* Aksenfeld himself points out that he wrote these in 1842. Hence, we must conclude that the author's first works were *Seyfer Khasidim* and *Der Ershter Yidisher Rekrut* which were composed several years after Levinsohn's two anti-Hasidic brochures, *Divrei Tzaddikim* and *Emek Refa'im*, were published and his *Hefker-Velt* began to be circulated in numerous copies.

We pointed out previously (p. oo) the national-social motives which considerably strengthened patriotic moods in Levinsohn. The same thing is noticeable in Aksenfeld. Because these motives also played a certain role among the *maskilim* of the later generation, it is worthwhile from the cultural-historical point of view to dwell on them at some length.

Aksenfeld had occasion to observe in the Ukraine the contempt and scorn with which the Polish landowners, the degenerate representatives of the feudal, decaying class, regarded the Jewish middleman, the Jewish saloon-keeper. As purveyor to the military during the Napoleonic wars, he also had the opportunity to become acquainted with certain representatives of the Russian nobility who served as officers in the army. That the Russian noblemen of Alexander I's era also regarded the Jewish middleman and *Luftmensch* with the greatest scorn can be clearly seen from the previously quoted memoirs of one of the most humane and cultured of them, Prince Dolgoruki.[10]

However, Aksenfeld saw the members of the Russian nobility not in the role of feudal barons and estate owners who exploit the peasant deprived of all rights, but in the role of commissioned military officials who participated in the process of "capitalist accumulation," i.e., gathering capitalist wealth. In this historical process they were strongly aided by the energetic and enterprising Jewish purveyors and their assistants. It is natural that under these circumstances the feeling of contempt of the feudal nobleman for the Jewish broker could not be disclosed; on the contrary, this

10. I. M. Dolgoruki, *Slavnï bubnï za gorami.*

feeling was weakened to a significant degree through the sentiment of solidarity in the joint "enrichment process."

Naturally, Aksenfeld at that time was not in a position critically to anaylze this phenomenon. Hence, in his *Shterntikhl*[11] he comes to the following conclusion:

A Polish landowner is mainly (one cannot say this of all of the landowners; there are also some better ones) stuffed with great arrogance. Only he considers himself a man in the world; the peasant, for him, is equivalent to a horse, an ox, or a cow. Peasants were created for the sake of working for the nobleman. Jews, after all, are not his slaves, so he considers them instruments. They, too, are in the world only for the landowner's purposes. Indeed, when the landowner needs the rich Jew's favor, to lend him money, the Jew is, for him, like the shoemaker; he must have him because he requires boots. Once he has his boots, the shoemaker is no longer a *shoemaker*. How much more so is the Jewish innkeeper and shopkeeper, for the arrogant landowner, more despised than a dog of the streets. He mocks him, ridicules him, beats him, slaps him whenever he wishes. To insult and curse him is merely a common custom. "Jewish rogue" or "Jewish cur" is used in the same way as "Hey, mister." A middleman who hangs about a Polish landowner hears even cruder words from him: "Dog! Get the hell out of here immediately!" A pull on his earlock or his beard is a little joke, and when he pays him for his trouble he throws the gulden to the ground: "There you have it, cur." To be able to endure such a thing one must, indeed, be a thoroughly base man, a drunkard, a libertine."

Our Russian officials are quite different people. The bitter, puffed-up Polish boastfulness, the Polish arrogance, is not present in the Russian. A Russian, when he knows a Jew and has dealings with him several times, calls him "brother" or "dear brother." He even likes the middleman when he serves him loyally (yes, yes, indeed, he simply likes him). Especially when he becomes acquainted through business connections with a Jewish merchant for some time, the greatest Russian becomes the Jew's good friend (yes, yes, a good friend).

Levinsohn's influence is especially prominent in Aksenfeld's attitude toward the Hasidim and their *rebbes*, on the one hand, and toward the traditional rabbis, on the other. Aksenfeld considers it his life-task to battle against Hasidism, to turn away, to quote his own words, "the Jews from the mystical and dreamy Hasidic manner of life and to tear away from the *rebbes* that aura of sanctity with which the benighted public has surrounded them." Toward the rabbis, however, he has an attitude of great respect. Pinkhes the "Red One" laments in *Der Ershter Yidisher Rekrut* that "since the *rebbes*, the *gute Yidn*, have invaded the country in large numbers the

---

11. *Dos Shterntikhl*, Chapter Eight.

traditional rabbis are no longer willing to live in a small town." To this the enlightened Aharon Baal-Makhshove replies that he considers it a good deed that he drove away from the town the *rebbe* "who used to take away the last *groschen* from everyone." He observes in this connection to the leaders of the community that the money that the *rebbe* "cost the town—if you were willing to spend it on more essential things, you could have a rabbi, a decent scholar, in the town and beadles who are not drunkards."

Levinsohn in his *Hefker-Velt* sets over against the *rebbes*, who take contributions from the smugglers and enter into partnerships with them, the Lithuanian rabbis. "Among us," says the traveler, "the rabbis have issued an excommunication forbidding smuggling; the rabbi and *kahal* take the smuggler and denounce him to the police . . . Our rabbis have taught in *Yoreh Deah* [a part of the *Shulḥan Aruch*] that it is a great good deed to denounce a smuggler to the government so that he may 'be dealt with according to the law,' because he is a troubler of Israel."[12] In Aksenfeld, too, (in *Di Genarte Velt*) the Hasidic *rebbe*, Leib Shpitzenitzer, makes common cause with Yidel Peklmakher (Smuggler). But Reb Baani, the rabbinic judge of the town, exclaims forcefully:

This (i.e., smuggling) is in fact plain thievery according to the law of the Torah, for among us Jews, in the *Shulḥan Aruch*, 'the law of the state is law.' What the emperor has forbidden us to do is as much prohibited as what God has forbidden us in the Torah . . . Yes, you have no mercy on a thief and say, 'He should not have stolen—he deserves it!' I say that in the case of the smuggler this should also be said; he is a common thief. It is forbidden to have mercy on him.[13]

Over against the avaricious and enormously extortionate Mottl of Chernobyl (in *Kabtzen-Oysher Shpil*), who reminds one of Levinsohn's wonder-worker in the second part of his *Hefker-Velt*, Aksenfeld places (in *Man Un Wayb, Shvester Un Bruder*) the rabbi of Wimisl, Rabbi Solomon Cohen, who is "a great scholar, a great saint, a great sage." The latter explains to the wealthy Noah Englander: "God has always conducted me throughout my life in the paths of honesty. So shall I now take illegal profits? God forbid! The Lord will continue to lead me in honesty. A caftan with a bit of bread and borscht, only from God Blessed be He, not from any man's gift—God forbid!—suffices for me."[14]

Aksenfeld's contemporaries stress particularly that in all of his

---

12. *Di Hefker-Velt*, 31.
13. *Aksenfelds Verk*, I, 313.
14. *Man Un Vayb*, 42.

numerous works actual events are described. The publishers of his works (at the end of the 1860s) point out in the preface to *Di Genarte Velt*: "In his theater pieces we see stories that happened or that may happen among Jews. In all his tales and novels we encounter people who actually lived or who are still found now among Jews." Zederbaum also declares in his necrology on Aksenfeld[15] that "all his novels and plays are true stories, and the characters are portraits of people who were actually known but, naturally, so represented as to be suitable and that everyone might find therein a moral lesson and recognize the defects of quite similar people."

Gottlober, who read practically all of Aksenfeld's writings in manuscript, also considers it important to note that the author describes true events. So, for instance, in the tale "Der Moyfes" a true story that happened with the rabbi of Savran is described, and the hero of the long novel *Mikhel Der Oyzerkir: A Yidisher Gil Blas*, is, according to Gottlober, "an actual person with the same name; I myself knew this man in Odessa." Aksenfeld himself writes of his works in the introduction to the previously mentioned "roster": "Some of the books are comedies, some are true stories well told, some are about libertines and convicted swindlers and their bad end. People who will laugh as they read these stories will, at the same time, hear moral instruction and proper conduct and, indeed, all kinds of useful knowledge as well."

In the author's petition to the minister of education Uvarov, submitted in 1841, he points out that the earlier writers enjoyed no success in their battle against the noxious influence of the Hasidim because they "used to write their works in Hebrew or German. How could their works have any effect, when the common people for whom they were intended understand neither of these languages?"[16] Hence, he found it necessary "to employ another method; to write in the language comprehensible to the ordinary Jewish public, to invent comical and, at the same time, instructive events from real life, to attract the reader with a story so that everywhere the truth might appear, but in the finer form of a more interesting narrative. This difficult task I have assumed."[17]

In order that "the truth might appear everywhere," Aksenfeld endeavors most faithfully to portray his characters, whom he takes from real life, with their manner of speech, their attire, and all their gestures. M. Wiener in his thorough work on Aksenfeld[18] rightly characterizes him as a "naively primitive realist." The author was

15. *Kol Mevasser*, 1866, No. 26, 402.
16. *Filologishe Shriftn*, II, 46.
17. *Ibid.*
18. *Aksenfelds Verk*, I, 52, 85.

not endowed with the eye of the true artist who knows the "secret of brevity" and understands how, out of the plethora of minute detail, to obtain the most typical and colorful. Sholom Aleichem, for instance, had even in his youth the understanding of how to give us[19] a clear picture of one of his characters with the following brief description: "Reb Zechariah, a scribe, a tall Jew, always wrapped in a green shawl." We do not even speak of Mendele Mocher Seforim who so ingeniously manages with a few strokes, rendering a couple of characteristic gestures, to revive before us the extraordinary characters of Glupsk and Tuneyadevka.

Aksenfeld, however, endeavors to present with protocol-like fidelity all the details of the appearance, the dress, and the manner of speech of his characters. But from the sea of individual details no unitary portrait emerges. The reader's eyes are literally dazzled, and only gradually, through their behavior and conversation, do the figures swim out from the haze and begin to obtain more concrete, prominent forms. So, for instance, Aksenfeld portrays the *parnas hodesh* Reb Shelomo Psiayokhe:

A Jew of some fifty years, reddish, with two long reddish earlocks, with no beard at all. He has the voice of a woman and a small, wrinkled forehead. His cheeks are furrowed; he has gray, foolish eyes, a long nose, a wide mouth. He goes about dressed in an old, torn, once mohair man's frockcoat instead of a smock. The lining, of blue sateen, is seen hanging out everywhere, and it holds the whole garment together, ungirdled. He wears a four-fringed undergarment of white piqué, but very dirty, and an old velveteen headcovering full of feathers. He always strokes his beard when he talks, even though he has no beard.[20]

And here is the picture of the other *parnas hodesh* Velvel Gilivate:

A tall, aged Jew, with a gray beard, quite long and narrow, also with gray, quite long earlocks. In the middle of his very wrinkled forehead he has a large growth. The growth, too, is red. A short, thick nose filled with tobacco. Thick mustaches that cover his mouth, and a long, swarthy neck. He goes about dressed in a new velveteen caftan with a narrow lapel and in a very old *shtrayml*, or fur hat. Behind a whole piece of the *shtrayml* is missing, and so it always moves with the side that is defective toward the front. The top is completely torn. He is girded with a dyed silk sash that was once red silk and of which the color is fading. One still sees in it the former red coloration.[21]

At no lesser length does Aksenfeld portray the external appearance of the rich man's wife Yute in *Kabtzen-Oysher-Shpil:*

19. In the comedy "A Get."
20. *Aksenfelds Verk*, I, 149.
21. *Ibid.*

A thin, small, swarthy, pock-marked woman with a short little nose as if grown together on one side, and lacking front teeth in her mouth. The mouth is small, the eyes also tiny and gray. The little veil is fashionable. She wears a large head-band and pearls on her neck. Yellow pearls, but many—indeed, a whole strand. She wears a silk *laptikinashl* with its lace embroidery ripped off, a narrow, red, brand new bodice covered with lace, and a calico apron burned at one end. Two ugly hands. On one finger she has a narrow ring, on the other hand two of her fingers have been bent since childhood. She goes about in white socks with odd slippers. She speaks sibilantly, always with a hissing "s."

It is clear that precisely through the excessive plethora of details the figures become diffuse, and a clear picture does not emerge. On the other hand, however, through this highly detailed, primitively realistic manner of portrayal, Aksenfeld's works obtain a very significant ethnographic and social-historical value. Such protocol-like descriptions as, e.g., the portrait of the marketplace and the streets of the town of Nibivale (in the first and second scenes of *Kabtzen-Oysher-Shpil*) are a genuine treasure for the investigator of economic life in the Jewish pale of Russia in the time of Nicholas I. Also no lesser value pertains to the fidelity with which Aksenfeld reports all the nuances and singularities of the folk-language that was spoken at that time in the southwestern region of Russia. Quite justifiably M. Wiener remarks: "The virtually ethnographic precision in the recording of the living speech gives Aksenfeld's language-reproduction (just as his life-style descriptions), aside from their literary significance, an especially great linguistic-historical value. His works are an important document for the language-history of that era."[22]

However, it would be erroneous to think that Aksenfeld's works possess merely an ethnographic and not any literary-historical value. The author had a passionately militant nature with a healthy social temperament and a keenly observant eye. His talent was primitive, raw, unpolished, but authentic and powerful. Aksenfeld's work represents a significant stage in the development of modern Yiddish literature, the first bold attempt to carry on an extensive, obdurate cultural battle for enlightenment, for new forms of life, in the language of the masses of the people.

We already know that, like all the battlers for Haskalah of Galicia and Volhynia, Aksenfeld was also a bitter opponent of the Hasidim and their *rebbes*. He himself points out that he wrote his first work, *Seyfer Khasidim*, so that the "wild hypocrisy" of the "so-called *gute Yidn*" might be clear "to the people. . . . They [the people] will have to feel contempt for the whole Hasidic sect." The battle

22. *Ibid.*, II, 71–82.

against this sect and "the so-called *gute Yidn*" is conducted in virtually all of his works that have been preserved—[23] in *Shterntikhl*, in *Di Genarte Velt*, and in *Kabtzen-Oysher-Shpil*. He also does not tire of disclosing, and covering with mockery and contempt, the old-fashioned, small-town way of life, with its modes of earning a livelihood hanging in air, its wild superstition, the crudeness and clumsiness stemming from terrible ignorance and backwardness.

Aksenfeld's ideal, naturally, as was the case among all the other *maskilim* of his time is to learn languages and sciences. "A young man who knows languages"—this, for the author, is the highest praise. His sharp observer's eye and social temperament, however, did not permit him not to notice that among "enlightened" people who "know languages" and have an attitude of hatred toward the backward, old-fashioned forms of life, crying social injustices are frequently committed. And the temperamental writer did not consider it possible to maintain silence about this. Here, however, he no longer employs his customary weaponry—mockery and laughter. After all, his own ideals, his own gods, are shattered. Hence, he must respond to this tragically, and he produces a tragedy. Very typical in this respect is his *Der Ershter Yidisher Rekrut*.

The ukase of 1827 regarding military recruits had to evoke keen soul-searching among the *maskilim* with an outspoken social temperament. According to the Haskalah program, it was, after all, obvious that if Jews wish to obtain rights equal to those of the rest of the population in the country, they must also assume all the obligations—among them, the duty of military service. The recruit decree, however, left the despotic hand of Nicholas I in an extremely rigorous, police-like style, and its implementation in life assumed grossly disgusting, criminal forms.

We already know how painfully Isaac Baer Levinsohn reacted to this ukase. He not only wrote his *Hefker-Velt* and submitted petitions to the government. He also witnessed how his townsman and relative, a *maskil* who had acquired renown as a great

---

23. Typical is the following tirade with which the enlightened entrepreneur Oksman, under whose name Aksenfeld himself speaks, issues forth in *Dos Shterntikhl*: "The plague-impudent Hasidim—make fun of the whole world. One need not know anything at all, and the Hasidic *rebbes* say explicitly that the main thing is only to be a Hasid, to believe of the *rebbe* that he stands with one foot here and with the other foot over the heads of the angels to reach God's trousers' buttons. This is what a Jew ought to know; everything beyond is all good for nothing. This affliction is the greatest misfortune for the Jews in Russian Poland. Every day Jews become more crippled. They cannot learn any Yiddish. They cannot write, and they are extremely impudent."

bibliophile,[24] became rich from the "kidnappers" and their vile deeds. He could not be silent about this, and he proceeded to pillory him in his *Toledot Peloni Almoni Ha-Kozevi* (see above, p. 27). Aksenfeld, too, could not remain silent about this great social injustice and therefore wrote his *Der Ershter Yidisher Rekrut*. "A comic-tragic novel" is noted on the German title-page of the first edition, published while the author was still living.

We know from his novel *Shterntikhl* (Chapter 14) of the strong impression made on the young Aksenfeld by the German bourgeois, middle-class theater with which he first became familiar in Breslau. In *Shterntikhl* the author lets the enlightened quartermaster's purveyor Oksman explain to the young Michal Matzevah the utility he derives from the theater:

The theater, after all, is more useful than a preacher's ethical instruction. Here, in the theater, when one enjoys the make-believe scenes, as you, Michal, call them, they inculcate moral teaching in the heart of everyone who sees and hears, as well as a demonstration that it is good to be honest and to follow good people—and that this way always turns out well. On the contrary, again, there is a demonstration that an arrogant man, a bad man, a libertine, even though it seems for a brief time that he shines, later comes to shame and contempt.

Aksenfeld, in fact, took as his model the German bourgeois comedies that he saw in Breslau and other German cities (and perhaps also in Odessa). He endeavors to underscore in his comedies the moral lesson "how good it is to be honest and to follow good (i.e., enlightened) people," with the firm belief that then "everything always turns out well." In his *Der Ershter Yidisher Rekrut*, however, Aksenfeld definitely casts off, in the sharpest and most decisive fashion, this bourgeois, optimistic moral lesson.

Written in the comic genre are the colorful scenes in which the author portrays how childishly and clumsily the community of Nibivale, with its two *parnassim* of the month, react to the recruiting ukase that has been received. But the play becomes tragic when Aaron Kluger, the wealthiest man in Nibivale, a person who carries great influence with the chief official of the town and who is also, according to the author's remark,[25] "learned in all kinds of sciences and languages," intervenes. Aksenfeld, who theoretically is in complete agreement with the other *maskilim* that Jews should fulfill their military duty equally with all others, understands very well, however, that the Jewish populace, which has for generations

24. Many of his books, which are rarities, are now found in the Asiatic Museum in Leningrad, and the author of these lines has frequently used them.
25. Aaron Kluger (also called Aaron Baal-Makhshove) figures in *Kabtzn-Oysher-Shpil*, too.

led a quite singular way of life, must consider the new ukase, which tears the recruit out of his own environment for all of twenty-five years, a grievous, bitter oppression. Hence, in our author's work, it is not only the benighted, foolish women who complain so intensely about the ukase but also Zipporah and Perele, of whom Aksenfeld asserts in his comment that they are "very beautiful, very clever, and very good."

"To take Jews as soldiers"—Perele laments,—"is this also not a persecution? It is certainly a bitter oppression!" Her husband, the worldly and modern-minded, wealthy merchant who carries on trade with Warsaw, gives her to understand in this connection: "It is obvious that one who desires to have equal rights with another must carry the burden equally with the other. At present, however, the Jews do not provide any recruits. Hence, the czar has ordered that the Jews should also supply recruits, and so they will obtain the right to live everywhere on equal terms with others and trade everywhere." To this, however, Perele responds:

But in the meantime it is very grievous for the mother and father when their child is taken away. Woe is me! How is this?—To take away a child! When I think of it, how would I feel—God forbid—if someone should wish to take away my child? I would certainly die. How does it help me that they also take children from another? It is dark and bitter for others, too. But for me it is very bad, worse than all the misfortunes in the world.[26]

"After all, he goes to be a soldier forever"[27]— Frumele, who is also characterized by the author as "a very beautiful, clever, good girl," exclaims. Pinkhes the Red One (*Der Royter*), who, according to the author's remark, "is liked in Nibivale" and who testifies about himself that "all of his years he moved about in Berdichev among the greatest people, learned how to write and read Russian and Yiddish, heard his fill among the men of Brody and other people who are competent and have been in the world and in other countries, aside from Petersburg and Moscow"—Pinkhes also regards the new ukase very critically. "We think," he argues,

that this is a persecution. Other, greater persons say that the czar has done Jews a favor thereby, so that, through it, Jews may have equal rights and a portion in the land . . . For the time being we still do not know what will come of this, but, in any case, we may not be opposed to the will of the czar, may his glory increase . . . I know that at first it is bitter; I know that Jews until now have been free of the obligation to supply recruits, and

26. *Aksenfelds Verk*, I, 161.
27. *Ibid.*, 189.

suddenly to bear giving a Jewish child as a recruit is very difficult. But do not forget that the decree has already been issued. How will your refusal be of any avail here? My heart is torn. I feel quite well what the bitterness is—that a mother should have to give away her son or that a father and mother should see their child taken as a recruit.[28]

Only the man of the "greater persons," the above-mentioned representative of the *haute bourgeoisie*, Aaron Kluger, who carries on large-scale business affairs and is exempt, along with his family, as a guild merchant from military duty according to the recruitment law, is highly satisfied with the new ukase, because he hopes that as a result of the recruitment law "Jews [i.e., Jewish guild merchants] will obtain the right to live everywhere and trade everywhere on equal terms with others." So he explains to his wife Perele that if "we did not have so many soldiers and regiments and generals, the French or some other enemy would take everything away, all of us and our fortune . . . Today, you understand, the mother and father must know that at the time a child is taken away from them to be a soldier, he is, in fact, going for them; otherwise, all would have to go to war."[29]

However, for the rich and for their fortunes, it was not their own children who went as recruits, but the children of the poor classes. Even in the year 1852, shortly before the abrogation of the *Rekrutshina* and the cantonist system, eleven merchants of the first guild and "honorary citizens," led by the well-known Yozel Günzburg, submitted to the government a memorandum in which the idea of dividing the Jews into "categories" or "classes" is especially endorsed: into "useful" citizens (i.e., in the first rank, merchants and other "productive elements") and into "harmful ones." In the interests of the "useful" citizens, these merchants of the first guild petitioned Nicholas and his ministers that the burden of the increased recruiting obligation should be placed on the "unproductive elements," i.e., on the classes of poor Jews.[30]

Aksenfeld, with his acutely observant eye witnessed the base, deceitful tricks wherewith the "useful citizens," the "important men" and leaders of the town imposed the recruitment obligation exclusively on the "harmful and unproductive elements," i.e., on the poor masses of the people. He could not be silent about this and expressed his indignation in his *Der Ershter Yidisher Rekrut*. He even had the courage to disclose the complete hypocrisy and vileness, not of the old-fashioned, overly devout people of the *kahal*, but of his Haskalah ideal, the cultured and modern large-scale merchant

28. *Ibid.*, 154.
29. *Aksenfelds Verk*, I, 162.
30. *Historishe Shriftn*, I, 782–787.

Der Ershter Yidisher Rekrut

Aaron Baal-Makhshove. When Aaron explains to his wife Perele the meaning of the new recruitment law, he points out that "a lot must be cast to determine who should remain at home and who should go as a soldier. This lot is made by each village, each town by itself, and they select whom to give as a recruit. Hence, we ought to consider the soldiers as precious men who go to war for our sake."[31]

These words, however, are nothing but hypocrisy and swindlery. The town of Nibivale casts no lots. Aaron Baal-Makhshove all by himself devises a trick intended to deceive Nakhman the Big One, the only son of his blind mother, into going as a soldier. And this Nakhman is by no means considered a "precious person" by Aaron Baal-Makhshove; on the contrary, he twice underscores that thereby they will be "rid of such a libertine from the town."[32]

What kind of person is this Nakhman the Big One, whom the highly cultured and clever Aaron declares a "libertine" of whom the town must be rid? In the list of characters Nakhman is described as follows: "He is in town a prankster, a plague, a handsome, clever youth, even possessed of virtues, but not a respectable person." Nakhman himself points out:

> If I wish, I can study and write,
> But I like to play jokes.[33]

He declares that for him "old and young, poor and rich, scholar and ignoramus, are all alike." We also know from the little song he sings that "all laugh at his pretenses and jokes" and that if he wishes "to terrify the whole town, he goes around at Passover time waking people for the recitation of *seliḥot* [penitential prayers recited before the New Year]." That he beats his own mother is something that was merely fabricated about him; it never happened, and his mother asserts that "he was a saucy boy, but a good boy."[34] "Yet he is a decent, good fellow," Frumele testifies about him.[35] The worst "trick" that the "prankster" committed was that when the *parnas ḥodesh* Velvel Gilivate "was going about the streets on his business, the jokester came up behind him and gave him a fillip on the lump on his face and then jumped away."[36]

31. *Aksenfelds Verk*, I, 162.
32. *Ibid.*, 176, 180.
33. "In addition, he also, alas, speaks Polish quite well," Pinkhes the Red One says of him (*ibid.*, 192).
34. *Aksenfelds Verk*, I, 195.
35. *Ibid.*, 190.
36. *Ibid.*

In short, we have before us Isaac Landa's *kundes*, or jester, several years later, when the latter had grown up and become an adult. Like Landa's *kundes*, Nakhman the Big One also grew up without a father, is gifted by nature, and feels bored and constricted in the melancholy alleys of Nibivale. So he squanders his awakened, undisciplined powers on pranksters' tricks, on singing ditties in the tavern before artisans' apprentices. Nakhman is also a visitor in the house of Aaron Baal-Makhshove; the latter makes merry with the clever, saucy youth. Nakhman even thinks that "Reb Aaron wishes to make a man out of me."

But the naive, good-humored Nakhman is mistaken. A wanton youth who sings songs in a tavern shocks the wealthy merchant who "carries influence with the highest official of the town," with Count Nibivalski himself. He considers Nakhman a libertine of whom the town must be rid as soon as possible. He deliberately dictates pranksters' couplets to Nakhman, so that the latter may sing them in the tavern and thereby provoke the overly pious householders of Nibivale against him even more strongly. He, the "important man" of the town, designates him as a sacrificial victim. Through a swindler's trick, at Aaron's initiative, they deceive the naive Nakhman; they convince him that the beautiful Frumele is in love with him and that her wish is that he, the only son who is exempt by law from military duty, should voluntarily enlist as a recruit.

The melodramatic ending, in which Frumele, the tender, only daughter, actually falls in love with the handsome, cheerful Nakhman and dies of grief, while her mother, the clever and good Zipporah, goes mad, is unimportant. Highly characteristic is Aaron Baal-Makhshove's last speech: "I have acted only with reason; I have forgotten that where the heart feels, there reason ends." Even the most grievous catastrophe does not bring him to any spiritual stocktaking. He is still certain in his mind that what he has committed with Nakhman the Big One was "done with reason" and, naturally, with justice as well. It is, after all, a matter of right that the decent town of Nibivale should be rid of such a "wanton libertine."

The following characteristic detail is also worth noting. Of all of the thirty works he had written,[37] Aksenfeld in his old age, at the first opportunity, printed first of all (along with the anti-Hasidic novel *Shterntikhl*) the play *Der Ershter Yidisher Rekrut*.

Here we touch upon Aksenfeld's profound life-drama, which is

---

37. In the abovementioned list Aksenfeld notes only twenty-six works. However, not mentioned there are the already printed *Dos Shterntikhl* and *Der Ershter Yidisher Rekrut* and, for reasons unknown to us, *Seyfer Khasidim* and *Matzes Bakin*, familiar to us from other sources.

not only of great importance for the author's biography but also has a definite cultural-historical significance.

"In many towns of our fatherland," relates a writer of that era Joachim Tarnopol,[38]

for instance, Warsaw, Vilna, Odessa, Moghilev, Berdichev, and the like, where there are whole groups of cultured Jews, there exists in these enlightened circles a special kind of literary entertainment: people pass the time in reading aloud, in the common Polish-Yiddish jargon, stories, dramatic scenes, whole pamphlets in verse or prose. In these booklets, which are declaimed before the entire assemblage, many foolish customs, obsolete superstitions, and false Hasidic ideas are ridiculed in an extremely sharp fashion.

The most interesting thing in this connection is that this literature of the *maskilim*, which was "written in the common jargon," remained, in largest part, a *written* literature and was circulated not in print but in a limited number of hand-written copies. Zederbaum, the editor of *Ha-Melitz* and *Kol Mevasser*, endeavors to point out the reason or—more correctly—the reasons for this phenomenon. "Some," he writes,

did it as a joke and in no way thought of publishing such writings; some were simply ashamed suddenly to become authors in the "poor jargon" which, it is desirable, should be completely forgotten by our Russian brethren, just as it no longer exists in Germany; some fulminated against cultivating—God forbid—the noxious jargon. The writers in this language were fully regarded as jesters. Who longs to play such a role?[39]

Old Zederbaum, however, does not note *all* the causes of this interesting phenomenon. He is silent about precisely the most important. It is clear that Aksenfeld did not regard his works written "in common Yiddish" as a "joke" and was, in general, not at all ashamed to become a writer "in the poor jargon." We have already noted that the temperamental Aksenfeld regarded the language of the masses of the people as the best weapon with the help of which it is possible to conduct the stubborn battle against obsolete forms of life, against Hasidism and superstition. It is obvious that his ardent desire was to circulate his works as much as possible, to make them available to the masses of the people in the widest fashion. And here the author's life-tragedy begins. The opportunity of printing his works was taken away from him. For all of twenty-five years he carried on the obdurate struggle. He strove

38. *Opit sovremennoi i osmotritelnoi reformi*, 86–87.
39. *Kol Mevasser*, 1869, No. 22, 247–248.

to disseminate his works, to make them accessible to the masses, and he lost the struggle.

We have already pointed out how difficult for Manasseh of Ilya and Isaac Baer Levinsohn was the battle with the Jewish printers who refused to allow "dangerous," heretical books to be circulated through the help of their presses. This battle, naturally, was conducted not only in regard to Hebrew books but also, and in still sharper fashion, in the realm of the popular book written in the language of the masses.

We observed in the preceding volume that the youthful Hasidic movement understood how to employ the folk-language as a powerful weapon and propaganda instrument in disseminating its ideas among the masses. However, not only Hasidic books—the Yiddish editions of *Shivḥei Ha-Besht*, Rabbi Naḥman of Bratzlav's *Sippurei Maasiyyot*, and the like—were distributed in many thousands of copies and went through one edition after another. The Old-Yiddish literature, which was suited to the old, patriarchal way of life, to the world-view of the common man, of the old-fashioned Jewish woman, did not by any means end with the eighteenth century; it did not cease to extend its thread further in the course of the nineteenth century,[40] in the era of the Haskalah movement.

The Haskalah literature for a relatively long time was not in a position to set aside the old-fashioned folk-literature and to take its place. Published in numerous editions were not only translations of the old morality books and of historical books such as *Josippon*, *Shevet Yehudah*, *Yeven Metzulah*, and others, but also, in very large number, "entertaining" stories, all possible kinds of tales and booklets of secular content. The renowned *Maaseh-Bukh* was transformed into Eliezer Pawir's *Sippurei Ha-Pela'ot*, in which the remnants of "Judeo-German" were already removed and the stories are related in an exclusively contemporaneous folk-language. The once so popular *Bove-Bukh* at the end of the eighteenth century was transformed into the *Bobe-Mayse*, which achieved the enormous popularity of a true book of the people only in the nineteenth century.[41] The same is also the case with *Tsenture Venture* and numerous other narratives of *A Thousand and One Nights*. Many new works, originals and translations, almost all anonymous, were also printed.

We have already noted in our first volume (In the Yiddish supple-

40. It is the merit of the scholar of language and culture, Zalman Rejzen, who, in a series of articles (*YIVO-Bleter*, Vol. I, No. 3; Vol. II, Nos. 4–5; Vol. III, Nos. 1, 3), especially stressed this phenomenon that is so important in cultural-historical respects.
41. In Vilna alone the *Bobe-Mayse* went through all of ten editions in the period from 1824 to 1860.

ments) that in 1825 there appeared at the Vilna-Grodno press a new, rhymed translation of the famous medieval *Mishlei Shualim*. In the same year there appeared at the same press a guide for letter writing under the long title *Mesadder Aggadot, Oder Eyn Nayer Lehrir Un Brifshteler Fir Yidishe Kindr Beyde Gishlekhtir*, about which the well-known folklorist Jehudah Elzet (Jehudah Leib Avida) writes that many of these letters are "literally a treasure for one who wishes to have an insight into the family-life of the people, its socio-economic strivings and efforts, customs, modes of dress," etc.[42] In 1830 in Vilna at the press of Isaac Dworzitz a *Kurtz Gefaster Robinzon* (Abridged Robinson Crusoe),[43] translated "after Herr Campe," was published. A year later a Yiddish reworking of Moses Samuel Neumann's biblical drama *Bat Yiftah* (published in Vienna in 1805)[44] was printed. At the same time there appeared in Vilna the unique work *Mordekhay Un Ester, Eyn Sheyn Vunderlikhe Historye Fun Eyn Khosn Mit Eyn Kale*.[45]

It is worth adding, as an interesting detail, that such publications would frequently appear serially. A whole set of such a series was issued in the 1820s and 1830s by the press of Sudylkow. Every booklet of the collection had its own special title-page, but the pagination was consecutive in the entire series. One of the series,

42. We quote according to Zalman Rejzen, *YIVO-Bleter*, Vol. II, Nos. 4–5, 373.

43. The full title (in English translation): "*Abridged Robinson*, a wondrous story that happened to the young Robinson who was called Crusoe, when he ran off to sea without the knowledge of his parents. And the misfortunes that befell him and how miraculously God helped him, because he improved himself greatly after this. It is a great lesson for young people that they should not act without their parents' permission. Reworked in abridgement."

In the copy we employed, under the short address "to the reader," it is merely noted: "from the translator." More remarkably, however, in the copy which Zalman Rejzen uses, the name of the translator is indicated under the introduction: Levin Behr Garmayza. As the reader observes from the title-page, the *Abridged Robinson* is written in somewhat "Daytshmerish" style. Several years earlier in Galicia a reworking of Defoe's narrative appeared in a purely popular language under the title *Robinzohn: Di Geshikhte Fun Alter Leb* (for a discussion of this reworking, which went through many editions, see M. Wiener, *Filologishes Zamlbukh*; Noah Prylucki, *YIVO-Bleter*, Vol. III, 36–44). This reworking is filled with maxims of an enlightening character to the effect that one ought to study languages and engage in productive work.

44. We have in our possession the Vilna edition of 1844. We present here the title-page (in English translation): "*The Daughter of Jephtha the Gileadite*. Told at length in the present fashion. A splendid story taken from the Book of Judges, how Jepthah the Gileadite, the Judge of Israel, sacrificed his only daughter Hannah as a victim, because he had taken a vow and wished to fulfill his vow; also the piety of the virgin Hannah. From the story is to be learned how a man must guard himself well before he lets words out of his mouth, as is written, *Shemor pithei pi'cha*, meaning, 'Guard the gates of your mouth.'"

45. In our possession we have this narrative under a somewhat different title: *Historiye, Eyne Sheyne Historiye Fun Eyn Khosn Ve-Kale, Vos Zikh Getrofin Hot In Salonike*. Since the title-page is missing, we do not know the place of publication and the year of the edition.

entitled *Sippurei Maasiyyot,* which was published in 1834, was reprinted several times in Vilna[46] after the presses in Volhynia were closed in accord with the ukase of 1836. Of the fifteen booklets which comprised this collection some of them, such as *Eldad Ha-Dani, Sefer Neshikat Mosheh, Sefer Maaseh Yeshurun, Gezerat Uman Ve-Ukraina,* and others, were reprinted from earlier publications; others, again, such as *Sefer Maaseh Tzedakah*[47] and *Sefer Maasiyyot Nehmadim,*[48] were taken from the Midrash and Gemara, interwoven with considerable additions from the newer, oral, narrative folk-creativity. A special place is occupied in this collection by the booklet *Mashal U-Melitzah*[49] to which attention was first drawn by Zalman Rejzen (*YIVO-Bleter,* III, 256-259). This is a rhymed translation of the poem *Torat Adam Ve-Korotav,*[50] a didactic work written in *makama*-style which appeared in 1819. To give the readers some notion of the style of the poem in the Yiddish translation, we present a short fragment of it:

And it came to pass, when I heard his words, I turned to him. He led me into his house. It was adorned with precious stones. Lovely vessels of gold and silver and gems stood in it. Beds and chairs studded with jewels and with silk bolsters over them. When I contemplated this well, I made my residence there and said: I always hoped for this—to live in such a room, to settle among great people. I wished this for myself all the time, and I forgot my father's house and remained dwelling there.

And it came to pass, when thirteen years had already gone by, they

46. In our possession is the Vilna edition of 1845 (with the censorship authorization of March 31, 1844).

47. On the title-page is noted: "In this book is related how a man gave away the clothing and jewelry, along with the dowry, of his daughter to a bride who was a stranger. Also how a man was a welcomer of guests and a great giver of charity, and how things went with him as long as he lived; and how he said his prayers with the patriarchs Abraham, Isaac and Jacob, and Moses and Aaron and King David, and his end was very good, and through the merit of charity the righteous redeemer will come quickly in our days. Amen. Selah."

48. On the title-page the moral of the little composition is noted: "In this book is related with many very lovely stories how God Blessed be He guides the just man in this world, and in the world to come his reward is beyond calculation and beyond measure. And the end of those who gossip is not good in this world, and in the world to come they have great punishment. Therefore, every man ought to remove himself from gossip and speaking ill and join the righteous and the pious, and in the merit of this, the righteous redeemer will come speedily, in our days. Amen.

49. The full title-page in English translation: "*A Book of Parable and Wisdom (Sefer Mashal U-Melitzah),* a wise lesson how a man should conduct himself in the world, that he should not make money the chief thing but devote himself to the Torah and fear of God, that he should purchase for himself eternal life. Then it will be well with him in this world and in the world to come, and he will live to see the redeemer come to Zion speedily, in our days. Amen.

50. The author of this little composition was a certain Aaron bar Yehudah Ha-Levi of the Volhynian townlet of Aleksenitz (see *YIVO-Bleter,* VII, 88).

handed me a letter from my father Abimelech through some one from my country to whom I was well known. In this letter was written: My son, I adjured you as soon as you were born that you should observe my Torah and my commandment and not depart from dear God. But you have not listened to my words and turned away from the good path. . .

In 1836, as we previously noted, all the Jewish presses were closed and, according to the new law, only two were to be opened—one in Vilna and the other in the southern region of Russia. But during the course of more than ten years the Vilna press remained the only one in the whole empire (outside of Crown Poland), because the authorization to open a press in Kiev was unrealized for a long time,[51] and only in 1847 was another Jewish press established in Zhitomir.

The monopoly of printing aggravated to a significant degree the deplorable condition of Haskalah literature. Freed of all competition, the press monopolists had the opportunity to raise the cost of printing on their own without hindrance, and to publish only those works which they believed useful and religiously proper. It is clear that in such a situation a writer with so militant a nature as Israel Aksenfeld's had to suffer most grievously.

As early as the 1830s, as soon as Aksenfeld wrote his first works, he attempted to have them published in Vilna. His *Seyfer Khasidim* was already furnished with the censors' approval. However, the printer of Vilna, who, as we have just seen, had so eagerly reprinted the series of popular books of the press of Sudylkow, refused to publish Aksenfeld's works that were written in such a sharp anti-Hasidic tone.[52] But the author would not yield. He submitted a petition to the minister of education Uvarov in which he related at length the purposes he aimed at in his work,[53] the great utility they might bring the common Jewish reader, and that the whole obstruction lies in the fact that the printer of Vilna refuses under any circumstances to print them. "Hence," Aksenfeld concludes his petition, "I allow myself most obediently to beg your excellency to prescribe whom one must approach in order to have my works printed without hindrance."[54]

51. On this, see P. Kon's work in the Warsaw *Bikher-Velt*, 1929, Nos. 3-4.

52. It is worth noting that the Vilna printer also had no desire to print even the second edition of Levinsohn's *Te'udah Be-Yisrael*, and only when Levinsohn threatened to complain to the authorities about the matter did the printer finally bestir himself and in 1856 issue his work from the press (see *Iggerot Ribal*, 1896, 15).

53. It is worth noting that in the petition to Uvarov, when he mentions his first work, *Seyfer Khasidim*, the following comment is set down: "A kind of Don Quixote."

54. See S. Ginsburg's article in *Filologishe Shriftn*, 43-54, and Y. Riminik's work in *Tsaytshrift*, V, 171-180.

The petition, however, did not produce any substantive results. Following the inquiry of the ministry of education, the censorship committee of Vilna carried on negotiations with the printers of that city and the latter set forth in writing the reasons why they could not publish Aksenfeld's *Seyfer Khasidim*:

The work is not composed in any pure language but in the speech that is used among the common Jewish people, and contains nothing but defamation of the Hasidic sect, with the sharpest accusations both against the sect itself and against its *rebbes*, and indecent, wanton, mocking expressions against their words and conduct . . . Especially do we find that the printing of this book at our press would produce great injury for us, because thereby the Hasidim, who form a large part of the Jews, would be mightily enraged against us and would cease to buy Jewish books from our press.

At the end the proprietors of the press indicate that they will print *Seyfer Khasidim* only on the condition that they obtain a direct command from the government. Then the guilt in regard to the Hasidic public would be removed from them. The ministry of education, however, did not assent to this.[55]

When Aksenfeld became convinced that, for the time being, there was no hope of having his works published, he applied to Uvarov with another petition: to permit him to print his works through lithography. This time Uvarov fulfilled his request. He informed the superintendent of the Odessa education district that, on his part, there is no obstacle to Aksenfeld's issuing his works by means of lithography in Odessa, where there is no Jewish press, provided that he observes the prevalent requirements of the censorship.

However, nothing came of this plan either, this time for purely economic reasons. Despite the fact that the monopoly of Jewish presses produced high prices for books,[56] a lithographed book had to cost ten times more than a printed book of the same size.

Aksenfeld, however, could not rest. He considered it his life's

---

55. For what reasons, see Ginsburg, *op. cit.*, p. 50.

56. So, for instance, in the region of Vilna, the price of festival prayerbooks which previously used to cost seventy-five kopecks rose to almost three rubles (see the above-mentioned work, 45). Gottlober also complains in a letter of his to Firkovich: "It is not hidden from your honorable highness that the children of Israel dwelt in our land many days without presses and without books, and the people's soul was bitter and they murmured in their tents against the two printers in Vilna and Zhitomir who placed a heavy, iron yoke on their backs and pronounced sentence on them as on a thief to pay double and four times and five times for every book which the soul of an Israelite wished to bring under the shadow of his roof."

task to enlighten the Jewish masses, to free them from superstition and old mildew, and he could fulfill this task, according to his firm conviction, only through the *printed* word, through publishing his propaganda writings. In 1847 the second Jewish press finally opened—in Zhitomir. Its owners (the Shapiros), however, remained loyal to the pious Hasidic traditions of the well-known press of Slavuta and refused under any circumstances to pollute their press with heretical, anti-Hasidic works such as Aksenfeld's and those of men like him. Hence, there remained only one solution for him: to obtain authorization to open his own press. The writer was not discouraged by the failure of 1841. In 1852 he submitted the same petition (for permission to open a press in Odessa for the special purpose of printing his works) to the minister of internal affairs. Upon inquiry to the deputy of the governor-general of Odessa and Bessarabia, a reply was received that the latter has nothing against this proposal, provided that Aksenfeld's works be reviewed by the censorship committee of Odessa with the aid of the administrator of the Jewish school of that city, B. Stern. The assistant to the minister of internal affairs then applied to the minister of education Shirinsky-Shikhmatov, requesting him to express his view on the matter. Shirinsky-Shikhmatov's reply was quite brief: Since, according to the law of November 27, 1845, only two Jewish presses are permitted (in Vilna and Zhitomir) Aksenfeld's petition cannot be granted.[57]

Soon after this categorical refusal, Aksenfeld sent a petition addressed to the czar himself regarding permission for him to open a Jewish press in Odessa. His hope for the "monarch's grace" ended with nothing.[58] However, Aksenfeld still did not lose courage. As soon as A. S. Norov took Shirinsky-Shikhmatov's place as minister of education, Aksenfeld again submitted (in June 1854) his request to the new minister. But this time he received the same answer once more—that, according to the law of November 27, 1845, his petition cannot be granted.[59]

In the first years of Alexander II's reign Aksenfeld's hope was reawakened. On October 22, 1859 the "Jewish Committee," with the assent of his "Imperial Highness," granted Zederbaum permission to issue a Hebrew newspaper in Odessa. Soon all the remaining official obstacles were removed.[60] This gave Aksenfeld new courage, and he submitted to the Odessa city chief of police a

---

57. See S. Ginsburg's work in *YIVO-Bleter*, Vol. II, 9-13.
58. See Y. Riminik, *op. cit.*, 173-174.
59. *YIVO-Bleter*, II, 12.
60. Regarding the piquant details as to how these obstructions were set aside, see our work *Istoriya Yevreiskoi Pechati*, 1915, 73–74.

request to open a Jewish press. "The only existing presses in Russia," the author complains, "are in the hands of fanatics who do not print what is, in their view, harmful, and even if they did agree to print my works, it is not to be expected that they will not spoil them."[61]

Once more Aksenfeld had no luck, and his request was not granted. In the meantime the year 1862, the terminus of the printing monopoly, drew near. In the seventy-five-year-old Aksenfeld the hope of carrying through his plan revived, and on October 5, 1861 he again submitted a letter of request regarding permission to open a press. The position of city chief of police was, precisely at that time, occupied by a new person, and this man was sympathetic to Aksenfeld's request. He concluded that it is necessary to provide the author the opportunity to publish his works "which are written in a plain language ("jargon") for the common people and thereby inculcate in them rational concepts and demonstrate to them the harmfulness and ridiculousness of Hasidism and its swindlerish wonder-workers." As a final decision, the chief of police transmitted Aksenfeld's petition to Count Stroganov, the New Russian and Bessarabian governor-general. For his part, the chief of police thereby noted that, in his view, "the opening in Odessa of a Jewish press is not only useful but even very essential as a means of cooperating in the moral development of the considerable segment of Jews who live in the cities."

This was Aksenfeld's first triumph. Finally he managed to break through the iron walls, to persuade the Russian bureaucracy of the necessity of his undertaking. Quite unexpectedly, however, a new opponent stepped forth not from the outside, but from the inside, in the person of the enlightened "learned Jew" of Odessa, Marcus Horowitz.

Count Stroganov, in all matters of "Jewish politics," used to take counsel with his "learned Jew," the pedagogue and educator of Jewish youth, Marcus Horowitz, a bitter enemy of Yiddish. As early as 1856 Horowitz wrote to Stroganov in his report about his tour of inspection of the New Russian region: "It would be very useful to discontinue the publication of works in the Yiddish language and to adopt the most effective means to the end that

---

61. See S. Borovoi's article in *Bibliologishn Zamlbukh*, 93-103. Also Gottlober, in the above-quoted, unpublished letter, complains especially about the printery of Zhitomir that it refuses to publish any Haskalah books. "And this latter (the printer in Zhitomir) has heavily distressed the people, for besides having raised the price he also withheld the property of his press from the exactness of proofreading . . . And besides this he has done much evil with the books of wisdom, which he has driven out completely from having a share in the property of his press and has not shown them any mercy."

Russian and German should become the generally used languages among Jews."[62]

We shall see below how this battler for enlightenment later (in 1862) tried to persuade the government to forbid printing books in "jargon."[63] Hence, it is not surprising that, with such an "advisor," Stroganov denied Aksenfeld's petition.

The seventy-five-year-old Aksenfeld finally lost hope of seeing his works printed in Russia, and so in 1862 published two of them in Leipzig—*Dos Shterntikhl* and *Der Ershter Yidisher Rekrut*. The aged author, however, knew quite well that in such a way it would be extremely difficult to hope that his works might be circulated among the masses of the common readers—chiefly because of the high price of books imported from abroad. Besides this, there was at that time in the southern region no censor of Jewish books; hence, it was necessary to bring books imported from abroad for censorship at Vilna or Kiev, where they would lie for a long time and not infrequently be completely lost.[64]

The rest of Aksenfeld's works remained in manuscript. In 1862 the writer applied to Gottlober[65] in a letter with the request: "Perhaps you will find a wealthy person who will be willing to believe you about the large profit he may obtain through purchasing all my writings. You will thereby confer benefit upon many individuals of our people." This letter did not have any practical results. The aged and indefatiguable Aksenfeld still made his last attempt: In October, 1863, he applied to the renowned surgeon Pirogov, who some time earlier had occupied the position of superintendent of the Odessa education district, with a request to provide him with the necessary means of publishing his works.[66] However, Pirogov at that time was abroad, and Aksenfeld therefore did not receive an answer for a long time. It was already not the writer himself but his friends who applied in 1864 to the Ḥevrah Mefitzei Haskalah (Society for the Promotion of Enlightenment) to purchase Aksenfeld's manuscripts.[67] This proposal also, as is known, remained unsuccessful. In the same year Aksenfeld moved to live with his children in Paris, where he died in 1866.

The sad fate of Aksenfeld's literary legacy did not change with the author's death. Before his demise Aksenfeld left all his writings

---

62. S. Borovoi's article in *Bibliologishn Zamlbukh*, 98.
63. See our work in *Voskhod*, 1903, III, 56-59.
64. See Borovoi, *op. cit.*, 96.
65. Just at that time Gottlober, on his part, wasted much energy in an attempt to obtain an authorization to open a Jewish press in Kamenets, but his lobbying was also unsuccessful.
66. See Riminik, *op. cit.*, 174-175.
67. See our work cited above, 96.

(approximately 300 printers' sheets) as a gift to his friend of many years, L. Murenish in Odessa. The author's friends and admirers in Odessa, led by Moses Zhvif, Abba Feldman, and Gedaliah Einimer,[68] established a fund to publish his works. However they managed to issue only three plays (*Man Un Vayb, Di Genarte Velt,* and *Kabtzen-Oysher-Shpil*). Aksenfeld's novels *Berdichever Yerid* and *Matzes Bakin* were already set up in type. Suddenly (in 1871) the renowned pogrom in Odessa broke out. The press was demolished, the type-composition scattered about, Aksenfeld's manuscripts disappeared completely,[69] and with them an enormously rich treasure of authentic images and portraits of Jewish family and social life in the first decades of the nineteenth century was lost.

More luck was enjoyed by Aksenfeld's younger contemporary and friend, the well-known battler for Haskalah, Abraham Baer Gottlober.[70]

Gottlober was a very unique, contradiction-filled personality. His father Hayyim Gottlob[71] and his grandfather on his mother's side were well-known cantors. Gottlober also was a singer, had a fine voice, and from a still unpublished letter of his we learn that for some time he even entertained the idea of becoming a cantor in a choir-synagogue.[72] He himself used to compose melodies for his songs and sing them to listeners and admirers. In him there was a spark of the ancient *Gesellekeit-Leute* with their cheerful witticisms and couplets, with their strong thirst for the joy of life, men whose life-program consisted of

---

68. See *Kol Mevasser*, 1869, No. 36, 258.
69. Sholom Aleichem indicates in a letter of his to Gottlober that he has a manuscript of Aksenfeld's "Di Moyren." Where the manuscript is now is, unfortunately, unknown to us.
70. Born in Staro-Konstantinov in 1811, died in Bialystok in 1899.
71. On the title-page of Gottlober's unpublished drama of his youth *Amnon Ve-Tamar*, it is noted: "From the young Abraham Ber Ha-Kohen Gottlob." And further on: "I am today nineteen years old—A. B. Gottlob." Also in his abovementioned album there are several acrostics with the name Gottlob. Only in later years did he change his name to Gottlober.
72. "For many of the worthies of Brody," he writes in this letter, "gave me their testimony that I have talent and a reputation in music . . . And all of them unanimously say that there is nothing better for me than to have myself chosen as a teacher for the time being in the school, and in connection with this work I will teach the laws of music in Brody as is proper to sing in choirs in the house of the Lord. Nevertheless, when I came and found there the cantor mentioned above, I refrained from words and put a bridle on my mouth without talking about it. And now, after the cause has been removed, I said I will speak my words into your ears, and now perhaps it will be proper in your sight to speak to the ears of the sage, the director, and to the ears of the elders of the community, and if they will happen to want me you will write to me and I will come to you, and you might ask also of Abram who heard my voice whether I am fit for this work. Let me know your gracious answer on all these things, so that I may know."

> Let us glory lustily, let us carouse again
> Whole days and whole nights through.

As a reward for their "entertaining" witticisms they demanded:

> Short sermons and long baked meats.
> Bring here the best victuals . . .
> Give us wine without measure,
> We will still guzzle it all up.[73]

This man, by his character a typical scion of the ancient *Gesellekeit-Leute*, was very little suited to the role of a *maskil* and ascetic, following the pattern of Isaac Baer Levinsohn, Kalman Schulman, or Jacob Reifmann, who, with such humility and readiness for sacrifice, worked, struggled, and gladly went hungry. However, along with this, Gottlober was also a man of militant nature with a full-blooded temperament, and this compelled him to become Isaac Baer Levinshon's disciple, to set out on the thorny path which the ascetic battlers for Haskalah walked.

Gottlober's father, a man of learning, even a Hasid but not a fanatic, himself brought his little Abraham Baer *Tzohar Ha-Tevah* and *Talmud Leshon Ever* to learn grammar, and when the ten-year-old boy was not himself able to bite into these textbooks, the father was not at all opposed to the idea of having him helped by the *maskil* of Staro-Konstantinov, Joseph Weisner. Weisner had spent several years in Brody and there, as Gottlober relates in his memoirs, "drew from the wells of wisdom," and when he returned home, "he there kindled the light of pure enlightenment." In the year 1828, shortly after the decree regarding the recruitment of soldiers among Jews was issued, Weisner wrote a mourning-play on the subject entitled *Kol Bochim.* "Weisner's influence on me," Gottlober writes, "was very great. I became a completely different person. He told me about Moses Mendelssohn, familiarized me with Lessing's *Nathan the Wise*, explained to me briefly what a theater really is, interpreted to me everything that occurs in that book, in various scenes, and also told me the biography of Lessing and how he used to associate with Mendelssohn."[74]

At the age of fourteen Gottlober was married off and moved to Chernigov to be supported by his wealthy father-in-law, an ardent Hasid of Ruzhin. The young bridegroom felt quite congenial in the cheerful Hasidic environment; he associated with young Hasidim, eagerly studied Kabbalah, and became interested especially in

---

73. See our *History*, Vol. VII, p. 314.
74. *Gottlober Un Zayn Epokhe*, 23.

Ḥabad Hasidism.[75] However, the youthful adherent of *Ḥabad* did not completely forget Weisner's instruction. He wrote poems and also attempted to put together textbooks of the Hebrew language.[76] For the time being, Haskalah lived quite amicably alongside Hasidism in him and did not result in any conflict. However, a great change was wrought by the journey that Gottlober made with his father to Jassy. On the way they stopped in Tarnopol, where Gottlober visited the battler for Haskalah Joseph Perl. This visit made a very powerful impression on the young man. "I suddenly became a different person," Gottlober says of this in his memoirs. When he returned to his father-in-law, the change was soon noticed. People incidentally became aware that he was reading heretical books, and they began to persecute him. News of the matter also reached the rabbi of Zhitomir and, at the latter's command, the father-in-law compelled Gottlober to divorce his daughter. The young couple in fact were very much in love. They already had a three-year-old boy who was very attached to his father. But this was of no avail. Gottlober had to part with his beloved wife, leave his father-in-law's wealthy home, and remain without any material support, for his own father died soon after his journey to Jassy. A short time later Gottlober's little boy also died.

Even decades later, when Gottlober mentions in his memoirs the family-drama that he lived through in his youth, his still unassuaged pain and indignation are very strongly discernible. "Vengeance!"—this became the dominant feeling of the deeply shattered author. He came to perceive in Hasidism the greatest enemy of modern life, of progress and enlightenment. From a gentle young man supported by his Hasidic father-in-law and a listener to Hasidic wonder-tales, he was turned into the ardent battler for Haskalah, the stormy flag-bearer and tireless propagandist, the fiery "missionary" for Haskalah, as he is described by Zederbaum.[77] For many years Gottlober traveled about from town to town, gathered young men around himself, preached the ideals of Haskalah, and summoned them to fight against the old way of life, against superstition and, above all, against Hasidism and *rebbes*.[78] He became in the southwest region of Russia the symbol of

75. See our *History*, Vol. IX, Chapter Four.

76. In an unpublished letter of his Gottlober notes: "When I was fifteen years old, I had already written two books, one called *Petaḥ Tikvah*, containing a brief introduction to the Hebrew language, and the second called *Moreh Sefat Ever*, containing all the elements of the science of grammar according to the great grammarians."

77. *Ha-Melitz*, 1882, p. 135.

78. In his letter to Zayberling of 1864, Gottlober writes: "Behold, all my days I worked and toiled to open blind eyes, which I did in Dubno, in Kremenets, Moghilev, Kamenets, Berdichev, Warsaw, Zhitomir, Odessa, and many other places." In his letter to Hayyim

terrible heresy. The author of these lines still remembers from his childhood years how in Volhynia the following was regarded as a curse: "You heretic, you *alef-bet-gimel* (the initials of Abraham Baer Gottlober)!"

However, from the cultural-historical point of view it is worth noting how this propagandist and battler for new forms of life becomes very conservative and backward as soon as it is a matter not of questions of religion and the religious way of life but of political affairs. It is sufficient to mention his Hebrew poem "El Ha-Shenat Ha-Yotze'et, Shenat 5518" (To the Year Ending-the Year 1848) in which he bids farewell to the stormy revolutionary year. This "thorough revolutionary and innovator," as one of his biographers attempts to certify Gottlober, praises and thanks God that finally this year disappears in which

> The earth was almost turned over,
> Only weeping and sighing was our portion.
> . . . .
> Sheol and Abaddon did you confer as a gift.
> And the servant revolted against his master.

However, when one speaks of Gottlober's literary activity, he must take into consideration the above-mentioned variety—more correctly, the ambiguity or duality—of Gottlober's personality. Two elements struggled within him: on the one side, the life-loving folk-singer and writer of couplets, the witty and gifted *jongleur* with his healthy, even if scantily polished, humor directed against the wealthy leaders, against the community council people and social injustice; and, on the other side, the *maskil*, the doctrinaire, with his puffed-up rhetoric, his hurrah-patriotism which frequently passes, in the constantly poverty-stricken author,[79] into plain servility and

Yehudah Katzenellenbogen of 1862, Gottlober writes: "For, from my youth to the present day, I was taught to carry on an offensive war with the fanatics who kindle the fire of religious conflict. Lo, fanaticism is the idol whose high places I removed everywhere, wherever the sole of my foot trod; against it and its army my hand has been stretched forth now more than thirty years. Before the hair on my beard sprouted, I began to smite in the camp of these Philistines with a great smiting, and I was not afraid of taking them on, for all these things are swindlery, and to smite them hip and thigh was a delight to me."

79. Even in the years when Gottlober was employed as a teacher in the Jewish government-schools, he constantly complained in his letters about his difficult material situation. From one of his letters we learn, for instance, how he pawned a year's issue of *Ha-Meassef* in order to borrow three rubles. He used to circulate his compositions to various men of wealth and thus obtain material aid from them. We have in our possession a letter of Gottlober's from 1846 to the well-known rich man of Berdichev, Jakob Joseph Halpern, requesting the latter to come to his aid because he has been robbed. And, indeed, on the copy of the letter is a note of Gottlober's: "I received two half imperials."

lackeyish submissiveness, with the petty aim of thereby begging a medal, a better paid teaching post, or simply some benefit.[80]

In both Gottlober's "faces" there was literary activity. One wrote Hebrew, the other plain Yiddish. The first wrote songs and poems by the hundreds, but the only ones that have a certain literary value are mainly translations of poems that he originally wrote in Yiddish. A certain significance also pertains to his translation of the celebrated monument of the period of the Enlightenment— Gotthold Ephraim Lessing's *Nathan the Wise*. Of all of his Hebrew works in prose, only his memoirs, which he wrote in his old age, have a cultural-historical value. On the other hand, an honored place is occupied in Neo-Yiddish literature by the folksinger and his Yiddish poems and satires.

It is easily understandable that in the "ambivalent" Gottlober there could not be any definite, consistent attitude toward the folk-language. The son of a cantor, he was attracted to the popular, pithy Volhynian Yiddish, the genuine folksong. This, however, was in total contradiction with the program of Haskalah, the ideas of the Berlin *Aufklärung*, on which Gottlober grew up and for which he fought courageously. In addition, the *maskilim* in the 1860s, when the policy of Russification was strengthened after the Polish uprising, set forth the motto of "Hebrew-Russians": "One people and one language, only with different faiths." Hence, Gottlober's attitude toward Yiddish is so filled with contradictions. The well-known passage in Gottlober's Hebrew article (*Ha-Melitz*, 1865, pp. 180–181), in which he issues forth with the following counsel, has been cited several times in Yiddish literature:

Let us ask the writers, the *maskilim*, not to be ashamed to speak to the people in the language which it uses. Let them remember that thus our sages did from ancient times, each in his land. And let them not say: How is this? How can we abandon our pure and lovely languages and begin to write a mixed and confused language, a language that has no structure or beauty? My dear ones! Do you not know that many languages at the beginning were in the same condition in which this language now finds itself? The writers and their works improve the languages and make them equal to the best.

Mentioning in his memoirs the incident between Mendel Levin (Lefin) and Tobias Feder,[81] he declares the latter a "fanatic" and in this connection notes: "Tobias Feder hated Yiddish because it is not a beautiful language, but this poet and grammarian did not

---

80. On this, in the next volume.
81. See our *History*, Vol. IX, pp. 217ff.

understand that a language is not born all at once, that the literature creates the language, that the people cannot conceive a language which they do not understand. And what is the result if we speak to the people in a language they do not comprehend?"[82]

The same writer who expressed these ideas, however, issued forth in public articles[83] and in private letters[84] against the "language of Babel," the ugly, mixed jargon which has no grammar and which must be exchanged as quickly as possible for "the language of the country" and become equal to the best.

Characteristic in this respect is a still unpublished letter of Gottlober's to the well-known *maskil* and linguist of Vilna, Joshua Steinberg. The latter reported to him that he intended to publish a newspaper "in simple German" (*bi-sefat Ashkenaz kalah*). Gottlober does not understand what Steinberg means by "simple German." He immediately warns him that if he really means *leshon Ashkenaz* (the German language), such a newspaper will have no effect, for no one will be willing to read it, nor will anyone be able to understand it. "I," Gottlober writes further, "have known for a long time that one can help our people and heal their wounds only if one speaks to them in their language; they will cast off this corrupted language only when, through it, they obtain open eyes. It will then become a battered willow-branch which one throws away when he no longer needs it."

Especially interesting in regard to Gottlober's attitude toward Yiddish is his letter[85] to a well-known lady first published by us. In this letter, written in "Daytshmerish," we read:

I return again to my poem. I called it my last, for I am firmly resolved to write nothing else literary in this wretched, ungrateful, and pregnant with misfortune language. It is a language without a literature, without grammar, without logic, without rhetoric, without philosophy and history, and—what is worst of all—without a nation. For, to tell the truth, although those who speak this language belong to a people which was once called "a wise and understanding people," they, nevertheless, presently no more deserve to be called a nation than the mythology once honored by the Greeks and Romans deserves to be called history. For both are remnants from very ancient times, their deeply imbedded rust has become more sanctifying and mysterious than their very essence. Hence, I wish to have nothing more to do with this newest language of the oldest nation, this most corrupt dialect of the holiest people, this godless barbarism of the most God-blessed community. I have achieved much in the same way which neither they nor those who handle it are worthy of, and what

82. A. Fridkin, *Gottlober Un Zayn Epokhe*, 174.
83. *Ha-Melitz*, 1863, 232.
84. *Reshumot*, II, 421.
85. *Literarishe Bleter*, 1930, No. 10.

reward have I obtained therefrom?—The mockery of the cultured (or half-cultured) that I have let myself be seduced by this common wench. The hatred of the ignorant masses who, instead of acquiring culture, consider me the devil of their infernal language and everything as diabolical howling, because they know their value and that of their language too well to attribute to it anything of good principle.

Gottlober, indeed, fulfilled, to a certain degree, his resolution that he "wishes to have nothing more to do" with this "godless barbarism," i.e., Yiddish, and that he has decided to produce "nothing more of a literary character" in this "unfortunate language." He himself notes in a letter of his to S. J. Fuenn in 1862 which has still not been published that he wrote much "in the language of the people" in his "earlier years." Almost all of Gottlober's poems and satires which, in their day, made his name so popular were written in the 1830s and 1840s. Later, especially in the years when he was a teacher in government-sponsored Jewish schools, he did not write anything in the "infernal language" aside from his reworking of Erter's *Gilgul Nefesh*. Only after the pogroms of the 1880s, when Gottlober, like many other Haskalah writers, became a penitent, did he again begin to write Yiddish (national-Zionist) poems which we shall have occasion to discuss later.

Gottlober indicates in his memoirs that the first impetus to "speak to the people in their own language" was given him by the Yiddish translations of Mendel Levin (Lefin), with which he became familiar in Bar at the home of Meir Reich. This was in the year 1830, and, indeed, from his own indications, we know that his play *Dos Dektukh* was written in 1838; his satirical poem *Dos Shtraymel Mitn Kapeloysh*, in 1841; the long satirical poem *Der Seim*,[86] in 1842; *Der Bidner Yisrolik*, which was so popular that there was—as Gottlober himself points out—no Jewish house in which the poem was not sung, in 1843; and *Di Gezeyre Daytshn*, at the end of the summer of 1845. In the same year he composed *Di Groyse Kintz, Oder Dos Bisele Mintz*. No later than the 1840s was his political satire *Di Deputatn*[87] undoubtedly written. That he also wrote *Di Farkerte Velt*[88] in the 1840s we learn from the above-mentioned letter to Fuenn in which he indicates that already in 1850, when he

---

86. The inspector of the government school of Dubno, Tanhum Rosenzweig, translated *Der Seim* into Russian.

87. First published by us in *Tsaytshrift*, V.

88. "A son of a cantor," writes A. J. Paperna in his memoirs about Gottlober (*Der Pinkes*, 1913, 187), "he inherited from his father a musical talent. He was a good prayer-leader and he sang his folksongs in the tone of the Jewish national music. These folktunes made his folksongs even more popular."

was in Vilna, he obtained the censorship authorization for the publication of this poem.

Gottlober's Yiddish poems obtained for him not only, as he complains in the "Daytshmerish" letter quoted above, the "hatred of the uncultured masses," but also enormous popularity. There was virtually no Jewish home in Volhynia and Podolia in which the people would not declaim his poems or sing them with the tunes that he himself wrote for them. As a result of this colossal popularity, a series of folk-reworkings of the author's poems was even produced eventually. The masses of the people considered them their own and remade them according to their taste and conceptions.[89]

Gottlober sang his poems not only "in the tone of Jewish national music," as A. J. Paperna notes; they were also produced in the rhythm and tone of the common folksong with its primitive simplicity, but also with its caustic humor, with its protest against social injustice.

It is worth noting that precisely the most hated foe, Hasidism, is touched upon very little by Gottlober in his poems and satires. Aside from the successful parody on the Sabbath hymns, *Ish Khosid*, the poet composed a longer poem, *Reb Itzik Ger*, which was apparently supposed to have an anti-*tzaddik* tendency. However, he did not complete it but interrupted it at the very beginning. On the other hand, Gottlober very eagerly discusses social motifs and makes the communal leaders, the Jewish "town fathers," a target of his satires. With what contempt are the Jewish intercessors, or "lobbyists," whom the communities used to dispatch so frequently to Petersburg in those times mocked in the poem *Di Deputatn:*

> In short, it remained thus
> That they chose the ass,
> The scholar, the master of the holy language,
> As the intercessor and *parnass* of the month.

But because it is, after all, not proper that the lobbyist or intercessor should go all by himself, a bunch of seven other deputies were chosen. The ox, the proper householder; the horse, the plutocrat; both councilmen, the wolf and the dog; the scoundrels, the mangy fellows, the skinflints, and the licensed rabbi, the bear—all these also came there.

Even the modern reader will read with pleasure Gottlober's satire *Di Aseyfe*—"an old story but a brand new one," as it is called in the subtitle. With biting humor both sides at the assembly are

89. For an extended discussion of this, see Z. Skurditzki's work in *Tsaytshrift*, V, 245–255.

portrayed; on the one side, the leaders, the men whose opinions are listened to, and on the other side, the poor people, the constant sacrificial victims who do not even have the courage to protest against the injustices and oppressions that are committed against them:

> So everything remained by agreement,
> The ordinance was written down in the community-register.
> Since for days and years
> There have been among Jews rich men and beggars,
> One must, after all, know what purpose each one serves.
> So we write it down now in the record:
> For tearing, for biting, for slapping, for beating,
> And for bearing all kinds of afflictions,
> Poor people must raise their shoulders.
> And the rich men—they are useful for assemblies and counsel;
> We must tell their praise without flattery:
> They excellently make an assembly.

A special interest is represented by the long poem *Der Seim*, in which the whole "band of town fathers" is so sharply and mercilessly disclosed. It is literally incredible that the *maskil* Gottlober, with his servile, patriotic Hebrew paeans to the "righteous ruler" (the Russian emperor) should permit himself to write in Yiddish such impudent lines as:

> The main thing we need to have from the king
> Is—that he should only bury us well.

The clever fox thinks "silently to himself:"

> I am, indeed, too small for the government.
> This is the misfortune, this the affliction:
> The world loves a big man, even though he is a fool.

And when they finally elected the lion as king, the conclusion follows:

> The forest is again conducted as it had been conducted:
> The weak lies still, the strong deceives;
> The big one is big, the small one is small—
> Well it is with him who has sharp teeth.

Such barbed allusions are encountered quite frequently in the poem, but all this only incidentally. Our folksinger hurls his pointed arrows mainly against the local "men of importance," the rabbinic judges, rabbis, and leaders of the community council. He refuses to know anything of fine, elegant manners. In the common, popular language he says to them:

> Why do you push yourselves, rats, in the heat?
> Because you have no sense, no wit?
> Pigs, donkeys, horses, bears,
> Why do you all wish to be community-council people?
> How does it come to you that you know all afflictions?
> Into the forest with you, you scoundrels!

A special place is occupied in Gottlober's work by his comedy *Dos Dektukh*. We know from his memoirs that his teacher, the *maskil* of Staro-Konstantinov Joseph Weisner, who himself composed a Hebrew play entitled *Kol Bochim*, aroused in the quite young Gottlober a special interest in theatrical works. The first, rather long play that Gottlober produced in Hebrew was a Bible drama in four acts entitled *Amnon Ve-Tamar*.[90] We have already noted in our article cited above (*Literarishe Bleter*, 1930, Number 10) the very limited literary value of this play, which has remained in manuscript. Years later (in 1867) Gottlober published his allegorical drama *Tiferet Li-Venei Vinah*, which is the weakest and clumsiest of all the numerous Hebrew allegorical dramas that were produced in the Haskalah era following the pattern of Moses Ḥayyim Luzzatto's *La-Yesharim Tehillah*. However the *maskil* and rhetorician in Gottlober, as we previously observed, was interwoven with the scion of the ancient *Gesellike-Leute*, the talented "jesters" and *Purim-shpilers*, with their healthy folk-humor and laughter. Thanks to this, the battler for Haskalah forgets words of moral instruction and grandiloquent rhetorical flourishes for a time; the upper hand is obtained by the "jester" who produces in his pithy Volhynian speech the popular three-act comedy *Dos Dektukh*.

Gottlober himself points out in his memoirs the great impression that was made on him in 1837 by Solomon Ettinger, when the latter read aloud to him his *Serkele*. Indeed, it was under this impression that he composed his own comedy. *Serkele*, however, served the battler for Haskalah Gottlober merely as a stimulus, not as a model. The model for *Dos Dektukh* was provided rather by Levinsohn's *Hefker-Velt* and Wolfsohn's and Euchel's *Familien-Gemälde*. Gottlober's hatred for the *gute Yidn* and swindlerish wonderworkers, his contempt for the crude, obsolete forms of life, for the

90. A. Fridkin's suggestion, *op. cit.*, 178, that *Amnon Ve-Tamar* is a "play about present-day life" is not correct. The error probably stems from the fact that Fridkin did not correctly translate Gottlober's Hebrew expression *al derech ha-hoveh*. This is not at all intended to mean that the present is portrayed in the work, but that it is written in dialogue form.

unnaturalness of the old-fashioned marriages, in which, for the sake of foolish family prestige, it was considered proper to betroth a daughter to a good-for-nothing, to a physical and mental cripple— all these find the sharpest expression in *Dos Dektukh*, are mocked with the lash of satire, and are ridiculed with a healthy folk laughter. The representatives of light and "enlightenment" in *Dos Dektukh* are not *raisonneur*-like figures of wood, as in Euchel, but life-loving personalities of the *commedia dell'arte*. They sing cheerful couplets, perform all kinds of prankster's tricks, and like all the *Gesellike-Leute* and "jesters" are quite content when they are given beer and wine "without measure."

It is truly deplorable that this popular book of comedy, this first example of modern Yiddish melodrama, remained unprinted for decades and wandered from hand to hand in corrupted and erroneous copies until in 1876 one Jozef Werblinski printed such a corrupted copy under his name. Here, however, we must correct the conclusion that we reached in this connection in our article cited above. There we explained the fact that Gottlober's Yiddish writings remained in manuscript for such a long time by the theory that "he had no desire to print his works written in Yiddish, and this not because of material obstacles but simply because he was ashamed to appear in public as a writer of jargon."[91] After we became familiar with Gottlober's extensive correspondence, which is still unpublished, we arrived at the conviction that the reason why Gottlober's Yiddish works were not published in their time is the same as that which also brought it about that Aksenfeld's works remained in manuscript. "A printing, a printing!," Gottlober exclaims in one of his letters; "This is my dream since my youth, since my childhood up until my old age." We have already noted that as early as 1850 Gottlober furnished his *Farkerte Velt* with the censor's authorization, but he did not have the opportunity of printing the work.[92] As soon as the term of the press-monopoly ended (in 1862) and *Kol Mevasser* began to appear, Gottlober promptly commenced to print his shorter Yiddish pieces. In 1865 he published in *Ha-Melitz* (No. 12) the following announcement:

I hereby proclaim that I am prepared to hand over for printing the following of my works in the folk-language: (a) *Dos Dektukh, Oder Tsvey*

91. Incidentally, it is interesting to quote Gottlober's remark (*Yidishe Folks-Bibliotek*, 1888, 257) about Yiddish: "In earlier times people did not know of the name jargon. Our language was called *Yidish-Daytsh* (Judeo-German). The name jargon also does not please me, because in fact jargon means an incomprehensible speech; it is wiser to keep to the name Yiddish or Judeo-German."

92. It is characteristic that Gottlober exclaims with pride in a letter of his to Pinhas Bernstein: "Say, my brother-*maskilim*, when did you not satiate your souls with fatness, whether I sang Hebrew or Judeo-German?"

Khupes In Eyn Nakht, a comedy in three acts (b) *Di Farkerte Velt*, (c) *Der Seim, Oder Di Groyse Aseyfe In Vald, Az Di Khayes Hobn Oysgekilben Dem Leyb Far A Melekh*. The last two works are written in a free rhythm that is called in German *Knüttelreimen* (doggerel verses). The first is written in prose, but it also contains poems, some of them in closed rhythm and composed for singing, and these will be published together with the notes of the melodies. These works of mine have already acquired renown and they are known to many *maskilim* and poets.[93]

With this achievement of his, composing a play with poems and songs, the author appears as a forerunner of Abraham Goldfaden, the creator of the modern Yiddish theater. When one evaluates Gottlober's merits in Yiddish literature, it must be mentioned that his beloved disciples, on whom his influence was very considerable, were the grandfather of modern Yiddish literature, Mendele Mocher Seforim, and the founder of the modern Yiddish theater, Goldfaden.

93. In a second announcement of Gottlober's in *Ha-Melitz* are mentioned two of his poems "Di Dubner Sreyfe" and "Di Blinde Yesoyme," which are not noted in the other sources.

CHAPTER SIX

Haskalah in Poland; Eisenbaum, Reifmann, Slonimski, Ettinger

[The Haskalah movement in Poland—The influence of the Berlin Haskalah—Friedländer's *Über die Verbesserung der Israeliten im Königreich Polen*—The "enlightener" Jacob Tugendhold—Anton Eisenbaum and *Der Beobachter an der Weichsel*—Mendelssohn's *Biur* in the Warsaw edition—The uniqueness of the Haskalah movement in Poland—Jacob Reifmann and his work—Ḥayyim Zelig Slonimski and his importance—Ephraim-Fishel Fishelsohn of Zamose and his *Teater Fun Khasidim*—Solomon Ettinger's years of learning and wandering—Ettinger the aesthete and master of the Yiddish language—His plays, parables and epigrams—Ettinger the *maskil*—Ettinger's life-drama—The battler for culture Tugendhold as censor—The works of Ettinger "improved" by the censorship remain in manuscript.]

N THE previous chapters we familiarized the reader with the "fathers of Haskalah" of Volhynia and Lithuania. In the present chapter we shall dwell on the Haskalah movement in the third important center—Poland.

Poland's position adjacent to Prussia and its frequent trade relationships with the important Prussian centers collaborated in bringing it about that the influence of the Berlin Haskalah was already noticeable in the upper strata of the Warsaw Jewish community when Warsaw was still the capital city of the Polish kingdom. This process was strengthened even more after 1795 when Warsaw, following the third partition of Poland, came under Prussian sovereignty. Trade between Warsaw and Berlin was considerably increased thereby, and many Prussian Jews opened their own businesses in Warsaw. It suffices to note that in 1799 thirteen Jewish banks, mainly established by Prussian Jews,[1] operated in the city. At the end of the eighteenth century a reformed "German" synagogue with sermons in German was founded,[2] and this synagogue continued to function even after Warsaw ceased to be a Prussian province and was transformed, following Napoleon's decree, into the capital of the Duchy of Warsaw. But the influence of the Berlin Haskalah was felt at the threshold of the nineteenth century in certain strata of the Warsaw community not only in the intellectual, but also in the legal-political, realm.

When applying with its petitions to the government concerning extension of Jewish civic rights, the community of Warsaw deemed it necessary to request support in this connection from the leaders of the Berlin community who were, after all, "close to the government." For its part, the Prussian regime also saw in the Jewish community leaders of Berlin the acknowledged supervisors of the Polish *Ostjuden*. At the end of the eighteenth century the Prussian minister Voss turned to David Friedländer with the request that the latter express his view concerning "The Jews' Regulation" of 1797. For this purpose Friedländer made a special visit to Poland in order to become familiar on the spot with the Jewish situation and later (in 1801) submitted a comprehensive *Denkschrift* to the minister.

Even after the Napoleonic wars, when Warsaw became the capital of the "Kingdom of Poland" under Russian sovereignty, the intellectual influence of the Berlin enlighteners on their "fellow-believers" in Warsaw was not interrupted. Shortly after the "temporary government" of the newly declared "kingdom" established (in 1815) a special commission assigned the task of considering the Jewish question in Poland, Bishop Malichevski applied in the name of some political leaders to Friedländer with the request that the latter express his authoritative opinion concerning the fashion in which the Jewish question in Poland may best be solved. Friedländer responded with a long *Gutachten* which he published three years later with some supplements in his work already known to us—*Über die Verbesserung der Israeliten im Königreich Polen*.[3] From his narrow, rationalist point of view, Friedländer was firmly convinced that the major obstacles preventing the intelligent solution of the Jewish question in Poland are the following two factors: (1) the fact that among the Jews dwelling there the Talmud is so strongly prevalent, and (2) the pernicious Hasidic movement which occupies such an honored place in the

1. J. Shatzky in *Historishe Shriftn*, 427.
2. See B. Weinryb's pointed article in *MGWJ*, 1922, 139-152.
3. See our *History*, Vol. VIII, 113.

country. It is quite understandable that not only Polish spiritual and secular officials found themselves in contact with the aged Friedländer, but also representatives of the Warsaw *maskilim*. They saw in the rationalist of Berlin the recognized intellectual leader, and they used to apply to him and his followers in regard to various cultural questions.

In 1819 the young Jacob Tugendhold opened the first secular schools for Jewish youth following the pattern of the Berlin schools. Tugendhold was descended from German Jews. His father Isaiah Tugendhold, a native of Breslau (born in 1755) was an admirer of the Meassefim and wrote letters with rhetorical flourishes in their style, as well as poems and commentaries on the Bible.[4] While still a youth, he settled in the little Polish town of Zoloshitz (near Cracow) and there spent his entire life.[5] His elder son Jacob already had a family when he left his birthplace Zoloshitz (in 1812) and went away to study in Breslau.[6] In 1817 Jacob Tugendhold settled in Warsaw, and a year later made his debut in Polish literature with an indignant response to an anonymous anti-Semitic brochure entitled *Sposób na Zydów* which had just appeared and in which the only possible rational means of solving the Jewish problem was declared to be the banishment of all Jews from the land. In his polemical *Jerobaal czyli mowa o Zydach*, written with youthful force, Tugendhold incidentally expresses his firm conviction that the new generation of the Jewish populace will be educated in the spirit of modern European culture.[7] In order to accomplish this, Tugendhold a year later established the just-mentioned modern schools with Polish as the language of instruction.

Here, however, great disappointments awaited him. The "Berliners," the enlightened bankers, manufacturers and large-scale merchants, who felt the necessity of European education and of new forms of life, at that time constituted a very thin stratum in Warsaw; the largest mass of the Jewish populace consisted of orthodox Jews, Hasidim, and plain people who still clung firmly to the old, isolated forms of life. The assimilationist tendencies which were then so strongly discernible in Prussia could have very slight influence in Poland because the economic structure of Polish society was still completely feudal. The Jew lived off the

---

4. A considerable segment of his manuscripts was burned during a fire in 1796. The remaining part of his literary legacy was published by J. J. Weissberg in a special collection *Divrei Yeshayah ben Yaakov Tugendhold* (Cracow, 1896).
5. He died in 1830.
6. See *Divrei Yeshayah* . . . , 16-19.
7. See *Perezhitoye*, I, 205, 211.

landowner and satisfied his concerns about a livelihood within the four cubits of his own little world. He could somehow come to terms with the landowner, and did not have any great interest in political and cultural-social questions because these, as a result of his social isolation,[8] still had not entered his consciousness.

It is therefore not surprising that Jacob Tugendhold, with his reformed schools, aroused great indignation in the orthodox circles and the pious leaders of the Warsaw community began to persecute him intensely and fabricated all kinds of slanders against him.[9] There was even a moment when Jacob Tugendhold was so terrified that he thought of fleeing from Warsaw.[10] The most interesting thing in this connection, however, is that both sides—Tugendhold and his father, on the one side, and the opposing party—applied, in regard to the controversy, with letters of complaint to the "prominent men" of Berlin, to the well-known communal leader Israel Jacobson and to David Friedländer's intimates.[11]

The three modern elementary schools (two such schools were soon especially added for girls) established under the direction of Tugendhold were merely the first step on the part of the *maskilim* of Warsaw to bring the Jewish populace close to modern culture. At the end of 1823 Anton Eisenbaum,[12] who had completed a Polish lyceum and was conversant with several European languages, established a bilingual newspaper, in Polish and Judeo-German, in Warsaw, *Der Beobachter an der Weichsel* (in Polish it was called *Dostrzegacz Nadwiślański*). The government commission for popular education which granted Eisenbaum permission to publish a Yiddish newspaper "in order to spread education among Jews" also, in this connection, assigned him a subsidy of two thousand Polish gulden on condition that the text in the paper be printed not only in Yiddish but in Polish as well.[13]

The newspaper,[14] according to its content, consisted of five parts: (1) official government decrees and ordinances, and reports about internal life in the country; (2) "reports from abroad," descriptions of foreign countries and of the life of Jews dwelling

---

8. J. Shatzky, *Historishe Shriftn*, I, 427.
9. Jacob Tugendhold's father complains in one of his letters: "For the leaders of the community of Warsaw sent me a letter . . . and the synopsis of the letter was an indictment of my son in the following language: 'That he does much evil against Jews and brought it about that he has manufactured a theater-piece to slander Jews' " (*Divrei Yeshayah* . . ., 78).
10. *Ibid.*, 65.
11. *Ibid.*, 77-81; see also Weinryb, *op. cit.*, 146-152.
12. Born in 1791, died in 1852.
13. *Kwartalnik Żydów w Polsce*, 1912, II, 59.
14. The first number appeared December 3, 1823.

there; (3) business reports; (4) biographies of great Jewish men, anecdotes, and stories; and (5) advertisements.

The newspaper had no success whatever, and this was brought about mainly by the editor himself. The arid "learned Jew" and "informer" Anton Eisenbaum was generally very little suited for the responsible role of a newspaper editor. Moreover, in order to "spread education among Jews," he set himself the task of displacing the "crippled jargon" with literary German. For this purpose he printed his newspaper in the following kind of "refined" *Daytshmerish:*

"לוט בריפען אויס סאלאניקא פאם 15 נאוועמבער האט דער שלעכטעסטע
אלער מענטשן זיינען פערדינטען לאהן בעקאמען. אבאלאבו פאשא פאן
סאלאניקא, וועלכער אים פאריגן יאהרע איבער 5000 פאמיליען האט אומברענגען
לאססען און דערנאך זיך ריהמטע דאס אויף זיינען בעפעהל אן איינציגען טאגע
1500 ווייבער אונד קינדער ערמארדעט ווארדען זינד — איסט ענדלעך זעלבסט
אויף בעפעהל דעם סולטאנס הינגעריכטעט ווארדען."

(According to letters from Salonika of November 15th, the worst of all men has received his merited reward. Abalabu-Pasha of Salonika, who, in the previous year, ordered the killing of over five thousand families and thereafter boasted that at his command fifteen hundred women and children were murdered on a single day, was finally himself executed at the command of the sultan.)[15]

The Polish Jews understood this kind of "Judeo-German" even less than the money-changer of Berlin, Reb Chenech, understood the enlightened language of Marcus.[16] Hence, there occurred with the *Beobachter* what had to occur: since no one read it, it did not survive even for a year, and with the forty-second number (published on September 29, 1824) it ended its drab existence unnoticed.

However, Anton Eisenbaum's "enlightening" work did not end with this. Two years later he became the actual head of the rabbinical seminary established in Warsaw in 1826. The language of instruction in this school was Polish. The only concession made in regard to the teachers of religious studies was that, if they do not have a perfect command of the Polish language, they are permitted for the time being to use German, but under no circumstance the Judeo-German "jargon."[17] Eisenbaum's two closest collaborators in the rabbinical seminary were the strongly assimilationist-

15. *Beobachter an der Weichsel*, No. 1.
10. See our *History*, Vol. VIII, 140ff.
17. See *Perezhitoye*, I, 224.

minded "enlighteners" Jacob Zentnershwer and Abraham Buchner, the teacher of Hebrew and Bible. Like David Friedländer, Buchner was also a convinced opponent of the Talmud and even wrote a special work entitled *Die Nichtigkeit des Talmuds*.[18] Hence, it can be no surprise that the rabbinical seminary during the whole course of its almost forty-year existence did not graduate a single *Rabbiner*.[19]

In order to "enlighten the Jewish masses," the *maskilim* of Warsaw undertook, in the 1830s, a cultural enterprise of broad scope. In 1835 the Warsaw *maskil* Moses Tanenboim published an announcement to the effect that he was preparing to issue the Pentateuch with the *Biur*, or commentary, in Mendelssohn's German translation. The edition was financed by the wealthy resident of Warsaw Theodor (Tevel) Teplitz, who became rich from farming various taxes, such as the excise on salt and kosher meat.[20] However, the edition, it appears, had no success. The orthodox masses had no desire to purchase the Pentateuch with "Moses Dessauer's" *Biur*. This is confirmed by the following fact: two years later, after the third volume of the edition had already appeared, when the publishers became convinced that their Pentateuchs have no sale, the "money-provider" Teplitz submitted a petition (dated August 21, 1837) to the commission (ministry) for internal and religious affairs in Warsaw.[21]

This petition is so characteristic that we reproduce the first part of it here verbatim:

The experience of long years in various lands has proven that the salutary intentions of a government in regard to the moral enlightenment of the Jews become timely and produce desired fruit only when one employs effective means of weaning Jews away from the corrupted language, i.e., from the Yiddish jargon. The most efficacious means of acquainting them with the language of the country, however, is to accustom them first to speak the German language correctly, because Yiddish is very close to it. Also there is no doubt that as soon as the Jew knows German, he gladly takes to the language of the country in which he lives, binds himself with more sincerity to the government, to the laws of the land, as well as to his countrymen of another faith. But the effectiveness of the means mentioned can only be achieved if a translation in the pure German language is to be found alongside the text of the books that have a religious

18. *Ibid.*, 230. After Eisenbaum's death, Jacob Tugendhold, who is already known to us, was appointed director.
19. *Ibid.*, 232.
20. A bit of a contribution to the cost of the edition was also given by the *maskil* of Vilna, Hirsch Kliatzko (see *Historishe Shriftn*, I, 777-778).
21. On this, see B. Weinryb's note in *YIVO-Bleter*, VIII, 85-88.

approbation of the scholars of the whole world and which, aside from the fact that it forestalls some of the fanatical interpretations of Holy Scripture, also helps the Jews become familiar with the German language.[22]

Only after this whole introduction does Teplitz pass to the main point: that there is no means of spreading this useful work other than that the commission should order the communities *(Dozor Rozniczy)* to obligate themselves to order one copy—and in the larger towns, several copies—of the Pentateuch for the study-houses. As it appears,[23] the government, in fact, fulfilled Teplitz's petition and compelled the Jews to purchase the Pentateuchs with Mendelssohn's *Biur*.

In Poland, we thus see, the enlightenment movement assumed quite singular forms. In the major city, Warsaw, an upper stratum of the *haute-bourgeoisie*—Jewish bankers, manufacturers, large-scale merchants, and their agents who, for the purposes of business, required European education, conducted themselves "in German fashion," and were assimilated to a considerable degree—was formed. The large masses of the Jewish populace in Warsaw itself and especially in the provinces, however, still behaved in the old way, and such "enlighteners" as Eisenbaum, Teplitz, Buchner, and the like had a very slight influence on them. Indeed, they could not understand each other; these were two completely different worlds.

Precisely in several smaller Polish centers—in places such as Zamosc, Szczebrzeszyn, and the like—there were *maskilim*, even if in rather small number, of a completely different kind. These were not bankers and businessmen but poor *yeshivah*-students thirsting for knowledge. The new ideas of neighboring Prussia reached, albeit in weak echoes, their castaway little towns and aroused in them the drive for light and knowledge. With great toil and effort, after years of poverty and want, they finally managed to attain the sources of European knowledge. However, they did not part, in their order of life and their whole conduct, from their own environment.

It suffices to mention one of the most typical and also one of the most important of these *maskilim*—the learned Jacob Reifmann.

Jacob Reifmann was born in 1818 in a village near Opatov (in the government, or province, of Radom). He spent his youth in Opatov where his father Tzevi Hirsh earned a living in poverty from

---

22. Weinryb's note in *YIVO-Bleter*, VIII, 87.
23. For evidence of this, see Weinryb's note that has been cited.

teaching. While still in his youthful years Reifmann, who was gifted with sound common sense, found *pilpul*, with its overly subtle ingenuities, repugnant. In the most confused text he sought simplicity, the plain, clear meaning. A new era began in his intellectual development when he moved after his marriage to Szczebrzeszyn (in the government of Lublin), where he became acquainted for the first time in his father-in-law's house with Maimonides' *Guide for the Perplexed*. With great diligence the young man studied medieval Hebrew philosophical literature. Without any outside help whatever he also learned German, which gave him the opportunity to become familiar with modern philosophy and with critical philology. Already in 1842 Reifmann came forth in Isaac Marcus Jost's *Zion* with his first scholarly article about several apocryphal books. His material situation was a very sad one. He spent his entire life[24] in great distress and suffered hunger and cold. To give the reader some notion of the difficult conditions under which this scholar lived, it is sufficient to present a brief quotation from a letter of his to S. Z. Halberstam: "Unfortunately, I am compelled to live in a room the size of a cage, and this together with children, rather little ones and bigger ones, and also with fowl which cackle and quack day and night, disturb me in my scholarly work, and do not let me fall asleep."[25]

Under such conditions did the sage of Szczebrzeszyn carry on his scholarly work in the course of fifty years. As an autodidact who had not obtained any systematic education, Reifmann was not much of a systematizer. His works, especially the larger ones, are not a little deficient in structure. Frequently quite extraneous questions that are not organically connected with the theme under discussion are interwoven. The extraneous matters in Reifmann, however, are never empty verbiage, but important material of scholarly value. Reifmann was incapable of transmitting the enormous knowledge that he had accumulated with such tireless diligence in a strictly systematic form, but he presents it to the reader in a simple, clear language, scientifically elucidated and grounded. The old-fashioned reader, the scholar, the *yeshivah*-student brought up on *pilpul*, obtained in Reifmann's works[26] a plethora of critically illuminated scholarly information about the most varied branches of ancient Hebrew literature: the Apocrypha, the Targumim, the classics of religious philosophy, historical

24. Reifmann died in 1895.
25. See the *Freidus Memorial Volume*, 8.
26. For the list of Reifmann's printed works, see W. Zeitlin, *Kirjath Sepher*. For the 300 of his works that were printed in Hebrew and German journals, see M. Schwab, in *Repertoire*, 322. For the list of his unpublished works, see *He-Asif*, VI, 203-205; Russian-Jewish Encyclopedia, XII, 365.

books, and erroneous texts in old *Baraitot*, Midrashim, and responsa.

Of the reverence and feeling of gratitude that the tireless Reifmann aroused in his readers, a clear notion is given to us in J. L. Gordon's well-known poem which he dedicated to the scholar and in which he exclaims emotively:

> For wherever I turn, I see your spirit there,
> Explorer of the hidden chambers of the Torah by the light of the torch. . . .
> Ah, I have not forgotten you, my brother, and who can forget you?
> How many Jacob Reifmanns are there in the "marketplace!"

Not only among common readers, but also in the larger scholarly world, was the humble savant of the little town of Szczebrzeszyn highly revered. Virtually all the prominent Jewish scholars of his time—S. J. Rapoport, Tzevi Hirsch Chajes, Abraham Geiger, Isaac Marcus Jost, Reggio, Luzzatto, Fürst, Steinheim, Kirchheim, Senior Sachs, and others—carried on scholarly correspondence with Reifmann.

An even greater reputation was acquired by Reifmann's older contemporary Ḥayyim Zelig Slonimski.[27] It is indubitable that if Slonimski had grown up under different circumstances and obtained a regular education, he would have acquired great renown as a clever inventor in the technical-scientific realm. But he was brought up not in a technical school but in "Yekhiel Nikhe's" *kloyz* in his native town of Bialystok. There he was famed as an ingenious "mathematician." Out of all of the sections of the Talmud, he was chiefly interested in the passages having a relationship to mathematics and astronomy, such as the sanctification of the new moon and the like. When at the age of eighteen he married and moved to be maintained at the home of his father-in-law in Zabludow, he rummaged about there, too, above all, for mathematical works and was overjoyed when he managed to obtain Joseph Solomon Delmedigo's *Elim* and Raphael Hanover's *Techunot Ha-Shamayim*.

But these works could not assuage Slonimski's thirst for knowledge. Here the *maskil* Yeḥiel Michal Zabludowski,[28] one of the type of Haskalah pioneers of whom we wrote in the second part of the sixth volume of our work, came to his assistance. With his aid, Slonimski studied German and, as a result, acquired the

---

27. Born in Bialystok in 1810, died as a distinguished old man in Warsaw in 1904.
28. Zabludowski was born in 1803 and died in 1869. He published *Mishan Mayyim* (explanations of various legends in the Talmud and Midrashim) and *Mei Michal*, critical notes to obscure passages in the *Midrash Rabbah*.

possibility of becoming familiar with the newer works about mathematics and natural science. He also occupied himself a great deal with physics and chemistry. The *yeshivah*-student of Bialystok became a *maskil*, but a *maskil* of a very unique kind. He did not write any exalted rhetorical paeans to "Haskalah, the daughter of Heaven" and did not sing any odes to the "beautiful language, the only remnant." Poetry, in general, was as remote as the skies from this cold, critical-logical "mathematician." Nor did he battle against the Hasidim and their *tzaddikim*. Not struggle, but knowledge—as much knowledge as possible—was Slonimski's motto on his long lifepath.

"The basic purpose of *Ha-Tzefirah*," Slonimski many years later announced in the prospectus of the journal which he circulated in January 1862,[29] "is to spread the light of the necessary sciences, to demonstrate their beauty and utility." When he was only twenty-four years old he completed a comprehensive textbook on mathematics. However, because of lack of funds, he published only the first part under the title *Mosedei Hochmah* (Vilna, 1834).

Precisely in the following year the whole civilized world awaited a unique guest, the tireless cosmic-wanderer Halley's Comet, which, in ancient times, used to cast terror with its sudden marvelous appearance in the heavenly heights. The inhabitants of earth used to see in this unexpected guest the harbinger of bloody, misfortune-bringing events until the English astronomer Halley, Newton's pupil and admirer, came, calculated scientifically, and explored the path of this extraordinary celestial phenomenon. He demonstrated that it is a comet which wanders over the extent of the universe according to firmly established laws and embraces, as with a belt, on its elliptical path in the course of seventy-five years, the whole space of the sphere of the sun and its planets, including Earth. According to the formula that Halley set forth, in 1835 this heavenly guest was to be found in its wanderer's path so close to our planet that the inhabitants thereof would easily be able to observe it in the darkness of the night. All the newspapers wrote much about this, and the rumors about the expected Halley's Comet even penetrated into the Jewish streets, the Jewish study-houses. It was then that Slonimski found the best opportunity to come forth with his *Kocheva De-Shavit* (1835), in which he acquaints the reader with the elements of modern astronomy, with the laws of Kepler and Newton, and the nature and paths of the comets. The work made Slonimski's name very popular in the Jewish quarter.

Soon his name also became known in the outside world. For a new calculating machine that he invented, the Russian Academy of

29. We shall speak of the journal *Ha-Tzefirah* in the next volume.

Sciences awarded him the Demidov Prize. The same year Slonimski visited Berlin and there made the acquaintance of many scholars and scientists. He, the plain *yeshivah*-student, acquired such substantial scientific knowledge that it evoked the astonishment of the world-famous scholar Alexander von Humboldt, with whom he became acquainted in 1858.[30]

Slonimski made himself known in the scientific world with several other discoveries in the field of physics.[31] Not in this, however, lies the chief significance of this figure. Not as an inventor, not as a talented popularizer or as a representative of education and science, did his name enter the history of Jewish enlightenment. Slonimski utilized his great knowledge above all in disseminating useful information among the old-fashioned Jewish public, which spent all its days in the "tent of Torah" and had such a slight notion of the modern sciences. He was not at all willing to content himself with the fact that the secrets of the distant heavens with their infinite worlds and planets had been disclosed before his eyes; he also strove that the light of all of the strange worlds that had been revealed should illuminate the Jewish Pale of Settlement, that it should become bright and clear in all the corners of the old Jewish study-house.

Slonimski is virtually the only one among the old *maskilim* who was extremely popular *among all* strata of the Jewish reading public. He alone understood the secret of throwing a bridge over from the old to the new. And *this* bridge was trusted by all, so assuredly and cautiously was it constructed. Even the orthodox could not get over their surprise at how ingeniously Slonimski calculated, "according to the laws of mathematics," the "foundations of intercalation,"[32] how he explained so simply and so comprehensibly to them, the scholars and eager students, whence the *kochevei de-shavit* (the comets) derive, familiarized them with the *Toledot Ha-Shamayim* (History of the Heavens),[33] with the development and the movement of the planets. And Slonimski had a masterful understanding of how to veil the true scientific content in such a purely Jewish form that it was in no way to be recognized that this is something new or strange, and not a simple continuation of what is written in the old sacred books.

---

30. Out of a feeling of gratitude to the great scientist, who took a very warm interest in him, Slonimski composed in Hebrew the Humboldt-monograph *Ot Zikkaron*, in which he presents the content of Humboldt's famous work *Cosmos*.

31. As, for instance, transmitting through a wire four telegrams at one time.

32. The conjectures that Slonimski expressed regarding the calendar reckoning prevalent among Jews called forth in Hebrew literature a "thirty years war" in which all of the Jewish "reckoners" and expert mathematicians, such as Pineles and others, participated.

33. The work was published in 1838.

While the orthodox regarded other *maskilim* as destroyers, as "sinners against the covenant," Slonimski was *their* Slonimski, the simplifier, the explainer. Slonimski did not carry on any war with the "rebels against the light," did not make any reproving speeches, and did not praise to the skies the "divine daughter Haskalah." He merely accustomed the orthodox, the men with the obsolete world-view, to see in the secular sciences, in European science, above all—wisdom, not heresy.

When Slonimski later began to issue the weekly *Ha-Tzefirah* in which he printed popular articles about all kinds of scientific matters—about telegraphy, chemistry, steam-machines, air balloons, electricity, and the like—and illustrated all these with woodcuts, it was not only young *yeshivah*-students who were already "infected with heresy" but also the pillars of the Torah, the scholars themselves, who were delighted and derived enjoyment from it.

Jacob Reifmann and Hayyim Zelig Slonimski addressed themselves to the scholar, to the learned man; hence, they wrote exclusively in Hebrew. As in Volhynia, there were also in Poland *maskilim* who considered it their obligation to address the masses of the people, to write in the only language that these masses understood, namely, Yiddish. In this connection the following point is worth noting: In Volhynia the "language question" had no existence only in Aksenfeld; for him it was obvious that one must create for the people in the language of the masses. Levinsohn and Gottlober, in fact, regarded the "jargon" with contempt and used it only because they had no alternative. The Polish "Yiddishists," however, in general did not know of any "wrestlings" in regard to the Yiddish language. One of them, as we shall see below, went even further than Aksenfeld and wrote not only in the folk-language but even made the audacious attempt to raise this language to the level of a literary and artistic language.

We shall dwell here upon two of these writers both of whom grew up and were educated not in Warsaw with its two opposing camps, the half-assimilated *haute bourgeoisie*, on the one side, and the Hasidic, pious orthodox Jews, on the other, but in small centers of culture where Torah and "science," Haskalah and piety, still lived amicably side by side, as they did among those pioneers of Haskalah of whom we spoke in the sixth volume of our work (pp. ooo-oo).

One of these two writers, Ephraim-Fishel Fishelsohn, was until quite recently virtually forgotten. It is, therefore, understandable that we have very scanty biographical information about him. We know only that he lived for a long time in Lublin, was acquainted with Zederbaum, and on friendly terms with Solomon Ettinger.[34]

34. H. Borodianski in *Historishe Shriftn*, I, 632-633.

Max Erik brought our attention to some correspondence of Fishelsohn's in *Ha-Melitz*[35] in which he signs himself a man of Zamosc. Like New Zagare, Zamosc also was renowned as "a city of knowledge," as a center of culture. From there came Mendelssohn's teacher Israel Zamosc,[36] the author of *Netzaḥ Yisrael*, and the poet Issachar Behr Falkensohn.[37] In Zamosc also the poet Aryeh Leib Kinderfreund[38] was born and spent his youth. There also lived the *maskil* Joseph Zederbaum whose son later played such a significant role in Jewish journalism.

Apparently, Fishelsohn had a certain connection with Galicia. In any case, on the title-page of his work *Teater Fun Khasidim*, which he wrote in 1843, the following note is added: "played in Lemberg." The work consists of two parts—a long Hebrew introduction which is, in fact, an independent satire and, after it, the "theater" itself, an anti-Hasidic satire written in Yiddish in rhymed lines. However, it appears that, out of fear of the Hasidim, the author did not have the courage to publish his work. Thus, it remained in manuscript and only in recent times did Dr. Ḥayyim Borodianski print *Teater Fun Khasidim*, but without the Hebrew introduction of which he gives only the content.[39]

The reader would be mistaken if he believed that this work actually represents a play that was "performed" in Lemberg. It is noted on the title-page that the "theater" is "divided into three acts." In fact, however, we have before us not a play but one of the "disputations" that were so popular in Old-Yiddish literature. In form and style Fishelsohn's *Teater* is quite similar to the mocking poem entitled "Di Bashraybung Fun Ashkenaz Un Polyak,"[40] already known to us. There the disputation is carried on by the Pole, the German, and the man of Prague, and in Fishelsohn's satire the following take part: the speculator Leibele Oyfgeklerter and his friend Israel, the Hasidim Reb Shmuel, Reb Shmayeh, and Wolf Holtau, and the *yeshivah*-students of the study-house. The author's ideal is the theoretician Leibele Filozof. In his mouth he places his own demands and desires. The *maskil* Leibele in no way distinguishes himself with his behavior, with his whole mode of conduct, from the orthodox masses. Immediately at the beginning it is indicated how Leibele Filozof sits in the study-house "over the *Yad Ha-Ḥazakah* quite comfortably, cheerfully at the head of the table, clad in prayer-shawl and phylacteries." The work testifies

---

35. Vol. 1, No. 5, 78.
36. See our *History*, VIII, p. 13.
37. *Ibid.*, p. oo.
38. See Vol. X, p. 91.
39. *Historishe Shriftn*, I, 649-694.
40. See our *History*, VII, p. 296ff.

that the author himself was also quite familiar with medieval philosophical literature. He frequently quotes Maimonides, Baḥya's *Ḥovot Ha-Levavot* and Joseph Albo's *Ikkarim*. Of the newer Haskalah writers he mentions only the "splendid rhetorician" Naftali Herz Wessely (his *Sefer Middot* and *Shirei Tiferet*).

Like the chief hero of the *Teater*, Leibele Filozof, so also the author believes firmly in the persuasive power of common sense and of logical arguments. Hence, he strives to convince the Hasidim how foolish they are in that they, such poor people, carry away their last penny to the *rebbe*. With caustic irony he portrays how the misguided, ignorant Hasidim regard with the greatest contempt all who do not belong to their band.

The Hasid Reb Shmuel declares:

> We Hasidim will ride on your backs.
> We precious Hasidim will live, and you will be cast out afar.
> We with our *rebbe* will sit in Paradise,
> And you, libertines, will sweat in the dark.
> You will suffer terrible afflictions there in Hell.
> Really there would be no great loss, if you just dropped dead—I
>   assure you.

Leibele issues forth with a complete act of accusation against the Hasidim. He lists all the wrongs with which the *maskilim* of that era used to charge the Hasidim and exclaims at the end:

> No! Such Hasidism is like the melted snow;
> It is worth just as much as an empty egg-shell.

Leibele attacks with special anger the *rebbes* and *gute Yidn*:

> Oh! Dismal are the years and the days
> For him who accustoms himself to walk in such a path.
> Does he not understand by himself that the "ransom" to the *rebbe*
>   does no good at all?
> It is no more than that the *guter Yid* sucks out the little blood
>   [left]—
> They can do the work well, quite cleverly,
> But as for help—like hell! Just as much as a fly . . .

Like Levinsohn and Aksenfeld, Fishelsohn also stresses that the cult of the *tzaddik* paralyzes the active will among the Hasidism. They always rely on the *rebbe*'s miracles, do not think of any effective work, are content with pernicious means of earning a living that hang in the air, and cheating the peasant is, among them, not at all a wicked deed. Leibele Filozof in this connection especially emphasizes that one must not forget "that the gentile works hard and bitterly," and he preaches to the people:

> Just think, from the time that he [the peasant] is born
> Until, poor soul, he is lost from the world,
> His bitter work and the great toil,
> At the end the Jew comes and takes it away from him.

The author is sure that the young people will no longer allow themselves to be caught in the net of Hasidism, and he concludes the *Teater* with the statement that the *yeshivah*-students who were present "reflected upon the words they heard from Leibele" and concluded that Leibele

> Is quite clever, truly, in philosophy,
> And our beggarly Hasidim
> Are, indeed, idlers, great fools . . .

From the quotations that have been given, the reader may become convinced that Fishelsohn writes in a purely popular speech that is strongly colored with the peculiarities of the Polish dialect. Fishelsohn's Yiddish is absolutely free of "Daytshmerish" expressions. On the other hand, however, it is mingled with Slavisms, insofar as these made themselves at home in the spoken folk-language. His lines flow freely and easily, but refuse to know anything of meter and rhythm. Fishelsohn does not have in mind any aesthetic purpose, any art. For him the main thing is the moral lesson. His sole object is to enlighten, to free people from "foolish superstitions." But other goals were set for himself by Fishelsohn's friend to whom he dedicated his *Teater Fun Khasidim*, Shelomoh Hirtz of Zamosc, or Solomon Ettinger, who is so well known in Yiddish literature.

Ettinger was born in Warsaw at the end of 1800 or the beginning of 1801[41] into a prestigious rabbinic family. Becoming an orphan while still a child, he was raised by his uncle Mendel Ettinger, who was rabbi in Lentshne. As a result of his brilliant capacities, the young Solomon was renowned as an excellent student. At the age of fifteen he was married off, and he moved to Zamosc to be maintained at the home of his wealthy father-in-law Jehudah Leib Gold. We have already spoken[42] of the significance of Zamosc as a

---

41. On differences of opinion regarding the determination of Ettinger's year of birth, see M. Weinreich, *Shloyme Etingers Ksovim*, 585-588; M. Wiener in *Bibliologishn Zamlbukh*, 1931, 125-127.
42. Above, p. 183; see also J. Shatzky, *Pinkes*, 1928, pp. 281-282.

center of Haskalah. Hence, it is not surprising that the talented young Ettinger soon began to associate with the local *maskilim*, became familiar with the Haskalah literature, and gradually studied German. One must, in this connection, point to the following characteristic feature: the young *maskil* did not write high-flown Hebrew rhetorical pieces, but obtained a reputation with his Yiddish witticisms, epigrams, and mocking-poems. He was also a good draftsman and made portraits of friends and acquaintances.

Several years later his father-in-law died, and Ettinger, who, in the meantime, had already become burdened with several children, began thinking about a source of livelihood. He traveled to Odessa, where his wife's prosperous brother lived. The brother-in-law, who had a woman from Brody as his wife, received the young *maskil* in extremely friendly fashion but did not succeed in finding employment for him. Ettinger's new acquaintances in Odessa, who had close relationships with Galicia, advised him to go to Lemberg to study medicine. The young man arrived at the medical institute of Lemberg around 1825 and completed his studies in 1830. The "cheerful Zalomo," as Ettinger was called among his colleagues, did not restrict himself to the study of medicine and the German language in Lemberg. There the idea of becoming a writer in Yiddish also matured in him.

In the very important document first published[43] by Max Weinreich and written in Ettinger's own hand—a prospectus for the edition of his works—Ettinger himself explains under what circumstances and for what reasons he decided to become a writer:

Some years ago I read in Lemberg two little books. One was called *Di Genarte Velt*,[44] and the other *Alter-Leib*.[45] Both little books were translated, and completely reworked from German into Yiddish . . . I realized that these little books pleased a great many people, namely, both those who were very knowledgeable and those who were ordinary persons. The first group, I conjectured, had to be pleased thereby because they saw something that they had not hitherto seen written in the Yiddish language; and the others—because they were reading a storybook. Whether these little books were made well or not, I do not wish for many reasons to say, but each person will himself realize that at least the plan of writing in the common Yiddish language had to please me, because I immediately made an experiment to test whether it is in my power also to write in this fashion and in this language. The first thing that I wrote were several parables and aphorisms (in German these are called *Epigramme*). I saw that they pleased the public greatly. They grabbed everything that I

43. *Shloyme Etingers Ksovim*, XXVIII-XXIX.
44. See our *History*, Vol. IX, p. 23.
45. See above, p. 150.

wrote and each one copied it but, as usual, full of defects and mistakes. When I saw this I took counsel with myself, and by myself devised many parables and epigrams and, finally, a whole theater-piece.

In the previous chapter we noted how Aksenfeld in a written statement of his (to the minister Uvarov) noted that he sets for himself the task of freeing his brethren from the errors in which they live, showing them the barbarism of their "superstitions," and especially "exerting himself to save them from the pernicious effect of the Hasidim."

These written statements of Ettinger and Aksenfeld show very clearly how completely different were these two most important writers of neo-Yiddish literature in the era before Mendele Mocher Seforim. Aksenfeld, with his militant temperament, intended above all enlightenment, the bringing of utility. Ettinger's is an artistic nature. The instinct of an artist arouses in him the drive to produce such things as will *please* and will prove popular among the people. He himself relates in his just-quoted prospectus how he used to give what he had written to be read by persons who were very competent and had already read a great many books in other languages, and then again to persons who were quite ordinary and knew nothing more than the Yiddish language, "in order that I might hear from each one what he will say about it. The competent and clever people praised it in their fashion, and the common people in their fashion."[46]

Ettinger is among the few of the *maskilim* of that generation for whom the question of language did not exist at all. The artist's instinct brought him to the conclusion that he could enjoy life to the full artistically only in the mother-tongue, the language of the masses of the people. And that this instinct did not deceive him is, indeed, proven by his literary attempts in German and Hebrew— attempts that are total failures, without the slightest literary value. Ettinger, naturally, understands quite well that the Yiddish language is still raw and slightly polished from a literary point of view and, in fact, notes in a letter to an acquaintance of his how difficult it is "to write something rich in genius" in a "verbally poor" language "for a nation that lacks mythology, world history, and natural history."[47] Hence, Ettinger, indeed, gave himself the task of setting aside this "difficulty."[48] He felt summoned to enrich the "verbally poor" language, to transform it into the suitable instrument for artistic creation.

46. *Shloyme Etingers Ksovim*, I, XXVIII-XXIX.
47. *Ibid.*, II, 567.
48. On Ettinger's achievements in the field of Jewish vocabulary, see Weinreich in *Shloyme Etingers Ksovim*, I, XXXI.

Very interesting in this respect is the following point. Aaron Wolfsohn-Halle, Eliezer Liebermann, and many other *maskilim* of that time noted that one must pray in a *pure* language,[49] i.e., either in Hebrew or in a European language, but not in the "corrupted jargon." Ettinger considers it superfluous to debate this question; for him it is clear that the believing person ought to pray in his mother-tongue. But, with his artistic sense, he feels that liturgical prayers must not be composed in the same style as one talks in the marketplace. Hence, he follows a quite different way than Mendel Lefin (Levin) in his translation of the Bible.[50] Ettinger projected a new translation of the prayerbook into Yiddish. This translation was to be a true literary achievement; unfortunately, however, he did not carry his undertaking through. Only a few fragments are preserved. So that the reader may have some notion of the artistic seriousness with which Ettinger approached this work, we here present two examples of his projected translation of the *Siddur*:

(1) מה טובו אהליך יעקב: ווי גוט זיינען דיינע געצעלטן, יעקב, דיינע וווינונגען, ישראל! און איך קום אַצינד מיט דיין גרויסן חסד אין דיין הויז אריין, און בוק זיך צו דיין הייליקן טעמפל מיט גרויס יראה. גאט! איך האב ליב דאס הויז, וואו דו וווינסט, און דאס ארט, וואו דיין כבוד רוט, און איך וויל מיך ניגן און וועל קניען; איך וועל קניען פאר גאט מיין באשעפער. און ווען איך בעט צו דיר, גאט, לאז זיין דעמאלט א באוויליקע צייט, און מיט דיין גרויסן חסד, מיין האר, ענטפער מיר מיט א ווארער הילף.

(1) How goodly are your tents, O Jacob, your dwelling places, O Israel! And I come now with Your great lovingkindness into Your house and bow toward Your holy temple with great reverence. O God! I love Your house where You dwell and the place where Your glory rests, and I wish to bow and will bend the knee; I will bend the knee before God my Creator. And when I pray to You, O God, let it then be an acceptable time, and with Your great lovingkindness, my Lord, answer me with true help.

(2) די תפילה „אני קראתיך כי תענני": איך רוף צו דיר, וואָרעם דו וועסט מיר ענפערן גאָט, נייג דיין אויער צו מיר, הער מיינע רייד. איך, איך זע דיין פנים פול מיט גערעכטיקייט, און תיכף, ווי איך דערוואך, וועד איך זאָט פון דיין געשטאַלט, וואָרעם איך פארזיכער מיך נאר אויף דיר, גאט! איך זאג תמיד: דו ביסט מיין האר, הער דאס קול פון מיין געבעט, ווען איך שריי צו דיר, ווען איך הייב אויף מיין האנט צו דיין הייליקן פּאלאַץ. גאט מיין האר, איך האב שוין צו דיר געבעטן און דו האסט מיך געהיילט; נאר צו דיר, גאט, וועל איך רופן, נאר צו דיר, גאָט, וועל איך בעטן. זאל ליכטיק זיין דיין פנים איבער דיין קנעכט און העלף מיר מיט דיין חסד, וואָרעם

49. See our *History*, Vol. IX, p. 249.
50. See our *History*, Vol. IX, pp. 215 ff.

צו דיר, גאט, האף איך, אז דו וועסט מיר ענטפערן, גאט מיין האר. הער צו מיין
געבעט, גאט, און פארנעם מיין געשריי, שווייג ניט צו מיינע טרערן, הער מיך צו,
גאט, און לייטזעליק מיך, גאט! און בלייב מיין העלפער!

(2) The prayer *Ani Keraticha Ki Ta'aneni*: I call to You because You will answer me. O God, incline Your ear to me, hear my words. I, I see Your face filled with righteousness and immediately, when I awaken, I am satisfied by Your form, for I trust only in You, O God! I say always: You are my Lord, hear the voice of my prayer when I cry to You, when I raise my hand to Your holy palace. O God, my Lord, I have already prayed to You and You have healed me; only to You, God, will I pray. Let Your face be radiant over Your servant and help me with Your lovingkindness, for in You, O God, do I hope that you will answer me, O God, my Lord. Listen to my prayer, O God, and accept my cry, do not be silent at my tears, listen to me, O God, and be gracious to me, O God. And remain my helper!

It would be a mistake, however, to think that the aesthete Ettinger, who, with colossal effort, polished every word, every expression, was completely free of enlightening tendencies and did not have in mind any moral lessons with his work. After all, one must not forget that Ettinger spent his youth in the environment of the *maskilim* of Zamosc and Galicia and lived all his days under the direct influence of the German enlightening literature. The influence of Lessing is discernible with special strength in his writing. Characteristic in this respect is the following point. The favorite genres in which Ettinger liked to write were dramatic works, then proverbs and epigrams; and, indeed, Lessing not only produced much in these realms but also wrote many treatises on "dramaturgy" as well as "on the fable."[51] And many of Ettinger's fables and epigrams are, in fact, reworkings of Lessing and of other German writers of the Enlightenment era.[52]

But the fact that Ettinger very frequently employs foreign themes for his parables and tales in no way diminishes their value, just as it does not diminish Krylov's or La Fontaine's fables, in which the theme is also mainly taken from alien sources. Ettinger always manages to clothe the strange material in a highly national garb, and it becomes a genuine work of art. It suffices, for instance, to mention his splendid satires *Vitele* and *Di Frume Bern*. In *Vitele* Ettinger employed Gellert's *Die Betschwester*. The German pietist

---

51. See Lessing's works *Hamburgische Dramaturgie* and *Abhandlungen über die Fabel.*
52. On Ettinger's borrowing of themes and reworking of foreign sources, see M. Weinreich in the introduction to *Shloyme Etingers Ksovim* and also in his *Bilder Fun Der Yidisher Literatur-Geshikhte*, 280-291; M. Wiener in his able work *"Di Oysgabe Fun Etingers Shriftn"* in *Bibliologishn Zamlbukh.*

Beate is transformed, under Ettinger's skillful hand, into the pious woman Vitele, with all her gestures and base hypocrisy; he portrays how "out of piety she refuses to give charity." Also in *Di Frume Bern* the theme is taken from abroad (from the French fable-poet Jean Pierre Claris de Florian). With Ettinger, however, they become truly "Jewish" bears. The satire carries an exclusively Jewish coloration with the authentically Jewish conclusion that such rabbinic judges (*dayyanim*) are "only foolish beasts."

The same is the case with Ettinger's numerous proverbs and parables. The themes or subjects are mainly taken from German fable-poets—Gellert, Lessing, and others. But Ettinger always succeeds in weaving the foreign theme into a genuinely Jewish national tapestry, and we obtain a truly *Jewish* fable with a truly Jewish moral lesson. As illustration, it is sufficient to mention Ettinger's fable "Di Tsvey Hener." This is in fact a paraphrase of Gellert's *Die beiden Wächter*,[53] in which it is related how two night-watchmen beat each other murderously because of their differences of opinion about the way in which one ought to call out: "*Verwahrt* (preserve) the fire and the light" or "*Bewahrt* (also, preserve) the fire and the light." In Ettinger the night-watchmen are transformed in Jewish fashion into two roosters who dispute obstinately about the right way of crowing: kikereki, or kookoorekoo:

> What, cries one, will he even distort words
> And crow "kikereki," not "kookoorekoo?"
> Wait, I will let him have it
> For crowing with errors!
> I, cries the other rooster,
> Have always crowed "kikereki;"
> Every rooster can testify for me,
> Who has heard the crowing of my grandfathers
> Whom you must immerse yourself in cleansing water ten times
> To mention their names—
> That they crowed "kikereki,"
> And not with crude errors like you!

And at the end comes this purely Jewish moral:

> Among our scholars and rabbis
> One also sometimes finds such fools
> Who almost tear each other's hair out
> And quarrel away for many years
> And insult each other for whole epochs
> Over what a letter may mean . . .

53. See M. Wiener, *op. cit.*, 129-130.

Thus, in consequence of the sensitivity of the realistic artist that Ettinger possessed, his fables and ingenious epigrams obtain at times a militantly satirical tone, and in places socially pointed, belligerent motifs are heard. It suffices to mention such poems as "Asuse" or "Der Rosh Hakohol," who boasts:

> For me everyone must have respect,
> Because I can "bury" everyone.
> I have no fear
> Of the rabbi's court,
> For the principle "There is justice in Israel"
> Does not apply in the case of a head of a community.
> I may do what I please,
> Everyone must be silent.

In his fables Ettinger also touches on the problem of raising children ("Dos Katshkele") and freqently pokes fun at the "family distinction" or "pedigree," so popular among Jews (the fables: "Dos Zekl," "Di Aseyfe," "Der Gildn")

Not without reason does he say:

> I laugh at everything that takes place,
> And if anything is missing
> About which to give a laugh—
> I myself laugh at myself.

This, indeed, Ettinger does in his epigrams. From his biography, it is known that he was not particularly happy in his family life; his constantly irascible wife embittered his life. So he complains, in fact, in his epigram "In Haybl":

> By his own wife to have one's life made miserable,
> Day and night to hear only wicked words—
> It is better not to have been born at all . . .

And in the epigram "Bay Mayn Geburts-Tog" the poet relates how he sits and thinks:

> Why has my hair
> Still not lost its complete blackness?
> It is, after all, now forty-three years
> Since I was born into the world.
> But I have a very small explanation:
> They become blackened along with me.

We pointed out previously how in Ettinger's parables and

epigrams the enlightening tendencies of that time are prominently discernible. The objective literary scholar, however, must not be silent about the fact that, along with these tendencies, there are also to be noted in Ettinger's poetic creations all the limitations of the householderly, *maskil*-like world-view. So, for instance, Ettinger in his fable "Di Tsvey Ferdlekh" comes to the moral lesson that one must certainly have a master over him and may not forget "that the master gives him to eat," and one who wishes "to be rid of the master" will have a bitter end, "like two other stubborn horses." In the long fable "Der Indik" Ettinger teaches us that one must not dream about distant places and foreign lands, because

> You must not forget the places
> Where your ancestors dwelled.
> There, where you were born,
> There shall you die.

Especially characteristic is Ettinger's fable "Di Shmates." We noted previously how Aksenfeld regarded the recruitment law. Ettinger, however, like many other *maskilim*, received with great enthusiasm the report that "they are now taking Jews for military service." He strongly reproves his brethren who regard the new ukase as a grievous oppression and "both young and old, all scream: Let us weep, let us lament, let us run to recite Psalms, let us take out the scrolls of the Torah; let us go 'tear up' graves" [i.e., implore the intercession of the saintly dead, thereby disturbing their rest]. And he lectures the Jewish recruit:

> Only obey the officers
> And diligently learn drilling.
> Only be ever prepared
> Even to run into the fire
> To carry out the king's plan;
> For the good men who go about in crowns
> Do know how to recompense everyone.

This limitation of Ettinger's world-view is also discernible even in his masterpiece, *Serkele*—the highest artistic achievement of the neo-Yiddish literature of the period before Mendele Mocher Seforim.

Serkele is a play of life-style. The central figure, Serkele, is a benighted, morally corrupt owner of a flour-shop who becomes, through swindlery, newly rich. Her brother, David Guthertz, a wealthy merchant, travels to distant countries and spends a rather long time there. Serkele thinks he has died abroad, and so she composes a forged will according to which Guthertz supposedly bequeathed his entire fortune to her and completely left out his own daughter Hinde. The newly rich woman treats the poor Hinde very badly and pampers her own only daughter—her vain, foolish daughter Freyde-Altele, for whom she seeks a distinguished match. The match is concluded with the aid of Yoḥanan Shadkhen with the swindler-speculator Gabriel, who steals from Serkele a chest of jewelry. Serkele casts the guilt on Hinde and her beloved, the student Marcus. In the last act David Guthertz returns from his distant journey. Serkele's intrigue is revealed, the speculator Gabriel is unmasked, and the play ends with three weddings at the same time.

Like Aksenfeld, Ettinger also constructed his play according to the model of the German bourgeois, or middle-class, theater repertoire of the 1820s. But with Ettinger's play the same thing happens as with his parables. As a true artist, he manages to create from a foreign theme and borrowed motifs a completely new, original work. Over a hundred years have now passed since Ettinger produced his "completely new theater piece," and to the present day *Serkele* belongs to the most artistic plays that Yiddish literature possesses. To this day the brilliant composition of Ettinger's play, the great mastery with which he portrays his figures, are marveled at. Euchel and Aksenfeld, for instance, endeavor to render with photographic precision the manner of speech of their old-fashioned characters whom they copied directly from real life. They note down with the greatest exactness all the speech-gestures which they overheard among the characters whom they portray. But Ettinger, as a genuine master of literary form, uses word-construction as a painter uses colors in order to render the most subtle nuances and peculiarities of his types.[54]

The speech style of Serkele, of Gabriel Hendler, of Yoḥanan Shadkhen, of Shmelke Troinayks, is artistically individualized; in every speech one senses the hand of an authentic master. But all this is merely in regard to the more or less negative characters, or in

54. In his thorough work on Aksenfeld, M. Wiener carries through the following excellent comparison between Aksenfeld and Ettinger: "Aksenfeld is sometimes more precise and detailed, up to minute points, in the realistic catching of the phrasing of his characters, imitating their manner of speech without special inventiveness and formulation. Ettinger, however, is incomparably superior to Aksenfeld as far as artistic authenticity, artistically harmonized naturalness, symmetry in construction and composition, and organically developed climax, are concerned. He is as much superior to Aksenfeld as an important, developed, realistic artist is superior to a naive, primitive genre-painter. Ettinger's humor is sharply pointed, polished, excellent, fine, organized with an expert and sure hand; his wit is gracious and playful. Aksenfeld's humor comes out, by comparison with Ettinger's, drawn out, palely parodying, and awkward, with the stress mainly on the comedy of gesticulation, and not on the more refined comedy of word" (*Aksenfelds Verk*, I, 64).

portraying common persons—for instance, servants and maid-servants. But where Ettinger tries to portray positive figures of his own enlightening milieu, he stands at the limit of his possibilities. His Marcus Redlich (a student who is preparing to become a doctor) is no less schematic and bloodless than Marcus in Euchel's comedy.

Besides *Serkele*, Ettinger conceived two other theater pieces, but he did not complete these, because he lost hope of seeing his works in print. Here we touch on Ettinger's life-drama. His works during his own lifetime suffered the same bitter fate as Aksenfeld's compositions.

We noted previously that Ettinger, as early as the beginning of the 1840s, reported in a special prospectus that he is soon handing over into print "a theater piece in five acts and parables and epigrams." He promises, along therewith, "that he will not be content with this" and will "still always deliver new things, namely, theater pieces, stories, parables, epigrams, and still other things of this fashion." But nothing came of all these plans. Ettinger's fate brought it about that in his own lifetime he would not see a single line of his printed.[55]

Crown Poland, in fact, did not know of any printing monopoly. In Warsaw alone there were at that time four Jewish presses. The censor of Jewish books was Ettinger's good friend, Jacob Tugend-hold, the enlightener and battler for culture who is already known to us. Nevertheless, Ettinger did not manage to realize his loveliest hope: through the printing press, to make his work accessible to a large circle of readers. It was not the printers with their fanaticism who were responsible for this, but, in fact, Ettinger's friend, the highly cultured censor Jacob Tugendhold. It sounds almost like an necdote, but in Nicholas I's Russia all of life consisted of such tragic anecdotes.

According to the constitution which Alexander I bestowed on Crown Poland, books could appear freely without censorship—with the exception of Jewish books. These had to be strictly censored because, after all, it is a well-known thing that they contain "the most pernicious teaching, and also such ideas as are in complete contradiction with the good intentions of the govern-

---

55. However, while Ettinger was still alive, his works were very extensively disseminated in numerous copies. The journalist Neimanowitz (Hanetz), well known in his time, writes about Ettinger's parables, poems and dramas: "They went about from hand to hand, until the manuscripts spread into all the towns of Poland. And in the long nights of the month of Tevet people used to read them in practically every family which had just become infected with intelligence" (*Ha-Tzefirh*, 1888, No. 19).

ment."[56] At the beginning of the 1820s, the Italian, very anti-Semitically-minded Father Ludvic Ciarini was appointed president of the censorship committee for Hebrew and Yiddish books. Ciarini, however, had no great knowledge of Hebrew, so that the actual censor of Jewish books was the secretary of the committee, Jacob Tugendhold. After the Polish uprising of 1831 the censorship became considerably sharper. Jews were suspected of siding with the Poles; from all sides denunciations were submitted against Jewish publications. And in 1837 a special committee whose task was to consider how to struggle against "the malicious fanaticism of the Jews" was convened. A new edition of *Ḥoshen Mishpat* (a part of the *Shulḥan Aruch*) was even issued, from which many "harmful passages" were thrown out.[57] Even worse were the censorship conditions at the beginning of the 1840s when the apostate Chersker, a grim enemy of the Jews, was appointed a member of the censorship committee.

Just a year earlier there was published at a Warsaw press, with the permission of Jacob Tugendhold, a new edition of the well-known *Shevet Yehudah*.[58] Soon a denunciation was submitted that the edition is filled with slanders against Christianity and with attacks on the Russian czar. Hence, application was made to the member of the committee Chersker to express his view. He concluded that the accusation is fully grounded and expressed the opinion that Tugendhold should be handed over to the court and his fortune confiscated. Through great effort Tugendhold managed to absolve himself of the denunciation. Chersker, however, carried his hostile policy in regard to Jewish books further.

Under such conditions it is quite understandable that Tugendhold kept on trembling and, out of fear of denunciations and slanders, was terribly severe and, in the most innocent texts, battled with the red pencil against sedition and blasphemy of God; he even concluded that it is not permissible to rely on the Vilna censor, and that the Jewish books transported from Vilna to Poland must be censored once again. To obtain some notion of how the timorous Jacob Tugendhold struggled against "sedition," it is worthwhile to compare the text of the *Bobe-Mayse* in the Vilna editions with the Warsaw edition of 1849 which Tugendhold censored. He was even afraid of the fact that in the story there are such "holy" titles as king, queen, duke—and the Hebrew *melech* and *malkah*—and so he changed them into Oriental titles or, wherever

56. See B. Weinryb's work, "Zur Geschichte des Buchdruckers und der Zensor bei den Juden in Polen, *MGWJ*, 1933, 273–300.
57. Weinryb, *op. cit.*, I, 287.
58. See our *History*, Vol. IV.

possible, erased them completely. When in the Vilna edition, for instance, it is related "the king was called by his name Duke Guidon," this is changed by the Warsaw censor to: "The *bashe* (pasha) was called by the name Guidon." The sentence, "The queen was named Brandaya," is improved to read, "The woman was called Brandaya." Brandaya, after all, killed her own husband—now, how can a "queen" do such a thing? "He was a rich king" becomes "He was a rich official," etc., etc.[59]

At virtually the same time as Tugendhold had to absolve himself from the accusation regarding the *Shevet Yehudah* edition, Ettinger's good friend Anton Eisenbaum, the editor of the *Beobachter an der Weichsel*, who is already familiar to us, submitted (on May 24, 1843) a petition to the curator of the Warsaw educational district requesting permission to print Ettinger's *Serkele* and *Meshalim*. "Such works," he wrote, "are accessible to all classes of Jews. They set forth in living colors the defects and ridiculous things, they portray excellently and comically the whole Jewish way of speaking, and therefore they can have a redemptive (*bardzo zbawienny*) influence on minds."[60]

In this connection Ettinger especially placed his hopes on the influence of Tugendhold, with whom he was on friendly terms. But he soon had to become persuaded how bitterly mistaken he was. The grim enemy of the Jews Chersker and the pusillanimous careerist Tugendhold vied with each other in demonstrating what strict censors they were. Tugendhold ruled over Ettinger's manuscript with the same wildly foolish barbarism as six years later he did in the *Bobe-Mayse* text. Also in Ettinger's parables, for instance, the word "king" must not be mentioned as an epithet for the lion. "Monarch" is changed to "rich man," "queenly green" is improved by the censor to "ace-green." "Freedom" is an overly dangerous word, so it is exchanged by the "enlightener" Tugendhold for "delight." Even the comic *Vogelfreiheit* in Friedrich's monologue in the last act is erased by the strict censor and improved to "joy." "Apostasy tricks" is exchanged by the censor for "thievish tricks." And a sentence such as "He who deals [i.e., goes into partnership] with his father-in-law sleeps with the bear" is found by the censor to be overly frivolous, and instead of "sleeps" he inserts "sits." But the censors are not content merely with hundreds of "improvements" in Ettinger's text. They throw out whole stanzas from the poem "Asuse," many lines in other poems, and erase completely such epigrams as "Die Nekome," "Der Doktor Grind."

---

59. See N. Prylucki's article in *YIVO-Bleter*, III, 358-370 and our note, *ibid.*, IV, 187-188.
60. See *Shloyme Etingers Ksovim*, XXXII, 588.

Ettinger, who polished every word with such painstaking precision, was beside himself. He pours out all of his bitter heart in a Hebrew letter to a friend of his:

. . . to print the book with the improvements that the censor people have ordained I refuse, even if they were to print it for me without cost. For do my lips there—God forbid—speak evil against God and His messiah, against the kings of the earth, against their assistants, judges, and overseers? Does my tongue speak against the ways of morality, that these people have marked up my manuscript with red marks, erased, and mutilated it from beginning to end, corrupted its beauty, transformed its harmony into disgustingness? And furthermore—after all, I know that these people are cultured men who seek after knowledge, and they are goodhearted and have always been at peace with me. So I ask: What have they realized, to deal so badly with me? My book is free of any sinful thing, and if there is some defect in it, they could, after all, explain to me where I have failed, and I would either erase it or improve it . . .[61]

Through the fact that Ettinger lost hope of seeing his works printed, his drive for creativity was also weakened. He did not complete the larger works that he had conceived. With all his energy he betook himself to realizing the ideal of his youth— becoming a colonist and drawing a living from agriculture. Four kilometers from Zamosc he purchased sixty-five acres of land and settled on them with his whole family. However, he did not enjoy length of days there; in 1856 he died. But Ettinger was much more fortunate with regard to his literary legacy than Aksenfeld. Five years after Ettinger's death his comedy *Serkele* appeared in the small Prussian town of Johanisberg (in 1861) and was later several times reprinted. In the 1860s part of Ettinger's parables and epigrams were printed in *Kol Mevasser* and in the *Warschauer Jüdische Zeitung*. They were first published in collected form in 1889. In modern times (1925) the scholar of language M. Weinreich published a lovely textual-critical collected edition of all of Ettinger's writings with a great deal of effort and diligence.

Ettinger died at the very boundary of a new era. In the same year that he ended his life-path there also ended, under the thunder of the cannon at the walls of Sebastopol, the leaden, thirty-year reign of Nicholas I. The defeat at Sebastopol demonstrated most clearly how backward and rotten the economic foundations of mighty Russia were. The "epoch of great reforms," which also found a loud echo in the Jewish quarter began. Of this in the next volume.

---

61. *Etingers Ksovim*, 568.

Addenda

Note to page 65. On the critical situation in which the *maskilim*-literati found themselves after the ukase of 1836 regarding printing when, in the course of more than ten years, only a single Jewish press functioned in all of Russia, a quite clear picture is provided by the letter of the poet Adam Ha-Kohen Lebensohn written in 1843: "One must scream out," he writes in this letter, "at the great harm and injustice that was produced against the enlightenment of Jews in our lands by the fact that only a single printery was left remaining. Just as it is impossible that a star of the South Pole should shine over us here, so it cannot be conceived that a work which has to do with science and education should come forth from this press. They are not even capable of satisfying the large Jewish public with the necessary numbers of prayerbooks and *tehinnot*. Not even a single work of the earlier codifiers or of the old commentators, which is their greatest desire, has this single press managed to publish—so, what is there to speak of about science, knowledge of language, and culture?" (We quote according to S. Ginsburg, *Historishe Verk*, I, 55–56).

To page 93. The original text of Benjacob's "memorandum" about the rabbinical seminary of Vilna is published in *Fun No'entn Over*, I, 1937, 27–39.

Note to page 99. This legend to the effect that Mendel Landsberg supposedly composed *Sefer Ha-Kundes* was apparently quite widespread in the circles of the *maskilim*, and in the necrology after Landsberg's death, which was printed in *Ha-Melitz* (1866, No. 5), Zederbaum considers it necessary to point out that the deceased "in the days of his life wrote the booklet *Seder Avodat Ha-Kundes*."

Note to page 105. The manuscript of Eichenbaum's unpublished *Techunat Ha-Misparim* is in our archives.

BIBLIOGRAPHICAL NOTES

The Haskalah Movement in Russia

CHAPTER ONE

RABBI MANASSEH OF ILYA

On the Haskalah movement in general in Russia, see Lucy S. Dawidowicz, ed., *The Golden Tradition: Jewish Life and Thought in Eastern Europe* (1967); M. Erik, *Etiudn Tsu der Geshikhte Fun Der Haskole* (1934); L. Greenberg, *The Jews in Russia* Vol. 1 (1944); H. S. Kazdan, *Fun Ḥeder Un Shkoles Biz CYShO* (1956); I. Levitats, *The Jewish Community in Russia, 1772–1844* (1943); J. Meisl, *Haskala: Die Geschichte der Aufklärungsbewegung unter den Juden in Russland* (1919); D. Patterson, *The Hebrew Novel in Czarist Russia* (1964); J. S. Raisin, *The Haskalah Movement in Russia* (1913); Z. Rejzen, *Fun Mendelssohn Biz Mendele* (1923); J. Shatzky, *Kultur Geshikhte Fun der Haskole in Lite* (1950); I. Sosis, *Di Geshikhte Fun Di Yidishe Gezelshaftlikhe Shtremungen in Rusland In 19. Yohrhundert* (1929); S. Spiegel, *Hebrew Reborn* (1930); and B. D. Weinryb, "East European Jewry (Since the Partitions of Poland, 1772–1795)," in L. Finkelstein, ed., *The Jews: Their History, Culture, and Religion*, 3rd ed., I (1966), 321–375.

The largest part of Rabbi Manasseh of Ilya's literary remains were destroyed in a fire in 1884, but some extracts were included in the second volume of *Alfei Menasheh* (1904), published by his grandson Isaac Spalter.

A biography of Manasseh of Ilya, entitled *Ben Porat*, was written by one of the first Lithuanian *maskilim*, M. Plungian, and published in Vilna in 1858.

On Manasseh and his work, see also B. Katz, *Rabbanut, Ḥasidut, Haskalah*, 2 (1958), 187–203; J. Klausner, *Historyah Shel Ha-Safrut Ha-Ivrit Ha-Ḥadashah*, 3 (1953), 25–32; R. Mahler, *Divrei Yemei Yisrael Ba-Dorot Ha-Aharonim*, 4 (1956), 63–68; Z. Rejzen, *Fun Mendelsohn Biz Mendele* (1923), 183–260; S. Rosenfeld in *Ha-Tekufah*, II (1918), 250-88; and S. I. Stanislavski, in *Ha-Shiloah*, XVIII (1908), 274–77.

CHAPTER TWO

ISAAC BAER LEVINSOHN

David Bernhard Nathanson's biography of Isaac Baer Levinsohn, *Sefer Ha-Zichronot*, went through nine editions between 1876 and 1900.

On Levinsohn's *Te'udah Be-Yisrael* and *Bet Yehudah*, see L. S. Greenberg, *A Critical Investigation of the Works of Rabbi Isaac Baer Levinsohn* (1930), which includes a bibliography and a complete list of the works of the great pioneering figure of Haskalah in Russia.

For further discussions of Levinsohn and his work, see M. Erik and A. Rozenzweig, *Di Yidishe Literatur in 19. Yohrhundert, Ershter Bukh: 1800–1881* (1935), 38–50; D. M. Hermalin, *Yitzkhok Ber Levinsohn: Zayn Biografye, Zayne Sforim . . . Un Virkung Oyf Zayn Dor Un Zayne Nokhfolger* (1916); J. Klausner, *Historyah Shel Ha-Safrut Ha-Ivrit Ha-Hadashah*, 3 (1952), 33-115 (includes bibliography); J. Lestschinsky, *Dos Yidishe Ekonomishe Leben In Der Yidisher Literatur, Heft I: Ribal Un Aksenfeld* (1922); P. Lipovsky (Ben-Amram), *Rayon Ha-Avodah Ba-Safrut Ha-Ivrit* (1930), 23–31, R. Mahler, *Ha-Hasidut Ve-Haskalah* (1961), Index; J. S. Raisin, *The Haskalah Movement in Russia* (1913), 204-13; Z. Rejzen, *Fun Mendelssohn Biz Mendele* (1923), 235–286; idem, "Tzu der Geshikhte Fun Der Yidisher Haskole-Literatur," *YIVO-Bleter* I (1931), 193–207; A. Shaanan, *Ha-Safrut Ha-Ivrit Ha-Hadashah Le-Zeramehah*, I (1962), 187–90; N. Shtif, *Di Eltere Yidishe Literatur (Literarishe Khrestomatye)*, 1929, 21–35; S. Spiegel, *Hebrew Reborn* (1930), 167–72; and M. Waxman, *A History of Jewish Literature* 3 (1960 ed.), 202–13.

CHAPTER THREE

LEVINSOHN'S COMMUNAL ACTIVITY; MAX LILIENTHAL

The third edition of Levinsohn's *Di Hefker-Velt*, published in Warsaw in 1903, contains a *"Lebens-Beshraybung Fun Ribal,"* 3-29.

Levinsohn's *Efes Damim* was published in an English translation in London on the occasion of the Damascus blood libel (1841) by L. Loewe under the title *Efes Dammim: A series of conversations at Jerusalem between a patriarch of the Greek church and a chief rabbi of the Jews, concerning the malicious charge against the Jews of using Christian blood.*

Efes Damim was translated into German from the Hebrew under the title *Die Blutlüge*, with a foreword and notes by A. Katz (189-?). It was also translated into German from the Russian by M. Friedländer under the title *Das Damokles-Schwert* (1884).

On Max Lilienthal's educational activities in Russia, see S. M. Dubnow, *A History of the Jews in Russia and Poland*, 2 (1918), 50–59; S. M. Ginsburg, "Max Lilienthal's Activities in Russia: New Documents," *Publications of the American Jewish Historical Society* (1939), 39-51; J. I. Hessen, "I. B. Levinsohn and Dr. M. Lilienthal" (in Russian), *Perezhitoye* III (1911), 1-37; idem, *Die russische Regierung und die westeuropäischen Juden. Zur Schulreform in Russland 1840-44. Nach archivalischen Materialen* (1913); idem, *Istoriya Yeyreyev v Rosii* (1914), 224-230; D. Kahana, in *Ha-Shiloaḥ*, XXVII (1913), 314-22, 446-57, 546-56; I. Loeb, "M. Lilienthal et la Russie," *REJ*, IV (1882), 308-319; D. Philipson, "Max Lilienthal in Russia," *Hebrew Union College Annual*, XII-XIII (1937-38), 825-839; J. S. Raisin, *The Haskalah Movement in Russia* (1913), 171-181; L. Scheinhaus, *Ein deutscher Pionier: Dr. Lilienthals Kulturversuch in Russland* (1911); J. Shatzky, *Yidishe Bildungs-Politik In Poyln Fun 1806 Biz 1866* (1943), 71-80; P. Wiernik, "Max Lilienthal and the Educational Plans of the Russian Government," *The Jewish Forum*, I (1918), 540-49; and I. Zinberg, "Isaac Baer Levinsohn and His Time" (Russian), *Yevreyskaya Starina*, III (1910), 504-541 (deals extensively with Max Lilienthal).

CHAPTER FOUR

M. A. GÜNZBURG, ADAM HA-KOHEN AND MICAH JOSEPH LEBENSOHN, ABRAHAM MAPU

Among the major works of M. A. Günzburg are two volumes entitled *Devir* (1844 and 1862) which include letters by Goethe, Börne, and Heine; a translation of the letters of Sir Moses Montefiore's personal secretary, Dr. Eliezer Halevi, who accompanied the Anglo-Jewish philanthropist on his first trip to Palestine; and essays on the little-known Jewish communities of the Arab countries, Ethiopia, and China. Günzberg was also the author of an interesting autobiography *Aviezer* (1864), written in the style of Rousseau's *Confessions*, as well as *Ittotei Rusya* (1839), *Ha-Tzarefatim Be-Rusya* (1843), on the Russian invasion of France in 1812, and *Pi Ha-Ḥirot* (1845) a history of the wars of 1813-1815. In

1911 J. Fichman edited a selection of Günzburg's writings, *Ketavim Nivharim*.

On Günzburg, see J. Fichman, in M. Günzburg, *Ketavim Nivharim* (1911), Introduction; J. Klausner, *Historyah Shel Ha-Safrut Ha-Ivrit Ha-Hadashah*, 3 (1960 ed.), 120–70; D. Magid, *M. A. Günzburg, 1795-1846, und seine literarische Thätigkeit . . . Eine biographische Skizze* (1897); idem, *Rabbi Mordechai Aharon Günzburg* (Hebrew, 1897), includes bibliography; J. S. Raisin, *The Haskalah Movement in Russia* (1913), 213-21; and S. L. Zitron, *Yotzrei Ha-Safrut Ha-Ivrit Ha-Hadashah: Toledoteihem, Yetziroteihem, Signonam, Ve-Erech Pe'ulatam* (1924), 114-142.

Jacob Eichenbaum's collection of Hebrew poems and translations, *Kol Zimrah* (1836), was one of the first books of poetry to be published in the Haskalah era. His long poem on chess *Ha-Kerav* (1839) was translated into Russian. Only a part of Eichenbaum's textbook on mathematics *Hochmat Ha-Shi'urim* was published (1857). His poem *Ha-Kosem*, which was originally published in installments in *Ha-Melitz*, also appeared as a book (1863).

A six-volume collection of the poems of Adam Ha-Kohen Lebensohn and those of his son Micah Joseph was published in 1895 under the title *Kol Shirei Adam U-Michal*. A photo-offset edition of selections from Adam Ha-Kohen Lebensohn's *Shirei Sefat Kodesh*, vols. 1-2 (1895), was issued in Tel Aviv under the title *Mivhar Shirim Adam Ha-Kohen Lebensohn* (1966).

Joseph Klausner discusses Adam Ha-Kohen Lebensohn in his *Historyah Shel Ha-Safrut Ha-Ivrit Ha-Hadashah*, 3 (1953), 171-227 (see pp. 190-92 for an annotated list of the poet's works, and pp. 171-73 for a bibliography).

On Lebensohn, see also J. Fichman, *Anshei Vesorah* (1938); M. Michaeli, *Ha-Adam U-Fa'alo* (1963), 43-62; N. H. Rosenbloom, in *Perakim*, II (1959), 151-71, III (1962), 141-167; A. Shaanan, *Ha-Safrut Ha-Ivrit Ha-Hadashah Li-Zeramehah*, I (1962), 200–06; H. N. Steinschneider, in *Kol Shirei Adam U-Michal* (1895), 6–16; and S. L. Zitron, *Yotzrei Ha-Safrut Ha-Ivrit Ha-Hadashah* (1924), 5–34.

Kalman Schulman wrote an abridged Hebrew translation of Eugène Suë's *Mystères de Paris* (1857-60) which was very popular and went through several editions. He was also the adapter and translator of a nine-volume history of the world, *Divrei Yemei Olam* (1867-84) based on Georg Weber and other German historians. In addition, Schulman translated some of Josephus' work from German into Hebrew (1861-63), and published a series of books and compilations on the history of Palestine and its surroundings, *Toledot Hachmei Yisrael* (4 vols., 1873-78).

On Schulman, see J. Klausner, *Historyah Shel Ha-Safrut Ha-Ivrit Ha-Ḥadashah*, 3 (1953), 361-88; A. Shaanan, *Ha-Safrut Ha-Ivrit Ha-Ḥadashah Li-Zeramehah*, I (1962), 219-22; idem, *Iyyunim Bi-Safrut Ha-Haskalah* (1952), 141-48; and G. Kressel, *Leksikon Ha-Safrut Ha-Ivrit Ba-Dorot Ha-Aḥaronim*, 2 (1967), 890-92.

Micah Joseph Lebensohn's poems were first collected and published in *Kol Shirei Adam U-Michal* (1895). A new edition of his poetry, letters and translations, *Shirei Michal, Iggerotav Ve-Targumav*, edited, with an introduction, by J. Fichman was published in 1962.

On Micah Joseph Lebensohn, see Fichman's introduction to *Shirei Michal* (1962), 7-39; idem, *Anshei Vesorah* (1938); H. Bavli, *Ruḥot Nifgashot* (1958), 9-14; J. Klausner, *Historyah Shel Ha-Safrut Ha-Ivrit Ha-Ḥadashah*, 3 (1953), 228-68; P. Lachower, *Toledot Ha-Safrut Ha-Ivrit Ha-Ḥadashah*, 2 (1943), 115-33; M. Michaeli, *Ha-Adam U-Fa'alo* (1963), 63-72; and S. L. Zitron, *Yotzrei Ha-Safrut Ha-Ivrit Ha-Ḥadashah* (1924), 83-113.

Abraham Mapu's collected works, *Kol Kitvei Avraham Mapu*, were published in Tel Aviv in 1950. The author's letters were issued under the title *Michtevei Avraham Mapu* by B. Dinur in 1971. English translations of Mapu's novel *Ahavat Tziyyon* have appeared under various titles: *Amnon, Prince and Peasant*, tr. by F. Jaffe (1887); *In the Days of Isaiah*, tr. by B.A. M. Schapiro in 1902 (the same translation was published later twice, in 1922 and 1930, under the title *The Shepherd Prince*); and *The Sorrows of Noma*, tr. by J. Marymont (1919).

Outlines of the plots of the three novels and brief extracts in English translation from *Ahavat Tziyyon, Ashmat Shomron*, and *Ayit Tzavu'a* are given by D. Patterson in his excellent book *Abraham Mapu: A Literary Study of the Creator of the Modern Hebrew Novel* (1964), 111-167.

On Mapu, see R. Brainin, *Avraham Mapu* (1900); J. Fichman, *Anshei Vesorah* (1938); idem, *Alufei Ha-Haskalah* (1952); J. Frank, "Le-Toledotav Shel Mapu," *Ha-Shiloah*, XXXIV (1918); J. Klausner, *Historyah Shel Ha-Safrut Ha-Ivrit Ha-Ḥadashah*, 3 (1953); 269–360 (includes bibliography); idem, *Yotzrim U-Vonim* (1925), 176–198; J. A. Klausner, *Ha-Novelah Ba-Safrut Ha-Ivrit* (1947); D. Patterson, *Abraham Mapu: A Literary Study of the Creator of the Modern Hebrew Novel* (1964); idem, *The Foundations of Modern Hebrew Literature* (1961); idem, *The Hebrew Novel in Czarist Russia* (1964); idem, "The Use of Songs in the Novels of Abraham Mapu," *Journal of Semitic Studies*, I (1956); idem, "Epistolary Elements in the Novels of Abraham Mapu," *Annual of Leeds University Oriental Society*, IV (1964); A. Shaanan, *Iyyunim Bi-Safrut Ha-Haskalah* (1952); L.

Simon, "Abraham Mapu," *JQR*, XVIII (1906), 406ff.; N. Slouschz, *The Renascence of Hebrew Literature* (1909); A. S. Waldstein, *The Evolution of Modern Hebrew Literature* (1916); and S. L. Zitron, *Yotzrei Ha-Safrut Ha-Ivrit Ha-Hadashah* (1924).

CHAPTER FIVE

ISRAEL AKSENFELD AND A. B. GOTTLOBER

Israel Aksenfeld wrote some thirty novels and plays. Unfortunately, most of them have been lost. His extant works were published in two volumes, *I. Aksenfelds Verk*, the first in 1931 and the second in 1938, under the editorship of M. Wiener. These volumes contain studies on Aksenfeld by the editor, as well as by A. Yuditzki and A. Margolis.

On Aksenfeld, see *Leksikon Fun Der Nayer Yidisher Literatur*, I (1956), 160–64; Baal-Makhshoves, *Geklibene Verk* (1953), 92–94; S. Borovoi, *Bibliologisher Zamlbukh* (1930), 93–103; idem, in the collection *Mendele Un Zayn Tsayt* (1940), 172–196; S. Ginsburg, *Filologishe Shriftn Fun YIVO*, 2 (1928), 42–54; S. Lastik, *Di Yidishe Literatur Biz Di Klasiker* (1950), 160–175; S. Niger, *Dertseylers Un Romanistn*, 1 (1946), 52–60; Z. Rejzen, *Fun Mendelssohn Biz Mendele* (1923), 355–418; J. Shatzky, in *YIVO-Bleter*, XXIII (1944), 134–137; N. Shtif, *Di Eltere Yidishe Literatur* (1929), 72–99; M. Wiener, in *I. Aksenfelds Verk*, I (1931), v-xvi, 3–142; and idem, *Tzu Der Geshikhte Fun Der Yidisher Literature In 19 Yohrhundert* (1940).

A collection of Abraham Baer Gottlober's works in Yiddish, *A. B. Gottlobers Yidishe Verk*, edited by A. Fridkin and Z. Rejzen, was published in 1927. An anthology of his Hebrew poems, original and translated, appeared in *Kol Shirei Mahalel* (1890).

On Gottlober, see *Leksikon Fun Der Nayer Yidisher Literatur*, 2 (1958), 9–13; A. Fridkin, *A. B. Gottlober Un Zayn Epokhe* (1925); M. Erik and A. Rozensweig, *Di Yidishe Literatur In 19. Yohrhundert* (1935); H. S. Kazdan, *Fun Heder Un Shkoles Biz CYShO* (1956), Index; J. Klausner, *Historyah Shel Ha-Safrut Ha-Ivrit Ha-Hadashah*, 5 (1955), 286–344 (includes bibliography); S. Lastik, *Di Yidishe Literatur Biz Di Klasiker* (1950), 200–205; S. Niger, *Dertseylers Un Romanistn*, 1 (1946), 60–63; I. Riminik, in the collection *Mendele Un Zayn Tsayt* (1940), 221–225; D. Sadan, *Ka'arat Egozim* (1953), Index; P. Shalev-Toren, *A. B. Gottlober Ve-Yetzirato Ha-Piyutit* (1958); J. Shatzky, *Geshikhte Fun Yidn In Varshe*, 3 (1953), 279–281, 311; N. Shtif, *Di Eltere Yidishe Literatur* (1929), 119–42; Z. Skudetzki, *Tsaytshrift* (Minsk), V (1931); and A. Zeitlin, in *YIVO-Bleter*, XXXVI (1952).

HASKALAH IN POLAND: EISENBAUM, REIFMANN, SLONIMSKI, ETTINGER

On Jacob Tugendhold, see A. Levinson, *Toledot Yehudei Varshah* (1953, 117–18; J. Shatsky, *Geshikhte Fun Yidn In Varshe* (1947–53), Index; and B. Weinryb, in MGWJ, LXXVII (1933), 280 ff.

On Anton Eisenbaum, the editor of *Der Beobachter an der Weichsel*, see I. Zinberg, in *Perezhitoye*, IV (1913), 119–48; J. Shatzky, *Geshikhte Fun Yidn In Varshe*, (1947–53), Index; *Entziklopedyah Shel Galuyyot, Varsha*, I (1961), 240–46; Z. Rejzen, *Leksikon Fun Der Yidisher Literatur, Prese Un Filologye*, 2nd ed., 1 (1926); E. N. Frenk, *Tzukunft* (March, 1924); and N. Mayzil, *Tzukunft* (March, 1924).

For a list of Jacob Reifmann's most important published books, see the entry on him in *The Jewish Encyclopedia*, X (1905), 366. Some of his writings were published in recent times by N. Herskovics in *Hadorom* (1964–69) and by N. Ben-Menaḥem, *Iggeret Bikkoret Al Seder Ha-Haggadah Shel Pesaḥ* (1969) and *Iyyunim Be-Mishnat Avraham Ibn Ezra* (1962).

On Jacob Reifmann, see J. A. Klausner, *I. L. Peretz Ve-Yaakov Reifmann* (1969) and G. Kressel, *Leksikon Ha-Safrut Ha-Ivrit Ba-Dorot Ha-Aharonim*, 2 (1967), 867.

Among the better known of Ḥayyim Selig Slonimski's publications are *Mosedei Ḥochmah*, on the fundamental principles of higher algebra (1834); *Sefer Kocheva De-Shavit*, essays on Halley's comet and on astronomy in general (1835); *Toledot Ha-Shamayim*, on astronomy and optics (1838); *Yesodei Ha-Ibbur*, on the Jewish calendar system and its history (1852); *Metziut Ha-Nefesh Ve-Kiyummah Ḥutz La-Guf*, a defense of the immortality of the soul based on scientific arguments (1852); and *Ot Zikkaron*, a biography of the great German scientist Alexander von Humboldt written for his eighty-eighth birthday (1858). Two collections of Slonimski's most important articles from *Ha-Tzefirah* and *Ha-Karmel* were edited by J. L. Sossnitz and published under the title *Ma'amarei Ḥochmah* (1891–94).

On Slonimski, see A. A. Akavia, in *Davar Yearbook* (Hebrew, 1955), 387–96; S. Bernstein, *Be-Ḥazon Ha-Dorot* (1928); 90–120; J. Klausner, *Historyah Shel Ha-Safrut Ha-Ivrit Ha-Ḥadashah*, 4 (1953), 123–25, 130–31; G. Kressel, *Leksikon Ha-Safrut Ha-Ivrit Ba-Dorot Ha-Aharonim* 2, (1967), 504–07; E. R. Malachi, in *Bitzaron* (Heshvan-Shevat, 1963); N. Sokolow, *Ishim* (1958 edition), 135–52; and S. L. Zitron, in *Ha-Olam*, from Nos. 49–51, 1928 to No. 33, 1930.

On Ephraim-Fishel Fishelsohn, see *Leksikon Fun Der Nayer Yidisher Literatur* 7 (1968), 391; R. Mahler, *Der Kamf Tzvishen Haskole Un Khasides in Galitzie* (1942), passim; S. Niger, *Dertseylers Un Romanistn* (1946), 48; S. Lastik, *Di Yidishe Literatur Biz Di Klasiker* (1950), 180–182; and Z. Zylbercweig, *Leksikon Fun Yidishn Teater*, vol. 3, 2129–2130.

Solomon Ettinger's collected works, *Ale Ksovim Fun Dr. Shloyme Ettinger*, edited by Max Weinreich in two volumes, were published in 1925. A selection of his works, *Geklibene Verk*, was edited by Max Erik and published in 1935.

On Ettinger, see *Liksikon Fun Der Nayer Yidisher Literatur*, 6 (1965), 574–583; Z. Rejzen, *Leksikon Fun Der Yidisher Literatur, Prese, Un Filologye*, 2nd ed., 2 (1927), 725–39; N. Auslander, *Di Eltere Yidishe Drama Un Ir Kinstlerishe Oysshtatung* (1927), 46–54; idem, *Etapn Fun Der Literatur-Antviklung In Onheyb 19. Yohrhundert* (1928); G. Bader, *Draysik Doyres Yidn In Poyln* (1927), 474–77; M. Erik, *Geklibene Verk* (1935), 7–33, 370–74; A. Fridkin, *Avrohom Gottlober Un Zayn Epokhe* (1925), 176–78, 304–10, 337; A. Goldberg, *Undsere Dramaturgn* (1961), 53–82; B. Gorin, *Yidishe Dramaturgn in Rusland*, I (1929), 89–131; S. Lastik, *Di Yidishe Literatur Biz Di Klasiker* (1950), 183–196; I. Manger, *No'ente Geshtalten* (1938), 35–44; Z. Rejzen, *Fun Mendelssohn Biz Mendele* (1923), 271–285; I. Schipper, in *YIVO-Bleter*, III (April–May, 1932); N. Shtif, *Di Eltere Yidishe Literatur* (1929), 36–71; S. Turkov, *Shmu'esn Vegn Teater* (1950), 134–150; M. Weinreich, *Bilder Fun Der Yidisher Literatur-Geshikhte* (1928), 280–91; and M. Wiener, *Tzu Der Geshikhte Fun Der Yidisher Literatur In 19. Yohrhundert* (1940), 161–213.

Glossary of Hebrew and
Other Terms

Glossary of Hebrew and Other Terms

Aharonim (Hebrew for "later ones"): A term used to designate relatively recent rabbinic authorities, as distinguished from earlier ones, known as Rishonim (see below). Aharonim usually refers to decisors and codifiers of the law subsequent to the compilation of Rabbi Joseph Karo's Shulhan Aruch (see below) in the sixteenth century, although occasionally the dividing line between Rishonim and Aharonim is placed as early as the eleventh century.

Amora (plural, Amoraim): The title given to the Jewish scholars of Palestine and especially Babylonia in the third to the sixth centuries whose work and thought is recorded in the Gemara of the Talmud.

Baal Shem (in Hebrew, "master of the Name"): A title given to persons believed capable of working miracles through employing the divine Name. The title was not uncommon in Eastern Europe in the seventeenth and eighteenth centuries, where it frequently implied a quack or imposter who produced magical amulets, pronounced incantations, etc.

Bet Ha-Midrash: In the Talmudic age, a school for higher rabbinic learning where students assembled for study and discussion, as well as prayer. In the post-Talmudic age most synagogues had a Bet Ha-Midrash or were themselves called by the term, insofar as they were places of study.

Dayyan: A judge in a rabbinical court who is competent to decide on cases involving monetary matters and civil law, as well as questions of a religious or ritual character.

Gaon (plural, Geonim): The spiritual and intellectual leaders of Babylonian Jewry in the post-Talmudic period, from the sixth through the eleventh centuries C.E. The head of each of the two major academies of Babylonia, at Sura and Pumbeditha, held the title Gaon. The Geonim had considerable secular power as well as religious authority, and their influence extended over virtually all of world Jewry during the larger part of the Gaonic age. The title Gaon is occasionally applied as a general honorific sense to a very eminent Judaic scholar.

Gemara: The second basic strand of the Talmud, consisting of a commentary on, and supplement to, the Mishnah (see below).

Guter Yid (in Yiddish, literally "good Jew"; plural, Gute Yidn): Another name for the Hasidic *rebbes* (see below), especially those to whom thaumaturgic or wonder-working powers were attributed.

Haskalah: The movement for disseminating modern European culture among Jews from about 1750 to 1880. It advocated the modernization of Judaism, the westernization of traditional Jewish education, and the revival of the Hebrew language.

Haskamah (plural, Haskamot): Approbations or authorizations by respected rabbinic authorities, sometimes inserted in Hebrew books. The practice of inserting *haskamot* became particularly widespread after the synod of rabbis in Ferrara in 1554 decided that Hebrew books should obtain prior approval by Jewish authorities in order to prevent suppression or censorship by the officials of the Church. Later, a *haskamah* was frequently solicited by the author of a book as testimony of his work's scholarly value and its orthodoxy.

Kabbalah: The mystical religious movement in Judaism and/or its literature. The term Kabbalah, which means "tradition," came to be used by the mystics beginning in the twelfth century to signify the alleged continuity of their doctrine from ancient times.

Kahal: The semi-autonomous Jewish community organization and government officially sanctioned by the Russian authorities until the middle of the nineteenth century.

Glossary of Hebrew and Other Terms

Kahal-Shtibl (In Yiddish, literally "the little room of the Kahal"): The office where the business of the Kahal (see above) was transacted.

Kolyz (Yiddish, from the German *Klaus*, "enclosure"): The Yiddish term by which the Hasidim frequently designated their synagogues.

Maskil (plural, maskilim): An adherent of Haskalah (see above).

Meassefim: The contributors to the Hebrew journal *Ha-Meassef*, the major organ in Hebrew published by the proponents of Haskalah (see above) in Germany in the last decades of the eighteenth century and the first of the nineteenth.

Midrash (plural, Midrashim): The discovery of new meanings besides literal ones in the Bible. The term is also used to designate collections of such Scriptural exposition. The best-known of the Midrashim are the *Midrash Rabbah, Tanḥuma, Pesikta De-Rav Kahana, Pesikta Rabbati*, and *Yalkut Shimeoni*. In a singular and restricted sense, Midrash refers to an item of rabbinic exegis.

Mishnah: The legal codification containing the core of the post-Biblical Oral Torah, compiled and edited by Rabbi Judah Ha-Nasi at the beginning of the third century C.E.

Mitnagdim: The opponents of Hasidism. They obtained this title after the issuance of an excommunication against the adherents of the Hasidic movement by Elijah, the Gaon of Vilna, in 1772.

Parnass (from the Hebrew term *parnes*, meaning "to foster" or "to support"): A term used to designate the chief synagogue functionary. The parnass at first exercised both religious and administrative authority, but since the sixteenth century religious leadership has been the province of the rabbis. The office of parnass has generally been an elective one.

Parnass Hodesh: A layman elected to serve as parnass (see above) for a specific month.

Rebbe: Yiddish form of the term rabbi, applied generally to a teacher but also, and especially, to a Hasidic rabbi.

Rishonim (Hebrew for "first ones"): In modern times, the term has come to be employed primarily in reference to the commentators on, and codifiers of, Talmudic law of the Gaonic era until the time of the composition of Rabbi Joseph Karo's *Shulḥan Aruch* (see below). Later authorities are referred to as Aḥaronim (see above). On occasion the dividing line between Rishonim and Aḥaronim has been drawn as early as the eleventh century.

Sefirah (pl. sefirot): A technical term in Kabbalah, employed from the twelfth century on, to denote the ten potencies of emanations through which the Divine manifests itself.

Shulḥan Aruch: The abbreviated code of rabbinic jurisprudence, written by Joseph Karo in the sixteenth century, which became the authoritative code of Jewish law and is still recognized as such by Orthodox Judaism.

Talmud: The title applied to the two great compilations, distinguished as the Babylonian Talmud and the Palestinian Talmud, in which the records of academic discussion and of judicial administration of post-Biblical Jewish law are assembled. Both Talmuds also contain Aggadah, or non-legal material.

Tanna (plural, Tannaim): Any of the teachers mentioned in the Mishnah, or in literature contemporaneous with the Mishnah, and living during the first two centuries C.E.

Targum (plural, Targumim): The Aramaic translation of the Bible. There are three Targumim to the Pentateuch: Targum Onkelos, Targum Jonathan, and Targum Yerushalmi.

Torah: In its narrowest meaning, the Pentateuch. Torah is also known in Judaism as the Written Law. In its broader meaning, Torah comprises as well the Oral Law, the traditional exposition of the Pentateuch and its commandments developed in the late Biblical and post-Biblical ages. In its widest meaning, Torah signifies every exposition of both the Written and the Oral Law, including all of Talmudic literature and its commentaries. The term is sometimes used also to designate the scroll of the Pentateuch read in the synagogue service.

Tzaddik: In Hebrew, the term means "a righteous man." It is a title given to a person renowned for faith and piety. The concept of the tzaddik became especially important in the Hasidic movement of the eighteenth century, in which the tzaddik was regarded as endowed with extraordinary powers and capable of serving as an intermediary between God and man.

Yeshivah (plural, Yeshivot): A traditional Jewish school devoted primarily to the study of the Talmud (see above), and rabbinic literature.

Index

Index

Fridkin, A., 16n, 18n, 41n, 81n, 163n, 167n.
Friedberg, A. S., 127n, 128n.
Friedberg, Moses, 86.
Friedländer, David, 172, 173, 174, 176.
Frume Bern, Di (Solomon Ettinger), 189, 190. ·
Fuenn, S. J., 24n, 40, 42, 78, 87n, 88n, 89n, 92n, 101, 164.
Fun Mendelssohn Biz Mendele (Zalman Rejzen), 14n, 25n, 103n.
Fürst, Julius, 179.

Gaon of Vilna. See Elijah ben Solomon Zalman.
Garmayza, Levin Behr, 151n.
Geiger, Abraham, 85n, 89n, 179.
Gellert, Christian Fürchtegott, 189, 190.
Gelot Ha-Aretz Ha-Hadashah (Mordecai Aaron Günzburg), 102, 103.
Genarte Velt, Di (Israel Aksenfeld), 137, 139, 140, 143, 158, 186.
Gezerat Uman Ve-Ukraina, 152.
Gilgul Nefesh (Isaac Erter), 25, 99, 164.
Ginsburg, S., 30n, 65n, 75n, 81n, 83n, 93n, 136n, 153n, 154, 155n, 199.
Goethe, Johann Wolfgang von, 18.
Gold, Jehudah Leib, 185.
Goldfaden, Abraham, 169.
Golitzin, Prince N., 30.
Gordon, J. L., 108n, 179.
Gotthelf, Jeremias (Albert Bitzius), 129.
Gottlob, Hayyim, 158.
Gottlober, Abraham Baer, 16, 17, 26n, 40, 58, 66, 79, 80n, 83n, 84n, 85, 91n, 98, 100n, 136, 140, 154, 156n, 157, 158ff., 182.
Gottlober Un Zayn Epokhe (A. Fridkin), 81n, 159n, 163n.
Graetz, Heinrich, 121n.
Groyse Kintz, Oder Dos Bisele Mintz, Di (A. B. Gottlober), 164.
Grünbaum, Tzevi. See Vladimir Fedorov.
Guide for the Perplexed, A (Maimonides), 107, 178.
Günzburg family (of Petersburg), 129.
Günzburg, Jehudah Asher, 102.

Günzburg, Mordecai Aaron, 41, 42, 43, 78, 79n, 87, 88, 89, 90, 91, 92n, 102ff., 111, 121.
Günzburg, Yozel, 146.
Gzeyre Daytshn, Di (A. B. Gottlober), 79n, 164.

Ha'amek She'elah (Manasseh of Ilya), 5, 6n.
Halberstam, S. Z., 178.
Halevi, Eliezer, 68.
Halevi, Jehudah, 123.
Halley, Edmund, 180.
Halom Over (Adam Ha-Kohen Lebensohn), 115.
Hamburgische Dramaturgie (Gotthold Ephraim Lessing), 189n.
Hanover, Raphael, 179.
Hannah (Biblical), 151n.
Harisut Troya (Micah Joseph Lebensohn), 122-123.
Hausfranzose, Der (Abraham Mapu), 128.
Hazon La-Mo'ed, 81n, 83n, 87n, 88n, 108n.
Hegel, Georg Wilhelm Friedrich, 134.
Heine, Heinrich, 113, 119, 122.
Hefker-Velt, Di (Isaac Baer Levinsohn), 25n, 26n, 55, 57, 58n, 136, 137, 139, 143, 167.
Hemlah, Ha- (Adam Ha-Kohen Lebensohn), 118, 121.
Herzen, Alexandr Ivanovich, 54n.
Hessen, J. I., 20n, 61n, 69n, 73n, 92n.
Historishe Verk (S. Ginsburg), 199.
Hochmann, Mordecai, 126.
Hochmat Ha-Shi'urim (Jacob Eichenbaum), 105n.
Holdheim, Samuel, 89n.
Horace (Roman poet), 128.
Horn, Meir, 18.
Horowitz, Marcus, 156.
Horowitz, Sheftel, 32.
Horwitz, Abele, 135.
Hoshen Mishpat (part of Joseph Karo's *Shulhan Aruch*), 195.
Hovot Ha-Levavot (Bahya Ibn Pakuda), 184.
Hoyzfraynd (A. S. Friedberg), 127n, 128n.
Humboldt, Alexander von, 181.